PREPARE
FOR
BATTLE

Also by Neal Pirolo

SERVING AS SENDERS

THE REENTRY TEAM

I THINK GOD WANTS ME
  TO BE A MISSIONARY

PREPARE
FOR
BATTLE

BASIC TRAINING
IN
SPIRITUAL WARFARE

Neal & Yvonne Pirolo

Emmaus Road International
Resources for Third Millennium Missions
7150 Tanner Court • San Diego, CA 92111 USA
858 292-7020 • Emmaus_Road@eri.org • www.eri.org

Scripture quotations are often paraphrases by the author. All references should be studied in their context.

The section on Prayer in Chapter 2 is adapted from the book, *Serving As Senders*, and is used by permission of Emmaus Road International. Chapter 6 is adapted from the book, *Principles of War*, (Ransom Press, 1964), used by permission. The allegory, *Battle Fatigue*, following Chapter 7 is used with permission.

Published by Emmaus Road International
7150 Tanner Court, San Diego, CA 92111 USA

Printed in the United States of America
ISBN 1-880185-06-7

Dedication

To the many
Warriors of the Cross
who have rendered unselfish service
"that they may please the One
Who has chosen them
to be a Soldier."
II Timothy 2:4

A Word of Thanks

The writing of any book is never the work of a single person. And how true that is of this one. The first word of thanks is for my wife, Yvonne, who has stood by my side for forty years of warfare against the enemy. And then her wanting to add her "Practical Insights" sections after each chapter has been a strong motivation to proceed. After months of grueling writing and rewriting, we had what we called a "first draft." Lisa Hoffman, our secretary, deciphered our long hand, and entered it into the computer.

Then Ruth Donan, offered to edit our work. A deep, heartfelt gratitude developed as she handed me chapter after chapter, having written more words in critique than I wrote in the book. I was pushed back to defend (or change) almost every paragraph. But it was the best thing that could have happened to assure accuracy to the Scriptures and His call on our lives to be Soldiers of the Cross. Her work was magnificent.

Doing a fine job on the grammatical editing, my brother Paul, labored long—trying to reeducate me in proper English. He also added new insight on a number of Scriptures and illustrations. To assure the accuracy of the Scripture references, Ramon Rose highlighted every one of them (over 700), and checked them on his computer. A word of thanks is given to Kevin Schmuki for his work on the cover design and the drawing in Chapter 1. Another word of thanks goes to a team of three—Jonathan Menn, Elizabeth Keggi, and Steve Erbach—who assisted with further editing for this printing.

And finally, but foremost, "unto Him Who is able to do exceeding abundantly above all that we can ask or think; unto Him be glory throughout all ages."

Ephesians 3:20

Contents

An Invitation

I hate war! The intrigue of battle is overshadowed by the sorrow of suffering. The adrenalin rush of an offensive is drained in the despair of destruction. There is not one aspect of the business of war that is "fun." It is unfair. No rules of decency are observed. Every cunning and crafty device of the enemy is brought against us in vicious assaults. Mayhem and death are the objectives of the forces of evil that he sets against us.

Let us "learn war no more." Isaiah 2:4 Let us "beat our swords into plowshares and our spears into pruning hooks." Micah 4:3 "Peace, brother."

However, consider Jude, the servant of Jesus Christ and brother of James. He begins his short letter, "To those who are sanctified by God the Father and preserved in Jesus Christ and called: Mercy unto you, and peace, and love, be multiplied." He's on a roll, expressing the good things of the Lord.

In verse three he makes a transition: "When I had in my mind to write to you, (I was going to talk about our common salvation. I was going to sit down and write a real nice letter about how great it is to be a Christian. You know, how much fun it is to rejoice in the Lord, to relish in all the promises of the Word—to just bask in His love.) But," Jude explains, "that's the kind of letter I was going to write to you. However, when I put quill to parchment, I realized it was imperative for me to write to you an exhortation—a battle cry—that you earnestly contend for the faith. We are at war, brothers! Evil men have crept in—ungodly men who are wreaking havoc, turning the grace of our God into lasciviousness and denying the only Lord God." Jude 1-4

> *(Here, and throughout this writing, I put quotes around Scripture that has been amplified and paraphrased, or possibly abbreviated. Scripture references are always included for you to "search the Scriptures" [Acts 17:11] to see if what we have said is true.)*

Likewise, the exhortation of this book, **PREPARE FOR BATTLE**, is given under the duress of a preference to talk about how much fun it is to be a Christian rather than it being a book to provide **Basic Training in Spiritual Warfare**. Yet, I feel this urgency to present some basic, practical, hands-on, Biblical instruction to prepare us for the battle that rages 1) within the soul of a Christian and 2) for the lost souls of the world.

Why? Because my hatred for the enemy of our souls is greater than my abhorrence of war.

There is a second reason for writing these pages. Among the plethora of books available on the subject of spiritual warfare, there are few that deal with *basic training.* There are many that deal with real and serious issues, but they seem to be written with the assumption that the reader knows the basics. Or they limit their discussion to a very narrow aspect of spiritual warfare. Some books on the subject are based only on experiences, sometimes even stretching consistency with Scripture. Others, lacking substance, seem to exploit the bizarre. In contrast to some, yet as a basic complement to others, then, the focus of this writing explores the foundations of spiritual warfare—Armor, Weapons, Attitude, Tactics of satan, Authority, Principles of War and Strategies for Battlefield Living.

War is Declared in Heaven
For reasons with which my own sinful nature can too easily identify, Lucifer was lifted up in pride and said, "I will be like the Most High." Isaiah 14:14 Rebellion and

anarchy—schemes contrary to God's will—interrupted and interposed themselves on all that would follow in human history. And Lucifer drew a host of the angels into his camp. See Matthew 25:41. When time began, God created man (male and female) in His own image, and placed them in a garden. But satan, that fallen cherub, was there to find willing allies. "You will be like gods," he assured them. See Genesis 3:5.

(Here, and throughout the book, you will notice that I do not capitalize the word, satan. This is to indicate and emphasize my disdain for the enemy. Likewise, you will note that every word used in reference to the Bible is capitalized to emphasize my reverence for the Word.)

Very early in the history of man, in the story of Job, we see the adversary going back and forth throughout all the earth. God questions him: "Have you considered My servant, Job?" This word *considered* is a military term meaning "to look at all aspects of an attack, to strategize for an attack." The answer that satan gives confirms to us that "checking Job out for an attack" is exactly what he was doing. See Job 1:6-9.

Centuries later Jesus says to Peter, "Simon, satan desires to have you to sift you like wheat." Luke 22:31 Still later, Peter warns us to "Be sober, be vigilant because your adversary the devil, as a roaring lion, walks about, seeking whom he may devour." I Peter 5:8 The True Lion cautions us, "Impostors will come claiming to be messiahs and prophets and they will perform signs and wonders, to seduce and deceive, even the elect, if that were possible." Mark 13:22 These warnings speak of an inner battle.

On the other hand, Jesus identifies His mission "to proclaim liberty to the captives." Luke 4:18, quoting Isaiah 61:1. Paul summarizes his own strategy, "I have been made all things to all men so that by all means I might win some." I Corinthians 9:22 Jude ends his brief letter by telling us "to pull the lost out of the fires of hell—out of the clutches of the enemy—hating the evil deeds of their flesh." Jude 22-23 Thus the battle rages. The powers of darkness are using every destructive weapon in their arsenal to thwart God's Plan of the Ages. And we are given the mandate to be on guard for ourselves *and* to rescue the perishing. The war declared in heaven is being waged on two fronts—in two arenas—on two levels: 1) Inwardly, the Christian struggles against "the lust of the flesh, the lust of the eyes and the pride of life." I John 2:16 2) And outwardly, the Christian struggles for the lost, to "open their eyes, turn them from darkness to light, and from the power of satan to God." Acts 26:18

The Inward Battle
On one battlefront, the incessant bombardment of the enemy entices, coaxes, and tempts us with "secret thoughts to sin." This is an inner struggle, a personal battle for the Christian to "mind the things of the flesh" rather than to "mind the things of the Spirit." Romans 8:5

Paul, in a moment of transparency, so clearly verbalizes: "For I know that in me—that is, in my sinful nature—there dwells no good thing. I have the will to do good, but I just don't know how to make it happen. The good that I determine to do—I don't do. And the evil that I determine not to do, I find myself doing. I delight in the Law of God, but I see another law warring against the law of my mind and bringing me into captivity to the law of sin...." Romans 7:18-23 This inner struggle going on in the minds of Christians caused Paul, the Apostle—and causes us—to cry out: "O wretched man that I am! Who will deliver me from this body of death?" Romans 7:24

Paul saw this sinful nature clinging to him—nose to nose, arm to arm, body to body—as he carried it with him wherever he went. To comprehend the graphic nature of this illustration, we must realize that this is one way they punished murderers in those days. That's right! They tied the dead body to the one guilty of the crime—nose to nose, arm to arm, torso to torso, leg to leg. I will let your own imagination draw this illustration to its conclusion. And after you recover, place the intensity of it to Paul's (and our) cry for freedom from this inner struggle—from this "body of death," our sinful nature.

The Battle For The Lost
In the other arena of this war, Christians are waging a battle for the salvation of lost souls. In opposition to God, some people are actively fighting *with* satan against that which is right. They have thrown in their lot with the diabolical schemes of the enemy to wage war against God and all that is good. They lobby to void society of righteousness. They ridicule scientific evidence that supports creation while religiously espousing as fact a hodgepodge of contradictory theories. They rewrite history to suit their pantheistic outlook on life.

Others are held captive as prisoners of war. They are people just "going with the flow." "Peace, brother. Live and let live!" they say, thinking that their existence begins and ends in this life only. Nothing else matters.

Then there are those lost ones who have never heard the name, Jesus. Missiologists say that there are in excess of two billion people alive today who have not even heard the Name of Jesus, and another billion or so who have not had a clear, culturally-relevant presentation of the Gospel.

Prepare for Battle!
We should realize that the principles contained in this book apply equally to warfare on both fronts.

• Our armor must be on at all times.

• The weapons we use are the same whether we are battling some secret sin or wresting one of God's precious creations out of the clutches of the enemy.

• Our attitude toward war must be the same when fighting in either arena.

• Our knowledge of the enemy's tactics will equip us for battle on both levels.

• Our exercising of spiritual authority through Christ will yield victory over sin in our own life as well as "opening the eyes" of non-Christians.

• We must learn how to apply the principles of war to spiritual battles in both arenas.

• Learning how to live on the battlefield will keep us by the side of our Commander-in-Chief. "Through God we shall do valiantly, for it is He Who shall tread down the enemies!" Psalm 60:12 As the *giants* of our day would rise up against us, with David we can say, "I come in the Name of the Lord of Hosts, the God of the armies of Israel." I Samuel 17:45

In short, the lessons of the following chapters will give us the resources to live in the victory Christ won for us on Calvary. Thus, to the degree we walk in that victory over our inward battles, we will have the confidence to help our fellow Christians find victory in their lives. And then we will have the courage to do battle together for the souls of men and women who are lost in this sinful world.

Let us **PREPARE FOR BATTLE!**

Ministering by His grace,
Neal & Yvonne Pirolo
San Diego, CA 92111 USA

1

SPIRITUAL ARMOR

"Put on the whole armor of God."
Ephesians 6:11

In secular war the first consideration must relate to the protection of the warriors. Throughout the years of history many different materials have been tried. Some armor was so scant that, though it allowed for mobility, it provided no protection. In the Middle Ages, the armor was so heavy a warrior had to be hoisted into the saddle of his steed. Lightweight, yet protective, is ideal.

In spiritual warfare, the goal is the same. In the war that is raging, we must remain mobile. Yet we must also be well-protected, for the battle is fierce.

Though various pieces of spiritual armor are mentioned throughout the Word, a rather complete list is given by Paul to the Christians in Ephesus. It is important to note that before he even mentions the five pieces of armor he twice emphasizes to put it *all* on.

*"Put on **the whole armor of God**, that you may be able to stand against the wiles of the devil. For we wrestle not against flesh and blood, but against principalities, against powers, against rulers of the darkness of this world, against spiritual wickedness in high places. Wherefore take unto you **the whole armor of God**, that you may be able to withstand*

in the evil day, and having done all, to stand."
                                        Ephesians 6:11-13

Note with equal emphasis that it is the armor of God. It is His provision for us. Isaiah rejoiced greatly, for Jehovah "has clothed me with the garments of salvation, He has covered me with the robe of righteousness...." Isaiah 61:10 Our combat is not against "flesh and blood," but against spiritual forces. Thus, our armor, our protection against the enemy, is not made of any materials of this world but is of spiritual fiber. See II Corinthians 10:4.

As Paul introduces this theme to the churches of Ephesus, he says, "Finally, my brethren, be strong in the Lord, and in the power of *His* might...." Ephesians 6:10 In ourselves we are no match for the enemy. Even the sum total of all the Christians in the world banded together in perfect unity would be no match for the enemy if they were to go out to fight for right only in the power of their own might. Paul prayed for the Christians in Colossae that they would be "strengthened with all might, according to *His* glorious power." Colossians 1:11 Jesus said, "Without *Me* you can do nothing." John 15:5 Paul acknowledged the truth in the converse: "I can do all things *through Christ* who strengthens me." Philippians 4:13

Before we carefully examine and become familiar with each piece of our armor, let us further note that armor is defensive. Though we are to fight an offensive battle, "overpowering evil with good" (Romans 12:21), our armor is for our protection. In the heat of battle we do not strip ourselves of one or another piece of armor and begin using it as a weapon. When we are trying to exhort our brother to purity in his life habits, we don't take off our helmet of salvation and begin beating him over the head with how "pure" we are and how sure we are of what we believe. The minute we allow any part of our spiritual being to be unprotected, the fiery darts of the enemy can find easy target. Injury to warriors so foolish is inevitable. And lastly, this armor has to fit us, individually. We cannot go out to fight for right suited in another's armor. The truth girded about *my* loins must be Truth from the Word that has become real in *my* life. When doing battle with the enemy we cannot say, "Well, my pastor and three commentaries say it is true." When we raise our shield of faith against the fiery darts of the enemy, this faith must have been tested, tempered and proven in the crucible of our own life experiences.

Who cannot remember David, the young shepherd boy? His father has sent him to take corn and bread to his brothers and to discover how they were doing in battle against the Philistines. He arrives at a camp held captive in fear—fear of one giant named Goliath. You know the story. Saul has raised the reward three times: All the riches one would desire, his daughter in marriage, and his father's house free of taxes! Still no one will volunteer to fight Goliath. But David says he will fight him.

His brothers try to send him home. The word gets out and finally reaches the ears of King Saul. After a lengthy discussion during which the king, too, tries to dissuade David, he finally says, "OK, go for it! But at least put my armor on."

Now remember, Saul stands "head and shoulders above all the men of Israel." I Samuel 9:2 David is just a stripling youth. But in obedience to the king, the armor bearers start dressing him in Saul's armor. On goes the helmet of brass. David probably has to look out through the mouth opening. And the coat of mail? There are no letters here for David. He tries to walk, but can't. He says to Saul, "I cannot go out with these, *for I have not proved them.*" See I Samuel 17. *"Not proved"* means they had not been made to fit him. And the armory tailor had no time to take in a tuck here or cut off a snip there.

In the same manner—now in the spiritual arena—the armor we put on for our protection must be proven by us—it must fit each of us—individually; personally. As we look at each of these pieces of armor, let's do so in this context: Does this armor fit me?

> *"Stand, therefore, having your loins girded about with* **truth***, and having the breastplate of* **righteousness***; and your feet shod with the* **preparation** *of the Gospel of Peace. Above all, taking the shield of* **faith***, with which you will be able to quench all the fiery darts of the wicked. And take the helmet of* **salvation***...."*   Ephesians 6:14-17a

The Loin Cloth of Truth
Truth is primary. Truth is unchanging. Truth is eternal. Today, however, the world is telling us all truth is relative. Whether scientific, legislative, or even historical, truth is as changeable as the people currently in authority.

The world is flat. No, it is spherical. No, it is pear-shaped. I remember the early days of space exploration. Each space launch was so unique that they carried continuous live coverage. And, of course, there were often "holds" on the countdown as this or that had to be repaired or adjusted. During those "holds" in the countdown, the radio or TV commentator had to have something with which to fill that time.

On one launch that I was following excitedly on the car radio, Cape Canaveral put the launch on hold. By phone the newsman began talking with a chap in England. He happened to be the president of the Society for the Preservation of the Flatness of the Earth! Yes, this was back in the "dark ages" of the 1960s, but I almost had a wreck as I wove across the freeway lanes in disbelief that anyone could still think the earth was flat!

When the newsman asked him what his society did with the beautiful pictures being taken from space showing the curvature of the earth, he said, "I will have to admit that they cause us a bit of a problem!" "Do you still believe the earth is flat?" came the next question. "Yes, we do. We will find some reasonable explanation for those pictures." I kid you not! That is exactly what the man said.

One probe of the rings of Saturn disproved 28 previously held *truths* about them. Each new discovery from every branch of science is more and more clearly pointing to a young earth and an infinitely creative force. Yet evolution is more and more emphatically being taught as truth. Even those who promote Intelligent Design, have not come to the full measure of Truth. By the world's standards, scientific truth is relative.

The foundational truths on which human governments are based prove to be relative. Pilate, trained and experienced in principles of government, reasoned with the Jewish leadership, knowing that their arguments were perversions of their own beliefs. Trying to find a way to release Jesus, he talked with Him. Jesus said, "Everyone that is of the truth hears My voice." Pilate, rising to go back to the people, obviously frustrated by this travesty of justice, asked of Him, "What is truth?" John 18:37-38

With the ebb and flow of conservative and liberal court justices, legislative truth is interpreted as relative. In one day the sanctity of life in the womb is subjugated to a "woman's choice" and the child created in the image of God is described as "fetal matter" although the same law books determine that the destruction of that "matter" is murder if done without the woman's choice! And people with other perceptions of *truth* have been fighting that *truth* ever since.

Historical truth is also deemed to be relative. When one form of government fails in a country, all that was expounded as truth by its leader is now relegated to the archives of error. The new regime tears down the statues of the deposed leader and finally buries his bones.

Cults, and even Christians, establishing dates for this or that to happen, have to "reinterpret" their historical truth to maintain a degree of credibility. Scoffers say, "Where is the promise of His coming? All things remain the same since the beginning of creation." II Peter 3:4 Yet, Truth says, "All of human history will be consummated in Christ." Ephesians 1:10

On a personal level, from those who choose to believe a lie, we hear, "Oh, that's beautiful. That's *your* reality," when they are confronted with Truth. As if truth could be true for one person and not for another.

The Bible is not mere scientific truth, yet there is not one scientific principle (not theory) in contradiction with the Word of God.

The Bible is not mere legislative truth, yet the principles of government that have paralleled the counsel of the Almighty through His Written Word have been found to yield justice and equity.

The Bible is not mere historical truth, yet the data of every new archaeological find builds evidence for the historical accuracy of every Word of God.

COBE probed the outer reaches of our Solar System looking for proof of the Big Bang theory. Instead, it sent back data suggesting an orderly, creative act. One sincere probe of the Word in any area of investigation will yield Truth. For Christ, the Living Word, said, "I am the Truth!" John 14:6

Study the Word. Let it be the milk and meat to mature you in Truth. See Hebrews 5:13-6:1. Jesus said,

"Abide (make your home, settle in, become comfortable) in Me and let My words abide (make their home, settle in, become comfortable) in you...." John 15:7 As well-studied in the Word as Paul was, he commended the Bereans for *not* simply relying on his words. But rather they "searched the Scriptures daily to see if these things he said were true." Acts 17:11

E.V. Hill, in a dynamic sermon focusing on the power of the Word to transform society, related the story of growing up in Sweet Home, Texas. His mother couldn't read. So, often she would ask her son to read the Word to her. Once in a while to try to trick her, he would substitute the Word of God with his own words. She would immediately stop him, saying, "That's wrong. That's wrong! That just doesn't sound like God!"

Likewise, may we become so familiar with Truth that when error—half-truths, perversions, distortions or full-on lies—are foisted on us, we can immediately stop them with "No! That just doesn't sound like God!"

There are some who in their attempt to know Truth begin to investigate error. They can easily become engrossed, then possibly enamored with the tantalizing tenets of that error. Their motive is right: To know Truth. But their method leads them astray as they read more and more about false teachings.

Instead of making a study of false teachings, consider the example of bank tellers in training: When it is time for them to learn how to detect counterfeit (false) money, the teacher does not bring out a hundred samples of counterfeit bills and point out all the errors. Instead, he gives each teller a stack of real (true) money. The tellers spend time pulling them—bill by bill—through their hands. Their hands become familiar with the feel of true money. Their fingers become sensitized to "truth." After a set time, the teacher slips in a few counterfeit bills. As the tellers pull the paper through their hands they are able to detect the false bills. Those bills just don't feel right. Likewise, may we be so sensitized to the Truth that when anyone would impose on us a counterfeit thought or doctrine, we could immediately stop him with, "That just doesn't feel right. That just doesn't sound like God."

Truth is the primary part of our defense as we go out to fight for right, armed with faith and a clear conscience. The compass of this writing does not include how to study Truth. And I admit that just *knowing* that Truth must "abide" in us is not enough. There are many excellent methods and programs available for getting the Word to "abide" in us, not the least being the Holy Spirit with us in our personal closet of prayer. Knowing this, that "when He, the Spirit of Truth comes, He will guide us into all Truth...." John 16:13

The Breastplate of Righteousness
In II Corinthians 6:7, as Paul was speaking of his own warfare, he said he was a minister of God "by the Word of Truth, by the power of God, by the armor of righteousness on the right hand and on the left." The upper part of our torso—our chest and back, our "comings and goings"—needs to be protected by the righteousness of Christ. See Psalm 139:5. Herein lie the two most vital life systems—the respiratory and circulatory.

A very simple definition of righteousness is "right relationships." In Luke 2:52 it says, "And Jesus increased in wisdom and stature, gaining favor with God and man." Even our Lord grew in developing right relationships with God and man. In Luke's record of Paul's statements in the Book of Acts and in his epistles, you find Paul continually talking about having a clear conscience before God and man. Notably, as he shared his final words with the elders of the churches of Ephesus at Miletus, he said, "I am pure from the blood of all men." See Acts 20:26. This was in reference, most probably, to Ezekiel's words in Chapters 3 and 33.

(You surely have noted by this point in the study that I am listing numerous Scripture references that I am but alluding to in context. I encourage you to be like a Berean and search these Scriptures to prove in your heart that what I am saying is true—more to the point: That you will develop a deep sense for the Truth of His Word.)

When Paul stood before Felix, he was able to use as a part of his defense the truth of his words, "I do my utmost to live my whole life with a conscience void of offense toward God and toward men." Acts 24:16 When we clear our conscience we get "a load off our chest." We are able to "breathe freely." With a clear conscience, we can look everyone straight in the eye and say, "To the best of my knowledge, *agape* love is the force that binds us together." We are not harboring some blame for their previous actions or words. We are not concealing some guilt for ill we did against them. And as far as we know, they are not holding anything against us.

In Matthew 5:6, Jesus said our desire for righteousness should be as intense as the physical drives of hunger and thirst. How long do we go without eating or drinking before we say, "I'm starving to death!" or "I'm dying of thirst?" We're a long way from literal death, but that speaks of the strength of these drives in our physical makeup. Thus, in the emotional/psychological/spiritual dimensions of our life, we are to have an equally intense drive to maintain right relationships with God and man. It is a part of our defense—a part of our protection in warfare.

Unresolved conflicts are like breaches in our breastplate. They are weak spots in our armor which leave us open and susceptible to the fiery darts of the enemy. It can happen when we say, "I can forgive everybody but _____. (You fill in the name.) There is no way I can forgive that gossiping rumor-monger for the way he hurt me." So you go out to fight for right with unforgiveness in your heart, you may be thinking yourself to be "armed with faith and a clear conscience." I Timothy 1:18-19 But wait! There is a chink—a weak spot—in your armor. I say it again, unforgiveness leaves a giant hole in your breastplate.

Then you begin sharing with a person. Sure enough, he is having a hard time forgiving someone. "How can I have victory over this?" he asks you. You know the Word. You know the specific instruction to bring him peace. You bring Truth to bear on the issue. And he may even go away with peace in his heart and a plan for resolving his conflict with his brother. But (and possibly unknown to him) you had been sharing it with less than true conviction because satan was launching a steady barrage of fiery darts (They feel more like atomic bombs!) through that opening, that weak spot in your breastplate of righteousness.

Am I saying that we cannot minister until we are "perfect?" No! But to the degree that we harbor unresolved conflict, we reduce our effectiveness as Soldiers of the Cross. And we open ourselves up to become casualties on the battlefield.

The Word also says, "As much as is possible, live at peace with all men." Romans 12:18 But if they will not make peace with us, there is not much we can do, except wait patiently for the Lord to work in their lives.

A minister friend of mine, through a terrible misunderstanding, found himself in a broken relationship with another minister. When my friend realized the cause, he did everything in his power to bring about a resolution. And because he has forgiven his brother, his own heart is at peace. But the breach remains a grievous issue, for the other minister will not allow a resolution.

Proverbs 10 and 11 discuss no less than 28 benefits to the righteous—the upright in heart. Read them. List them. Study them. Ask God, the Holy Spirit, to lead you into all truth regarding those benefits. They will then become a strong motivation for keeping a clear conscience. Proverbs 16:7 says that when a man's ways please the Lord (that is, he walks in right relationship with God and man), He will make even his enemies to be at peace with him! Right relationships give people no chance to slander your good name.

The breastplate of righteousness not only protects our respiratory system (so we may breathe freely), but also the most vital organ of our circulatory system, our heart. Our heart is safe when we have right relationship with God and man. Paul shows the importance of having a protected heart when he writes, "Our ultimate aim is agape love which flows from a pure heart and a good conscience and a genuine faith." I Timothy 1:5 Solomon knew the importance of a clear conscience when he said, "Guard your heart with all diligence, for out of it flow the issues of life." Proverbs 4:23

Right relationships with God and man are at the very core of Scripture. Of the Ten Commandments (Exodus 20:1-17), the first four primarily deal with our relationship with God; the remaining six primarily with our relationships with man. Jesus summed it up succinctly, so simply (for He was the Master of simplicity), "Love God; love your neighbor as yourself. All of the Law and the Prophets rests on these two commandments." Matthew 22:37-40 "The Kingdom of God is not a matter of meat or drink," Paul said to the Christians at Rome, but its very essence is "*righteousness*, peace and joy in the Holy Spirit." Romans 14:17

Our Feet Shod With The Preparation Of The
Gospel Of Peace
The focus of Paul's instruction here is on the *preparation* of the Gospel of Peace—knowing how to share, what to share and when to share the Good News; "being instant in season and out." II Timothy 4:2 This would assume, of course, that we are fully cognizant of what the Gospel of Peace consists.

"These boots were made for walking and I'm going to walk all over you!" were the words of a secular song of yesteryear. How tragic a thought. Yet, more incomprehensible is the unfortunate truth that often our presentation of the Gospel of Peace tramples all over the very one we wish to come to the Lord.

Once I was waiting to pick up my car at the shop. Phil, the owner, with whom I was building a relationship, is an Iranian. He is a cultural Muslim who thinks any person who sincerely follows what he believes will make it to his "heaven"—whatever he wants that eternity to be. His (American) wife Mary, who was preparing the billing for the customer in front of me, was being harassed by a well-intentioned patron who kept inviting her to church. Mary kept kindly refusing. After many—too many—exchanges, it became obvious that Mary was becoming irritated by the customer's insistence. In one final burst of exasperation, Mary forcefully expressed, "I'm an atheist!" Without batting an eye, without missing a beat, the customer said, "Well, if you ever change your mind, you're still welcome at our church!" Then she turned and walked out.

I apologized for her. But it gave Phil and Mary one more "reason" to be sure they wanted nothing to do with Christianity.

Paul told Timothy, "Study to show yourself approved unto God, a workman who needs not be ashamed, knowing how to use the Word of Truth to the best advantage." II Timothy 2:15 This requires us to do more than simply quote Scripture to people. Our lifestyle as well as our words are to be "seasoned with salt" (Colossians 4:6) so the unbeliever in Christ will become thirsty for the Living Water. We need to know where they're coming from. What their interests are. Where they're hurting. What Jesus are they rejecting. That means that we need to get them to ask questions. And it is usually our walk—not so much our talk—that draws out the questions. "How can you have it together in a world that's falling apart?" they will ask.

(No, I don't believe we have to build a relationship with people before we have the *right* to tell them their house is burning down. But I do believe there is a way to give them that news without their becoming so panicked that they die in the fire!)

Do you think the Samaritan woman who came to the well at noontime (instead of in the evening with the rest of the ladies) was hurting? Maybe she was not even allowed at the well in the evening because of her reputation. Onto this situation Jesus sprinkled some salt! And she asked the questions. See John 4:6-30.

On another occasion in that same auto shop, during the Gulf War, Phil was engrossed in the television monitoring of the conflict when I walked in. He asked, "Neal, what in the world is going on?" Before I could answer, he said, "No! No! Never mind. I know what you believe." But my influence on his life was obvious. And we were able to talk about all the injustices of war. And about the war raging in his own soul. Scripture tells us that we are to "have a quiet and reverent answer for the reason of the hope that lies within us." I Peter 3:15

We can readily agree with the world (and with Phil, my mechanic) that all paths do lead to God. All spokes do lead to the hub. His Word declares it: "As I live, says the Lord, every knee shall bow to Me, and every tongue shall confess to God. So then every one of us shall give an account of himself to God." Isaiah 45:23; Philippians 2:10; Romans 14:11-12 The Truth, however, encompasses a broader consideration. Every path but one leads to a God of justice and judgment. There is only one—through Jesus Christ—that leads to a God of mercy and grace. Even this concept of agreeing with unbelievers where we can is a "nail" in the shodding of our feet with the *preparation* of the Gospel of Peace.

Paul, in his first letter to the Christians at Corinth, distilled this Good News—this Gospel of Peace—into a succinct statement: "Christ (fully God-fully man) died for our sins according to the Scriptures, was buried, and rose again on the third day according to the Scriptures." I Corinthians 15:3-4 The Gospel is truly a simple message—so simple a child can understand it. In fact, Jesus said that "unless we receive the Kingdom of God as a little child we will not enter into it." Luke 18:17

Many years ago now, I participated in a prayer meeting in Lima, Peru. I was dumbfounded as Catholics and "Protest"ants—rather, Christians—were uniting their hearts in prayer on various matters of concern. I had never experienced anything like this before, and from my childhood prejudice against Roman Catholicism I was struggling! I would look up every once in a while and notice the stiff white collars, the black suits on the men, the full black habits on the women and the rosary beads hanging from their waists. Once when I looked up, it was just in time for me to focus on the face of a nun, her cheeks pinched by the tight, black wimple. Yet the sweetest expression was on her face as she said, "Thank you, Jesus, for the simplicity of the Gospel."

We clutter the Gospel with our culture and our "habits" of worship. (And I would not be theologically ignorant at this point to suggest that Roman Catholicism has no doctrinal error. But then neither would I be as a "blind guide" and encourage you to believe that "Protest"ants have sorted everything out either.) But when all the superfluous cultural and religious garb, and all doctrinal error are stripped away, the irreducible element is "believe on the Lord Jesus Christ and you will be saved." Acts 16:31 Jesus said to Nicodemus, "For God so loved the world that He gave His only begotten Son that whosoever believes on Him shall not perish but have everlasting life." John 3:16 "If you openly admit with your own mouth that Jesus Christ is Lord," Paul reasoned with his Jewish brethren, "and if you believe in your heart that God raised Him from the dead, you will be saved." Romans 10:9 Joel (quoted by Peter in Acts 2:21 and by Paul in Romans 10:13) who, by faith, had to look forward to the cross, simply said, "Whoever will call upon the Name of the Lord will be saved." Joel 2:32

Yet, not unlike Naaman who would have done some great and difficult feat to be healed of his leprosy—so much so that he almost refused to do the simple thing (See II Kings 5:10-14.)—we today often complicate the simplicity of the Gospel. Instead of our feet being shod with the preparation of the Gospel of Peace, we go out to battle with our iPod loaded with our favorite translation(s) plus every conceivable commentary. And, oh yes, we downloaded our Greek-English Interlinear New Testament for instant referral. And then to be sure, we take with us the latest arguments on whether Paul wrote the Book of Hebrews, if there were one or two Daniels, etc. Our feet, heavy with the weight, become mired in the "mud" of controversy. And we are no longer useful on the battlefield.

The questions that some theologians are spending their lives in ivory towers trying to find the answers to are not being asked by the lost of the world. Behind the world's façade of togetherness—lost in their wild pursuits of wealth, fame and happiness—at the root of their endless questions of "Where did I come from? Why am I here? Where am I going?" lies one simple question: "What must I do to be saved?"

Paul says it is for our protection against the enemy that we go out to battle with our feet shod with the preparation of the Gospel of Peace. And he lived his instruction: "For the Jews require a sign, and the Greeks seek after wisdom, but we preach Christ crucified...." I Corinthians 1:22-23 Earlier he had reminded them, "I was determined to know nothing before you, save Jesus Christ and Him crucified." I Corinthians 2:2

One more Biblical illustration should seal in our hearts and minds the vitality of this part of our armor. A battle was raging. There had been a rebellion in David's kingdom of the worst kind. His son Absalom was in revolt. And the armies of God were pursuing him. David remained at home. "And Joab blew the trumpet and the people returned." The battle was over. The news had to get to David quickly. "And Joab said to Cushi, 'Go tell the king what you saw.'"

But Ahimaaz, a faster runner, said, "Let me run!"

"No!" Joab ordered. "You don't have a message ready to give the king!"

"Please! Let me run!"

"OK! OK! Go ahead and run!" And Ahimaaz outran Cushi and arrived at the king's palace first.

He had a lot of things to say but the only question King David wanted answered was, "Is the young man Absalom safe?"

Ahimaaz could only respond, "I saw a great tumult, but I don't know what happened."

Stand aside (those of you without a relevant message), here comes Cushi. "Is the young man Absalom safe?" King David asks again.

"Let the enemies of my lord the king, and all that rise against you to do you hurt, be as that young man is." See II Samuel 18:19-32. Runners who bring the message that Paul did or didn't write Hebrews, runners who bring the message that there are one or two Daniels, one, two, or three Isaiahs, runners who are carrying every wind of doctrine, *stand aside!* The question the world is asking (in many different ways) is "What must I do to be saved?" The answer is found in "Jesus Christ who died for our sins according to the Scriptures, was buried, and rose again on the third day according to the Scriptures." I Corinthians 15:3-4 Paul, quoting Isaiah 52:7 said, "How beautiful on the mountains are the feet of them who preach the Gospel of Peace." Romans 10:15 They will be beautiful to the degree that they are shod with the preparation of the Gospel of Peace.

In summary, we must come back to the point that having our feet shod with the preparation of the Gospel of Peace is for our defense—our protection. Knowing how, when and what to share keeps us from "putting our foot in our mouth." There are many excellent methods and programs available for learning when, how and where to share your faith. A simple "Google" search will give you scores from which to choose. However, do not neglect having an intimate relationship with the Holy Spirit, Who will "...bring back to your remembrance all things that I have told you." John 14:26 May we, through our study of God's Word and through our experiences of sharing our faith, become "instant in season, and out." II Timothy 4:2

The Shield Of Faith

God's provision for our protection in battle is born out of His wisdom and, therefore, is perfect. This next piece of our armor is exciting. The shield of faith is that part of our armor that is moveable. There is a strap on the middle back side of the shield. We slip our arm through it and grab the hand-hold fastened near the edge. We are able to move the shield from side to side and up and down. It is our first level of protection, our first line of defense. It is able to quench some of the fiery darts of the enemy. Stop! That just doesn't sound like God! ...to quench *some* of the fiery darts? We had better check our translation. What does it say? All! Yes, ...*all* of the fiery darts.

However, I have read "living epistles," including the one I see in the mirror, and too often they read, "some." When does it read, "some?" "There just seems to be no way for me to have victory over this sin. Temptation comes and I just fall again and again. There is no hope for me." Whether or not you have said (or thought) that, I am sure you have heard it. In effect, whoever says that has rewritten Scripture to say the shield of faith can quench only *some* of the fiery darts of the enemy. But we are assured in the Word that by faith in Christ we are able to extinguish *all* of the enemy's fiery darts.

Yes, *extinguish!* Historically, the shields were made of wood overlaid with leather. Before a battle the warrior would soak his shield in water. Thus, when the flaming arrows of his enemy stuck in his shield, they were actually extinguished. May our faith be so thoroughly "soaked" with the Water of His Word that our shield extinguishes *all* of the enemy's fiery darts.

Another characteristic of faith has to do with its size. Some Christians arm themselves for battle with a postage stamp-sized shield—maybe even smaller! And they consume all of their energy "defending their faith." They are never able to take an offensive posture. They may have heard somewhere about mustard seed faith and gotten stuck wearing the seed in a plastic ball around their neck! The point of Jesus' story about faith being the size of a mustard seed was not to emphasize our faith remaining small. Rather, Jesus taught of the capacity of our faith to experience phenomenal growth. Even though a mustard seed is the littlest of herbal seeds, when planted, it grows into a very large tree so that even birds can nest in it. So if your faith is like a mustard seed (in other words, capable of such phenomenal growth), you can say to this mountain.... See Matthew 13:31-32 and 17:20.

But, you may say, I thought that "to each is given a measure of faith" (Romans 12:3) and that's it. Yes, we are given a measure of faith. But what do we do with that measure? Do we exercise it? Do we plant it? Do we bury it in a cloth? We find in Scripture: "Lord, increase our faith" (Luke 17:5); "We thank God because your faith is growing exceedingly." II Thessalonians 1:3 Each of these phrases in its context points to the growing nature of faith. And the formula for this growth is concise: "Faith comes from hearing the message, and that message is the Word of God." Romans 10:17 Thus, we are driven back to the Word, the Source of our sustenance, our very life itself.

You may one day look at what you believe you have the faith to accomplish. And being dissatisfied with that amount, you pray, "Lord, I believe. Help my unbelief." Mark 9:24 Get into the Word. Let your faith grow. Sometime later you do another "faith check." And though your faith has grown to believe God for greater things than before, you again are at a point of wanting more. So again you dig deeper into the message of the Word. And your faith grows. And you read and study and apply the Word to your life. And your faith grows some more. And the day will come when your faith is so large that your shield will cover you from the soles of your feet to the top of your head. You will be able to stand there against the enemy, knowing that that shield of faith is your protection, your defense, as you go out and overpower evil with good. With Paul you can shout, "I can do *all* things through Christ who is my strength!" Philippians 4:13 With the emphasis, of course, on "through Christ" and not on "my great faith." (And be sure to read that Scripture in its context to understand what the "all things" were that Paul said he could do.)

The Helmet Of Salvation
As vital as our shield of faith may be, no less important is our helmet of salvation. The battle is raging for our minds. The world is searching the human brain to identify the mind. Every conceivable discipline of study is postulating its unique opinion. Though not new at all, currently one of the most unusual thoughts being put forward is: "Consciousness (mind) is but an illusion!" I prefer the statement of Sir John Eckles, Nobel Laureate for his work in brain theory: "We have to admit that the mind is much more than a series of brain functions." Our "grey matter"—our brain—is part of our body. Our mind goes beyond the neurons and synapses and lobes and cortex. It reaches to the depth of "and man became a living *soul!*" Genesis 2:7 It may be a Bell racing helmet that can protect your brain in a cycling accident, but it is the helmet of salvation that protects your mind in warfare with the enemy.

At a person's salvation, the initial euphoria can be "mind-boggling." I'm saved! I'm free! I'm clean! I'm a newborn baby in Christ! The weight of sin is gone! I feel so light I could fly! And for some, that euphoric bubble of protection can last for a long time. That's great. It should. But even as the Galatians were being called foolish for trying to complete in the flesh what was begun in the Spirit (Galatians 3:3) and the Ephesians were being called back to their first love (Revelation 2:4-5), we too can become foolish and forget our first love.

There is a cinch strap that goes under our chin to hold the helmet securely on our heads. Pull that strap tight. "Be fully persuaded in your minds," Paul said. See Romans 14:5. Know what you believe and why you believe it before you get into the heat of battle. The heat of the battle is not always in the middle of the day. The vicious onslaughts of the enemy are unrelenting. Imagine yourself on a battlefield—let's say, somewhere in another country—another culture. You are sharing the Good News. Yet, in your mind's eye, you see the teeming millions who are not responding and are going to a Christless eternity. In the still of night just as you are dozing off, exhausted from the heavy warfare of the day, the enemy sarcastically mocks in your ear, "A God of love...Do you really think He will send all those people to hell?" Kerbam! A fiery dart that feels more like an atomic explosion blasts against the side of your head. Unless your cinch strap is tight, off rolls your helmet of salvation. And because you don't fully understand God's ways, you may find yourself entertaining the enemy's enticements to doubt an all-wise, all-knowing God. When you come to your senses, you have to put down your Sword and shield to get the helmet back on, leaving yourself even more defenseless.

Rather, when you hear the whine of the enemy's missile flying through the air, you would do better to point your own powerful "It is written..." statement of faith at his fiery dart. And then, like a laser beam of Light, the Sword of the Spirit which is the Word of God intercepts and destroys the enemy's attack. You are able to use that Sword because you know what you believe and why.

No, I am not saying you must be a theological genius before you go out to battle, but so that you "be not shaken in mind" (II Thessalonians 2:2), you must have some semblance of an apology, a catechism—a statement of what you believe and why. To simplify and thus clarify the process, I put my belief system into three categories:

1) Absolute Truth: I believe thus and so and here is the specific, unequivocal Word of God to substantiate this Truth.

Example: The virgin birth. (Isaiah 7:14; Luke 1:27) Anyone who believes in the inerrant Word of God—and if they don't believe that, they are already in big trouble!—must accept the fact of the miraculous conception of Jesus.

2) Reasoned truth: I believe thus and so because as I study the Whole Counsel of God, it *seems to me* that this is what the Word says. Yet, I acknowledge that others, many of whom know the Word (and Hebrew and Greek) far better than I, have studied the same Scriptures and have come up with another interpretation.

Example: I personally believe in a pre-tribulation rapture. As I study the Word, this seems to be the most reasonable sequence of events. But I realize others study the same inerrant Word of God and conclude a mid-trib or a post-tribulation rapture—even *no* rapture! And I have discovered that people of divergent cultures have come up with an entirely different scheme of "end times" doctrinal positions. If anyone wants to "debate" this issue with me, I simply say, "I'm a pre-tribber. I sure hope God is!" (Between the first draft and final editing of this writing, I have vacillated time and again over this "reasoned" truth. And do continue to do so.)

3) Cultural truth: I believe this because it fits comfortably into my cultural mores. There may be Scripture about it; there may be none. But I recognize it is largely a cultural decision.

Example: Unless forced into it by an extremely awkward cultural situation, I will not drink alcoholic beverages. I even acknowledge there is Scripture that says it is okay to drink alcohol in moderation. See John 2:1-10; I Timothy 5:23; Ephesians 5:18. But because my Christian sub-culture says it is "sin," and because I have seen what it does to a person caught in excess, and because I am aware how easily one can get caught up in that excess, I have determined it is in my best interest to *not* drink alcohol.

(I must admit that even in the three examples given, all Christians would probably not agree into which category they should go. And this results in more conflict.) But let's go on. Because you want to focus on the critical issues of life, as you develop your statement of belief, you will look back through your three categories and consider, "For which of these am I willing to die?" Let's put these three beliefs to the death test!

Third Category of Belief: You are ministering with a team of European Christians. After a wonderful evening service you're at the local cafe with them. In their rejoicing over the power of God at work in this outreach, they insist that you join them in a toast to the Lord. No, your 7-Up won't do. It has to be the wine they are all drinking. Seeing the inevitable is before you, would you rise up in "righteous indignation" and "fight to the death" your insistence that you not drink alcohol? I wouldn't. I would be a little disappointed in their insensitivity to my culture. But, we are in their country, so... "Bottoms up!" You see I have decided that drinking—or not drinking—alcohol just is not worth dying for! Though I do believe it is best for me to not drink, I have and I would. (One time I decided *to* drink was when I was leading a communion service at an Anglican home church group in Singapore. Until the common cup was being passed around, I hadn't even thought about the fact that this would be the "real stuff!")

Second Category of Belief: The war is raging for the souls of men; you are part of a witnessing team on Castro Street in San Francisco. As you are declaring the Good News of emancipation to those held captive, Michael, a homosexual "evangelist for Christ," strikes up a conversation. Your partner takes the lead. You are praying. Somehow the subject gets around to "the rapture." To your chagrin, your partner starts sharing his "mid-trib" position. Are you going to divert your spiritual fire power from the critical issue of the soul of this man and engage your partner in a battle—to the death—on this subject? Are you willing to die for your eschatological position? I'm not.

First Category of Belief: To write a believable story about denying the virgin birth has had me at wit's end! It is inconceivable to me (no pun intended) that in this world of "live and let live" that a time could come when I would be forced to deny the virgin birth.

Yet, there are signs of ecumenism that suggest its possibility. A world religious leader recently proclaimed that "all of us (snake worshippers, fire worshippers, spiritists, animists, witch doctors, Hindus, Buddhists, Muslims and Christians) are praying to the same god." (I left the word "god" intentionally uncapitalized.)

Persecution of Christians today is unprecedented. More Christians were martyred for their faith in the 20th Century than in all previous centuries combined. And this century is not looking any better.

The issue is: Will you die for your belief in the virgin birth? I will!

Now, I am no more anxious to die than the next person. In fact, I am going to fight death to my dying day. But here is the point. There are certain Truths for which I will die. Having grappled with those issues of Absolute Truth, my mind is protected. The "cinch strap" is pulled tight.

However, there is another advantage. I have also determined that I will *live* for the beliefs for which I am willing to die! Come now let us reason together that we not be shaken in mind. As we listen to sermons, as we listen to Bible study tapes, the radio, TV or a friend who has come up with a *new* doctrine, whether a wind of doctrine or some "deep theological something," ask yourself the question, "Will I die for this?" If not, then don't clutter your mind trying to wrestle to the ground some issue that cannot be resolved by our finite minds. David acknowledged that there were things too high for him to consider. See Psalm 139:6. Paul said, "We see through the glass darkly. At present all I know is a small fraction of the Truth, but the time will come when I shall know as fully as God now knows me." I Corinthians 13:12 Yet we do not sit back and let our brains vegetate. On issues of life we are to be "fully persuaded in our mind." Romans 14:5 We want to experience the fullness of the Scripture (as incredible as it may sound), "We who are spiritual have the very mind of Christ." I Corinthians 2:16 Or as Paul said to the Philippian Christians, "Let this mind be in you, which was also in Christ Jesus...." Philippians 2:5 Thus, the instruction of Romans 12:2 becomes critical: "Don't let the world around you squeeze you into its mold, but let God renew your mind from within."

Renewal of the Mind
The battle for our mind is such a critical issue, I believe it is important to look at yet another aspect. We are only too familiar with the methods of our society to squeeze us into its mold—to conform us to the ways of the world. The advertising media will spend more than a million dollars a minute to get us to listen to their messages. They create the "needs." Then they supply a plethora of products to meet those needs—only to offer us "new and improved" versions long before the first ones are paid for.

To step off this treadmill is to fall into the loving arms of our Lord who will by His Spirit renew our thinking—our very method of thought-processing.

Let's study this diagram. Yes, it is a picture of you and me! Not too glamorous—a little chubby around the middle—without arms or legs, but it will do to illustrate the process of renewing the mind.

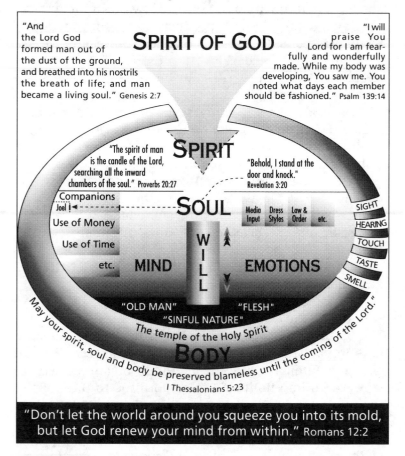

"And the Lord God formed man out of the dust of the ground, and breathed into his nostrils the breath of life; and man became a living soul." Genesis 2:7

"I will praise You Lord for I am fearfully and wonderfully made. While my body was developing, You saw me. You noted what days each member should be fashioned." Psalm 139:14

SPIRIT OF GOD

SPIRIT

"The spirit of man is the candle of the Lord, searching all the inward chambers of the soul." Proverbs 20:27

"Behold, I stand at the door and knock." Revelation 3:20

Companions
Joel
Use of Money
Use of Time
etc.

SOUL

Media Input   Dress Styles   Law & Order   etc.

MIND   WILL   EMOTIONS

SIGHT
HEARING
TOUCH
TASTE
SMELL

"OLD MAN"   "FLESH"
"SINFUL NATURE"
The temple of the Holy Spirit

BODY

May your spirit, soul and body be preserved blameless until the coming of the Lord.
I Thessalonians 5:23

"Don't let the world around you squeeze you into its mold, but let God renew your mind from within." Romans 12:2

Graphic artist Kevin Schmuki

First, notice our body. It is very good. It is the highest creation of God. Admittedly, it is our temporal dwelling. It is only for a certain period of time. Then it will return to dust. It is our earth suit. As astronauts need space suits, we—the real us—need earth suits. It is not evil or bad. Yes, it is of the molecular structure of the earth, but it is also the temple of the Holy Spirit. It is our eternal being's home on earth. Each cell is a "universe" of life—a miracle of the creative genius of God! The Psalmist David declares, "I am fearfully and wonderfully made." Psalm 139:14 Moses penned the words describing the creation of the first human: "And the Lord God formed man of the dust of the ground (body) and breathed into his nostrils the breath of life (spirit) and man became a living soul." Genesis 2:7 And Paul prayed for the Thessalonians that their "whole spirit and soul and body be preserved blameless until the coming of our Lord Jesus Christ." I Thessalonians 5:23

Now I realize that a simple two-dimensional drawing cannot show all the nuances of relationship and integration of our being. Why, even the Word declares that it is only the Sword of the Spirit that can penetrate deeply, making a distinction between the soul and the spirit and is able to discern the thoughts of the mind and the intents of the heart. Hebrews 4:12 But let us go on to what we might understand.

The spirit of man is that eternal meeting place with God. It is His breath of life. It is the home of our beliefs. The motivations of love and fear reside here. All the Fruit of the Spirit that grows out of our love relationship with Jesus finds its origin here. Galatians 5:22 The deep, settled peace that Christ said He would leave us with is found here. John 14:27 It is our spirit that came alive in God through Jesus Christ. Ephesians 2:1-6 It is often referred to as "the inner man." See Ephesians 3:16; Romans 7:22; II Corinthians 4:16.

The soul of man is that part which allows us to relate with ourselves and others—our consciousness. We relate through our senses of sight, hearing, touch, taste and smell (utilizing our body, of course). Our mind (thoughts) and our emotions (feelings) vie for dominance as our will (volition) tries to moderate, based on input from the spirit or (unfortunately) from the "flesh."

Yes, though we have been reckoned dead to sin (i.e. put in God's ledger column labeled, death), we have an "old man" or "sinful nature" to deal with while we remain on this earth. "In this *flesh*," Paul declared, "there dwells no good thing." Romans 7:18

Some people say that they have plenty of "will" power. It is "won't" power that they need. A unique characteristic of our will is that it is the "choice" of all decisions. And thus, in our diagram, it is a moving part. It moves up and down at "will" as our mind or emotions convince us to "mind the things of the Spirit" or "mind the things of the flesh." Romans 8:5 So we can willfully move our will down (sealing off the "old man") and we mind the things of the Spirit. Or, equally, by an act of our will, we can seal off godly motivations, grieving the Spirit of God (Ephesians 4:30), limiting the Holy One of Israel, by our unbelief (Psalm 78:41; Hebrews 3:19) and mind the things of the flesh. So either the Spirit of God within our spirit becomes the motivation of our conscious level of living or that bottom doorway is open, and guess what? We cry with Paul, "Oh, wretched man that I am!" Romans 7:24

But God wants more of a relationship with us than that our spirits be alive in Him. He ordained that "we should become conformed to the image of His Son." Romans 8:29 Thus begins the process of the renewing of the mind so that we will utilize the wealth of resource rightfully ours in having the mind of Christ.

Christ stands at the door of our soul and knocks, "If

any man will open the door, I will come in and have supper with him." Revelation 3:20 I am not ignorant of the wide usage of this verse as a "salvation" Scripture. Nor will I "die" to argue a point contrary to that. However, in the context of this passage, Jesus is speaking to Christians. Thus, I believe the door at which He is knocking is the door to our soul. By an act of our will, we open the door. We sit around the table of fellowship, for we have been invited to a banquet of wisdom and understanding. See Proverbs 9:1-6. The Bible is a Book of diverse figurative language, but follow carefully. When we open the door to Him, any desire to mind the things of the flesh is blocked off. Then the Lord ignites (Psalm 18:28) the "spirit of man (through our reading of His Word) which becomes the candle of the Lord, and He begins searching all the inward parts (rooms) of the belly (soul)." Proverbs 20:27

Let's say He is dealing right now in your life relating to your friendships. Certainly as you came to Christ you found friendships with a whole new set of people—the family of God. But you don't just ignore your worldly friends. It's just that you have a different relationship with them now. You don't sin with them anymore, for sure. So He brings the search light to the door of the room labeled "companions." And He knocks. But before you let Him in, you shove Joel, that one friend of the world that you just can't let go, under a pile of clothes in the closet. You lock that closet door and skip happily across the room to open the door on which Jesus is knocking. Together you begin sorting. "Yes, Lord, I know because of my previous intimate relationship with that person, I must stay far away from him, for now."

"Of this one," He says, "you will very soon have an opportunity to lead her to Me. Develop that relationship." Finally, he starts moving around the room, obviously looking for someone. "By the way," He asks, "where is Joel?" You know that Joel by this time is suffocating under that pile of clothes in your closet. Jesus is a gentleman; you now have a choice. You can either leave that closet door shut and "mind the things of the flesh" as you tell Him you don't know where Joel is. And the room will grow dim and your fellowship with Jesus will be diminished. Or you can cooperate with that renewal process, open the door, pull Joel out from under the clothes and talk with the Lord about him.

In this manner, He will deal with all areas of our life, whether it is the room full of our companions, our use of time, our use of money, our attitude toward law and order, our attitude toward media input, our dress styles, our sexuality...everything! Into every room of our soul He will eventually bring that candle (our spirit) to search out and expose to the Light of His Word those deeds that can only be done in the dark. And the Light of Life will light up our life, making us a witness of the transforming power of God.

As we allow this process to continue, we will not only be thinking the thoughts of Christ, but our very thought-processing will be renewed. Our cinch strap will be pulled tight, indeed. The gang says, "Let's go to that new movie." But you have read the reviews and immediately remember the words of David: "I will set no wicked thing before my eyes." Psalm 101:3 Your mind has been renewed with God's thoughts and you can easily say, "No, that's not for me." Every situation you face will be viewed through a renewed perspective.

Put on Jesus Christ
It is comforting to note that after having so thoroughly detailed the five pieces of armor, we can find the sum and substance of the subject in the words of Paul to the Christians at Rome, "The night is far spent, the day is at hand: let us therefore cast off the works of darkness,

and let us put on the armor of light...*let us put on the Lord Jesus Christ!"* Romans 13:12,14

Yes, as we gird up our loins with Truth, we are putting on Jesus Christ, for He said "I am Truth." John 14:6

Yes, as we put on the breastplate of righteousness, we are surrounding ourselves with Jesus Christ, for He is our righteousness; His Name declares it. See Jeremiah 23:6 and Romans 10:4.

Yes, as we shod our feet with the preparation of the Gospel of Peace, we are stepping into Jesus Christ, for He is the Living Word of God, expressed in the written Word. John 1:1

Yes, as we take up the shield of faith, we are putting on Jesus Christ for He will go before us and He is our rear guard as well. See Psalm 139:5; Isaiah 52:12; 58:8

Yes, as we pull that cinch strap tight, firmly positioning our helmet of salvation, we have put on Jesus Christ, for He is our salvation. "For there is no other name given among men whereby we must be saved." Acts 4:12

An exercise I find myself doing often: As I throw my legs over the edge of the bed to the floor each morning—sometimes even before my eyes are open—I see myself putting on each of the pieces of armor. I say a prayer with each action. As I am slipping my feet into the preparation of the Gospel of Peace, I might ask for an opportunity to give a quiet and reverent answer to someone for the reason of the hope that lies within me. As I clasp that belt of truth about my waist, I might ask for a clearer understanding of some doctrinal point. As I pull the cinch strap tight under my chin, I might gratefully thank Him for His sacrificial death that I may live. As I fit the breastplate to my chest, I ask God to protect my relationships. As I slip my arm through the strap of my shield, I thank God that my faith stands firm in Him.

PRACTICAL INSIGHTS

WHEN SATAN HASSLES CHRISTIANS

From my experiences, I have come to have a healthy respect for the awfulness of satan. He has been lying and deceiving and robbing and destroying for a long time. He is experienced. He isn't stupid. He knows he can't use the same tactics on Christians as non-Christians, nor the same lies on every person. He is far more subtle than that.

I am not saying that he does not, at times, use overt attacks to scare us; he does. It was our third night on a mission center in South America, and we had already sensed a heavy oppression over the whole area. On the way home from a meeting, my husband, Neal, had said that if we hadn't known for sure that this was where God wanted us, we would have been on the first plane out of there.

We were now in bed, and the light was out. We were talking about the heavy atmosphere on the center—and how it might be affecting the young people. I asked, "I wonder if the kids here have dabbled in any witchcraft or played with ouiji boards?" Well, Neal had fallen asleep while I was talking. But there was a voice that answered me! As clearly as if it had been audible, I heard, "Sure they have. And I'm going to get your kids, too!"

The presence of evil in the room was like a heavy blanket. I immediately did what I knew to do. I rebuked the enemy in Jesus' name and told him to leave—only he didn't leave! That was a first for me. So I told him again to leave—but he didn't. So, I decided to sing praise songs because I knew that the enemy hates to hear praise to God. However, I couldn't open my mouth because I felt that if I did, the evil spirit would come in through my mouth.

Now I knew in my head that that wasn't possible. But the thought was so strong—even though it was against what I believed to be true—that I didn't open my mouth. So, I began humming instead. I hummed praise songs for about ten minutes. And the evil presence was gone!

Unexplainable footsteps in the hall of the group house where we lived, apparitions—people seeing spirits materialize, a heavy awareness of evil—Yes! He can be overt in his hassles. Those experiences are easier to recognize and therefore, easier to deal with. However, to a far greater extent, he uses the more subtle, wear-you-out, tear-you-down, rob-you-of-your-joy approach. Too often we do not recognize them.

Without giving "paranoid" attention to the enemy, it is important to know, to discern and be aware of his tactics on a day-to-day basis. One of the major ways we Christians get attacked is through our relationships—especially with the people closest to us—our spouses, roommates, children, parents. He wants to destroy our witness and rob us of our fellowship. Jesus said, "By this shall all men know that ye are my disciples, if ye have love one to another." John 13:35 And satan knows that!

Chapter by chapter, through this study, I will share with you some practical insights from my experiences. But you must understand that they are *my* experiences (or those of friends). The more important thing for you to do as you read through these sections is to try to identify these types of experiences with the ones you go through. I would like you to keep four questions in your mind:

1) Has this (or something very similar) ever happened to me?

2) How soon into the situation did I recognize

the influence of the enemy?
3) How did I respond?
4) Could I have responded in a better way? If so, how?

I would encourage you even to write out the answers to these questions—particularly when you recognize recurring situations. It has been said many times that being aware of a problem is the first step towards resolving it. As you are giving your attention to this study and recording the answers to the questions I suggested, you will be getting a clearer picture of your problem areas.

You will be halfway to the solution. But what is involved in the other half? For we do want to live in the solutions God has provided for us. And that is the starting point: Our solutions are found in our trust and dependence upon God. He is sovereign. He is in control. He knows the end from the beginning and how everything in between "...will work out for good for those who love God and are called according to His purposes." That is where we usually stop. It is important to realize that the continuation of that thought is in the next verse. The "good" is that we "be conformed to the image of His Son." Romans 8:28-29 That is God's design and purpose.

While we were in South America, Paul, a friend of ours, was called to a tribal village. Everyone knew what the problem was: A witch doctor had placed a curse on a man named Juan, and he was dying. Otherwise a healthy person, he was now losing strength...and dying. The fact that the community was aware of the problem brought them halfway to the solution.

A group of Christians in the community asked Paul to come. He, along with others, began to pray. The curse was broken, and the man recovered instantly. Just as quickly another problem presented itself: the symptoms that Juan had displayed were now showing themselves in Paul! They realized that prayer for protection should have been made first. Before they prayed for Paul they asked for protection for themselves. The symptoms immediately stopped in Paul, and did not recur in any of the others.

When the hassles of satan are written in story form and we are able in a moment to read from the beginning to the end, it is a lot easier to recognize them than when we are going through the situation. A missionary family lived under a spiritual assault that no one seemed to recognize. It wasn't until fifteen years later that spiritual insight was given. As soon as the problem was known (first step to the solution), those of the family who prayed the prayer to break the power of satan found a new freedom to start walking in. Those who didn't, continued to struggle without victory.

The problem and the solution: The source of the problem can always be traced back to satan, the enemy of our souls. Jesus said of the devil, "He is a liar, and the father of lies." John 8:44 But it is important to sort through his methods and our vulnerability to them and learn to identify the source of the problem.

The solution, then, will always involve taking some action. Even such a basic command as "Stand still, and see the salvation of the Lord" (II Chronicles 20:14) is action to be taken. Sometimes standing still—or taking our hands off and trusting God to do it all—is the hardest. As you read through this study, you will recognize some of the most common types of spiritual attacks. Following each of them are practical Biblical solutions. Look for the problems that you identify within your life and then focus on the solutions.

There are three basic attitudes that are needed in every situation. Keep these key points in mind as you read about the specific situations:

1) *Know that God is in control.* Satan is allowed to do his destructiveness only within the bounds of God's control. Though satan has his purposes, God's purposes will be accomplished. A "favored" son was sold to the Egyptians by his brothers out of their feelings of envy and hatred toward him. Years later he was able to say to them, "You thought evil against me, but God meant it for good." Genesis 50:20 Even "the wrath of men shall praise You," the Psalmist declared. Psalm 76:10

2) *Learn to recognize the enemy.* Ask God for the gift of discernment of spirits so you will quickly recognize when the enemy is launching an attack. Learn his tactics. Be prepared to see trouble coming. Know what is going on. Be alert. Be on guard.

We all have established habits that just seem "natural" to us but leave us open for attack. When I am running late, due to leaving things to the last minute, it is an opportunity for him to instigate a crisis. Recognizing what is happening can help me respond in a godly way, instead of reacting in an ungodly manner.

3) *Keep your eyes focused on Jesus.* He is "the author (source) and finisher (goal) of our faith." Hebrews 12:2 "In all these things (tribulations, distress, persecution, famine, nakedness, peril or sword) we are more than conquerors through Him who loved us." Romans 8: 35,37 Another promise that should keep our eyes focused on Jesus: "Being confident of this very thing, that He who has begun a good work in you will bring it to completion at the day of His appearing." Philippians 1:6

2

SPIRITUAL WEAPONS

"The weapons of our warfare are...mighty through God."
II Corinthians 10:4

Our armor is secure. His truth abides in us. We are clothed in His righteousness. Our feet are ready to go over mountain and valley with His Gospel of Peace. He is our shield, for our faith is firmly placed in Him. He is our salvation. We are protected. The spiritual armor God has provided for us through Jesus Christ is able to withstand any attack of the enemy.

But are we ready for war? No. We are defensively prepared, but because we are to fight an offensive battle, we need some weapons. We would not dare take off any of our armor to use as a weapon. It would leave that part of our spiritual being open and vulnerable to the attack of the enemy.

The weapons of our warfare are numberless. Out of His boundless resources, "He has by His own action given us *everything* that is necessary for living the truly good life...." II Peter 1:3 Sometimes, to our surprise, these weapons are not what we would expect them to be. As God gave Gideon three rather unusual weapons to fight a secular war (See Judges 6 and 7), he may give us some unique weapons for spiritual warfare.

Consider the weapon given in Proverbs 15:1. When

a wrathful person is blasting us with every vile verbiage a wrathful person can express, the world teaches us to "fight fire with fire." So our natural (natural, that is, to our fallen, sinful nature) inclination is to begin railing back. However, the Word says "a *soft* answer" is the weapon that "will turn away that wrath."

Another Proverb (25:15) says that "*gentle* words will break the bones." Our mind thinks it would take a big hulk of a person to break bones! Not so in spiritual warfare. All that may be needed are "gentle words."

The consciences of those pious Pharisees was the weapon Jesus used when he said, "Let him who is without sin cast the first stone." John 8:7 As He wrote in the sand, I would not be surprised if He was listing the sins of the men from the oldest to the youngest. For "He knew all men. No one had to tell Him." John 2:24, 25

How's this for an unusual weapon? Another: Would you like your enemies to be at peace with you? Who wouldn't? Choose God's weapon: Make sure *your* ways please the Lord! See Proverbs 16:7. So, out of the abundant arsenal of heaven, God can equip us with weapons suited to any particular situation.

However, in this brief study, I would like us to look at (become familiar with, handle and use) the two main weapons Paul addresses in Ephesians 6:17-18: The Sword of the Spirit which is the Word of God, and prayer. As we prepare for battle, we need to develop a respect for the tools of war that will allow us to fight an offensive battle—without being offensive. Too many of us offend others too often, James 3:2 tells us. And that offense regularly comes from our improper use of the weapons of war. Let us therefore learn to use them correctly.

The Sword Of The Spirit, Which Is The Word Of God
As we hold the Bible in our hands, I trust we recognize

the awesome treasure that is there. I don't mean the leather and paper and ink, but the very heart of God which has been expressed in human language so that we may know and understand Him. We can read the Word with the assurance that it is Truth. When there is something we don't understand, the Word is not to be explained away. Instead, we must wait on the Lord for His illumination—whether we receive it today or maybe not until we are in Heaven.

The very first lesson to learn about this most powerful Weapon, the Word of God, is that it is the *Spirit's* Sword! "All Scripture," Paul assured Timothy, "is given by inspiration of God...." II Timothy 3:16 Regarding the prophetic passages, Peter (by inspiration of God) tells us, "...holy men of God spoke as they were moved by the *Holy Spirit.*" II Peter 1:21 I will belabor this point with one more Scripture, for I believe the proliferation of translations and the popularization of things Christian (e.g. "born again" may be referring to a true regeneration of a man's spirit or to a car that just got a rebuilt engine!) has produced a casual familiarity which often lacks reverence and respect for an awesome and holy God. On the Day of Pentecost, Peter quoted David, then said, "Men and brethren, this Scripture had to be fulfilled, which the *Holy Spirit* spoke by the mouth of David...." Acts 1:16 It is the Spirit's Sword! God's Word!

A second lesson to follow quickly on the heels of the first: He is the ammunition chooser and the guidance system. God is speaking in Isaiah 55:5-11: "For My thoughts are not your thoughts." That's a good place to start! We may think, "But, Lord, I used this very Scripture in an almost identical situation yesterday. And it worked! Why shouldn't I use it again today?"

He continues: "Neither are your ways My ways. For as the heavens are higher than the earth, so are My ways higher than your ways, and My thoughts than your thoughts." We do not know the hearts of men other than that they are "deceitful above all things and desperately wicked; who can know it?" Jeremiah 17:9 We must place our full confidence in Him to know the details of every specific situation.

He continues: "...*My* Word that goes forth out of *My* mouth shall not return unto *Me* void, but it shall accomplish that which *I* please, and it shall prosper in the things to which *I* sent it." Wow! God is saying that *He* will choose the Words (ammunition) and *He* will direct them to *His* target (guidance system). And they will accomplish *His* purposes!

Why must He be the ammunition chooser? As we flip through the pages of our Bible, our eyes catch familiar passages—promises, exhortations, assurances, commandments. Some may even be underlined or highlighted as we have chosen them to be particularly significant verses or passages. And we revel in them. We meditate on them. They become part of us. Unfortunately, as some people become familiar with the Word they begin thinking it is *their* sword! "I know what Scriptures to use in this situation," they think. And they pick up that Sword—it is very sharp—and they begin hacking away, bringing serious injury not to the enemy, but to the very one they were trying to help. Now it is going to take a lot of restoration by other people who are allowing the Holy Spirit to be the ammunition chooser in order to bring healing to that person. Or, more likely, the injured one will remain offended by the misuse of the Word. Solomon said, "A brother offended is harder to be won than a strong city." Proverbs 18:19

Why do we need a spiritual guidance system? The work of the Word of God in spiritual warfare is not some light, frivolous whitewashing over surface situations. The work of the Word is "quick and powerful—it is alive and active. It is sharp. It cuts more keenly than any two-edged sword. It strikes through to the place where the soul and spirit meet, to the innermost intimacies of a man's being. It exposes the very thoughts and motives of a man's heart." Hebrews 4:12

Scripture chosen and guided by the Holy Spirit gets down to where we really live. For example, it cuts out the root of bitterness rather than just dealing with a surface manifestation of that bitterness. See Acts 8:14-24. Nathan's "God-breathed" words, "Thou art the man!" to David brought a sincere, penitent change of heart. Not just, "Nathan, now that you know, please help me keep this covered up." See II Samuel 12 and Psalm 51.

As we pick up the Spirit's Sword and clasp our hand over the handle, feeling its balance, seeing the Light of Life reflect off its sharp blade, sensing the power of its thrust, readying ourselves for the heat of battle, we should always acknowledge that it is a very holy and significant battle we are entering. When we brandish the Sword, whether it is for a specific, "It is written...," thrust against the enemy, or Scripture that would prick the conscience of the non-Christian, or Words that would do delicate surgery in the heart of a Christian, it is truly a Holy War in which we are engaged.

Use The Word Against The Enemy
No better Biblical example of using the Sword of the Spirit as a weapon against the enemy could be given than that of our Lord Jesus Christ as recorded by Matthew. John the Baptist acknowledged Him as the Lamb of God who takes away the sins of the world. Jesus came up out of the waters of baptism. The Holy Spirit in the form of a dove rested upon His shoulder. A voice from Heaven like thunder said, "This is My beloved Son, in whom I am well pleased." Matthew 3:17

Then Jesus is led (Mark's Gospel says "driven") by the Holy Spirit into the wilderness. His public ministry

is about to begin. In three brief years His ultimate purpose in life will be accomplished. But now He is in the
wilderness being tempted by satan. He is fasting—no
food has passed through His lips for forty days and
nights. And when those days are ended, He feels hungry again. (Note: After several days of fasting, one loses
all sensation of hunger. But when one feels hungry
again, it indicates that death by starvation is close.)

It is then at this point that satan begins a trilogy of
temptations. He jeers, "*If* you are the Son of God, command that these stones become bread." In swift retaliation (though Jesus, fully human, knows that the hunger pangs He is now feeling mean that He is literally
starving to death), Jesus wields the Sword of the Spirit
with a specific, "It is written, 'Man shall not live by
bread alone, but by every word that proceeds out of the
mouth of God!'" Matthew 4:4, quoting Deuteronomy 8:3

In the context of this story we do not have evidence
that the Holy Spirit chose that passage for Him. However, by His own testimony elsewhere He said, "I say
nothing of Myself, but that which the Father has told
Me." John 8:28 So even Jesus, while here on earth, the
very Wisdom of God, the Living Incarnate Word, in
launching His offensive against satan did not just
think, "Hmmm! What would be a good Scripture to use
against him?" He depended upon God to be the ammunition chooser and the guidance system.

In his second attack, the tempter again taunts Jesus about His position, but adds Scripture to support
his temptation: "*If* you are the Son of God, cast Yourself
down: For it is written, 'He shall give His angels charge
concerning you; and in their hands they shall bear you
up, lest at any time you dash your foot against a
stone.'" Matthew 4:6, quoting Psalm 91:11-12 How dare the
enemy use the Word of God to attempt to support his
position. Yet he did! And he does—even today!

But again, using Words chosen by God and those Words being guided by Him, Jesus thrusts a death blow to that temptation: "It is *also* written, 'You must not tempt the Lord your God.'" Matthew 4:7, quoting Deuteronomy 6:16 Deuteronomy had been penned by Moses by the inspiration of the Holy Spirit.

Thus, when satan would use Scripture to support his temptations of us, we must be familiar with the Whole Counsel of God. It is the perspective of every Word of God that enables us to combat the enemy.

And to the tempter's third attack, Jesus rebukes him—"Be gone!"—and cuts short any contemplation of satan's temptation with a quick thrust of the Sword: "It is written, 'You must worship the Lord your God, and Him only must you serve.'" Matthew 4:10, quoting Deuteronomy 6:13

Then the devil left Jesus—"until his next opportunity." Luke 4:13 "And angels came and ministered to Him." Matthew 4:11

In our warfare against the enemy, not only do we want to have a specific "It is written" for the specific temptation he is apt to use, but we want that passage to be brief, so that the thrust can be quick and accurate. We do not want to spend undue time in lengthy conversation with him. The more quickly we're in and out of there, the better.

Let me illustrate: The thrust was a simple four-word statement. The speaker was Michael, the archangel. It is recorded in Jude 9. To catch the significance of this, however, let's fill in some background.

I believe Lucifer was one of the top three angels before he fell. If so, he, Michael and Gabriel were in a pretty close working relationship. They knew each other well. He might have even tried to persuade them to join him in his rebellion against God.

And then it happens. Lucifer, Star of the Morning,

Anointed Cherub, makes his move. He draws a third of
the angels of heaven with him in a revolt. Michael and
Gabriel are probably standing there and saying, "No!
Lucifer! No! Let God be God!" But in five rebellious assaults, he exercises his will against God. Therefore, he
is cut down to the ground. See Isaiah 14:12-14.

He is next seen in the Garden of Eden doing his destructive work, and all of mankind as well as the plant
and animal kingdom—the very earth itself—falls under
a curse. The world gets continually worse and worse
until all people are doing what is right in their own
eyes. And God destroys the earth with a flood, saving
only Noah and his family. But again, sin raises its ugly
head. Through the stories of Abram, Lot, Jacob, Esau,
Judah, Potiphar's wife, and even Moses, Aaron and Mir-
iam, we see the deceit and treachery of the enemy, and
mankind so often falling into his temptations.

And now Moses is dead on Mount Nebo. Michael
has been given the task of retrieving the body of Moses.
God has decided to bury his body in a valley in the land
of Moab so he cannot be found. But satan wants the
body, probably thinking that if he can bring it to the
children of Israel, they will enshrine and worship it.

So Michael has the body. And satan is trying to
snatch it away. They are fighting—contending—battling
it out! Now, think of all that Michael could have said in
truthful accusation against this once anointed cherub
who has wreaked such havoc in the earth. Yet, "He did
not dare to condemn him with mockery nor bring a single railing accusation against him, but simply said, 'The
Lord rebuke you!'" Jude 9 That's all! That's it! Four simple words did the job, for Scripture says, "No man
knows of his sepulchre even until today." Deuteronomy
34:6 We are not to give satan more time than he deserves. And all he deserves is a quick, sharp slash of
that two-edged Sword, "It is written...."

From whom did Michael take his cue? Probably from God, Himself. For, though recorded years later, we hear God using the same four words. The story is found in Zechariah 3. Joshua (not the one who followed Moses, but a High Priest) is standing before the angel of the Lord. God is about to do a great thing for Joshua. And satan is at his right hand to resist him. And the *Lord* says, "The Lord rebuke you!" Zechariah 3:2

Let's learn our lessons. If the Lord Himself uses quick, powerful, brief and accurate words to destroy the work of the enemy, how about us? May we have a stockpile of specific, "It is written's...!" that go to the heart of the matter, cutting him down to the ground.

Stockpile an Arsenal of Ammunition
Before we study how to wield His Sword with Christians and non-Christians, let's learn how to build a stockpile of useful "It is written's...." Jesus assured His disciples that the Holy Spirit would bring back to their remembrance those things that He had said to them. John 14:26 I believe that we can share in that assurance. See John 16:13; I John 2:20. But the Holy Spirit can't bring to our remembrance that which we have not studied. And since, in the heat of battle we do not have the time (nor probably the resources) to sit down and look for an effective, "It is written...," we need to build a cache of ammunition. We need to give the Holy Spirit an arsenal of artillery from which to choose.

If we go off to war with three favorite Scriptures, we might be able to get into the battle and be of some good. But pretty soon we are going to run into a situation that isn't covered by those three Scriptures. We need to know more of the Word of God. David said, "Your Word have I hid in my heart so that I might not sin against You." Psalm 119:11 And again, "In Your Law do I meditate both day and night." Psalm 1:2

By what process do we build this stockpile? By a process called meditation. Moses said we are to meditate in the morning when we get up, at night when we go to bed, as we are sitting around and while we are driving down the freeway. Wait a minute! They didn't know anything about freeways in those days. OK, the KJV says, "While you are walking by the way." Deuteronomy 6:6-7 Well, how many of us walk "by the way" today? I think we more often get from here to there on the freeway. So slip a cassette or CD of Scripture into your stereo system and begin the process of meditation.

The process of meditation involves several steps:

1) *Selecting the "It is written..." passage we will use.* Remember Joel? In the last chapter we left him in the closet, "hidden" under a pile of clothes. Remember also that our spirit is the candle of the Lord. Proverbs 20:27 As our spirit and the Lord are walking through the rooms of our soul and discussing one or another issue, we come to an area that we sense (or that He prompts us to recognize) needs some real work.

We open the closet door on which He is gently but insistently knocking. (For, though we are to "work out our own salvation with fear and trembling" it is "God who is working in us both to will and to do of His good pleasure." Philippians 2:12-13 And we talk about Joel.

Jesus knows our feelings about him. As God, He made those feelings; as Man, he experienced those feelings. Thus, "by virtue of His own suffering under temptation He is able to help those who are exposed to temptation." Hebrews 2:18; Also see Hebrews 4:15.

In our regular reading of the Word, then, we become sensitive to the Holy Spirit as He would choose to "neon-light" a particular "It is written..." for us to use against the enemy when he would dare to tempt us in that area. In this very personal time with the Holy Spirit, we ask Him to reveal to us what Scripture(s) He wants us to build into that stockpile of ammunition. It might be a verse, a paragraph, a chapter or Book.

2) *Understanding the specific "It is written..." passage chosen by the Holy Spirit.* Now we take that verse or passage and make it as personal as possible. We read it from many translations. We get the meaning of every word. We let them speak to us very personally. We study the cultural significance of the passage. We learn the symbolism if it is figurative language. We take out the "thee's and thou's" (all references to other people) and put in "I" and "me" and "my". We write the passage out in a new personal translation; not changing the content, of course, but in modern English that really speaks to our heart.

(I read and I teach from the King James translation and I like it. I've been in it a good number of years. It is very comfortable to me. However, some of the King James English just doesn't come through the way a more modern translation can. In developing my personal meditation translations, I usually use a mixture of King James, New King James, Phillips and the New Testament from 26 Translations. As you have been looking up the Scriptures in this study, you have probably noticed that many of them have been a paraphrase of my own rather than a direct translation. Yet, I trust you have also noted that in no case do I violate the context of Scripture.)

3) *Memorizing the personalized "It is written..." that is to become a part of our arsenal.* Using any number of memorization techniques, we need to get the passage clearly in our mind. We must think about it, remember the significance of each word and phrase, be able to recite the Scripture without struggling through it. However, the Bible does not say, "Your Word have I hid in my *mind* so that I won't sin against You." But the Word is to be hidden deep in our *heart!* See Psalm 119:11.

4) *Meditating on the specific "It is written..." that will be used by us in spiritual warfare.* Hiding His Word in our heart is accomplished through meditation. (We won't let satan's misuse of this word "scare" us away from this Biblical process.) The word meditate comes from the same root word as *ruminate* which is the technical term for a cow chewing her cud! And that's a good picture of meditating: "Chewing" on the Word—drawing all the nutritious, life-giving and life-sustaining "protein," "carbohydrates" and "enzymes" as we can—to develop the "innermost man." The nutrition goes into every cell of our spiritual being not at all unlike the action of physical food to our physical body.

With each new verse and paragraph and chapter, we are building our stockpile—that arsenal of spiritual ammunition to use in spiritual warfare—in our inward battle as well as in the battle for the lost.

Let me give a specific and personal illustration. In my "flesh," my tongue is every bit as vicious as James describes it. See James 3:2-12. After many personally painful and hurtful-to-others situations where my tongue wagged when it should have been dumb with silence, I began asking the Lord for help. I asked for a real concise "It is written...," for the tongue moves very quickly to destroy—even as a spark of fire. After some time, in the normal course of my Bible reading, I sensed that He was giving me Ephesians 4:29. (James gives a good description of how bad the tongue is, but he doesn't really say a lot about how to control it.)

Next, I began reading Ephesians 4:29 in a number of translations. That passage isn't too complicated. In fact, like most of His instruction, it is very simple—so simple that our "sophisticated" façades often miss the childlike relationship He desires us to enjoy with Him. I made it personal. Only five simple phrases—easy to memorize. But getting it deep in my heart that I might not sin against God took (is taking) a bit more doing. But now, more often than not, the Holy Spirit flashes that Scripture through my mind more quickly than I can say it out loud or read it. Like the keen two-edged Sword it is, it cuts off those thoughts from the enemy that would prompt me to use unkind words; second, it gives me good words instead; third, the words are suitable for the occasion; fourth, I focus on words that God can use; and fifth, they are words that will help other people. And there are the five phrases of Ephesians 4:29: "Let there be no more foul language, but good words instead; words suitable for the occasion, that God can use to help other people."

A critical lesson to learn as we are selecting our "It is written..." is to carefully study Scripture in its context so that we do not wield a sword of "half-scriptures." (The words "sword" and "scriptures" are intentionally left uncapitalized because "a text without a context is a pretext!" In other words, it is without value. Or worse, it becomes a distortion or perversion of Scripture, possibly leading many astray.)

Though I grew up in a Christian church, somehow I came to believe in phrases that suited a particular doctrine. One such "half-scripture" was, "Work out your own salvation with fear and trembling." Period. Exclamation mark! And so there was a lot of fear and trembling in my youthful relationship with God. Not until I was an adult and began reading my Bible more carefully did I come to know there was more to that thought, "...for it is God who is at work in you both to will and to do of His good pleasure." Philippians 2:12 *and* 13

Another example is Psalm 46:10. For years I "knew" it said, "Be still and know that I am God." Of course, it does. We have written songs with those words. We have beautiful plaques that inscribe it. But, again, as I came to understand the necessity to more carefully study the

Word of God, I saw that God has three things He wants us to know in that verse as we become still—as we quiet our souls—before Him: 1) I am God; 2) I will be exalted among the peoples; 3) I will be exalted in all the earth. It is a verse speaking of God's sovereignty—that He will be exalted among the peoples in all the earth.

Corollary to "half-scriptures" is the dangerous practice of out-of-context-scriptures. I work with a lot of pastors in the area of missions. We strongly encourage churches to work alongside of and with the nationals. There is no doubt that it is easier to go in and do your own thing, but Biblical models and historical record prove the former to be more effective in the long run. One particular pastor was struggling with that issue when he came upon a passage in Proverbs. It convinced him that he was not to work anymore with the nationals. It is found in Chapter 5:16-17, "Let thy fountains be dispersed abroad and rivers of water in the streets. Let them be only thine own, and not strangers with thee." From this passage, he determined to do his own thing in missions. It only takes a little reading before and after those verses to realize that this whole chapter is talking about loving your wife, not about missions!

Paul instructs Timothy (and thus, God instructs us): "Be diligent, concentrating on winning God's approval that you may emerge as a workman unashamed in rightly understanding and using the Word of Truth." II Timothy 2:15

Use The Word With Non-Christians
Having (and using) our growing stockpile of ammunition against the enemy, we also must be looking for an "It is written..." in each of our dealings with a non-Christian friend. As we are agonizing in intercessory prayer for him, "God, I know You must judge sin and unrighteousness, but hold off a little longer with Bill.

You know how I desire for him to become Your child. And Your Word says You want him as your child, as well." II Peter 3:9 (It is good to remind God of His Word. Many times men of Scripture did just that.)

In such a time of intercession for our friend, our natural inclination may be to look for a Scripture that will "really wake him up"—a real "hit-him-up-side-of-the-head" type! Something like the bumper sticker: "Get right or get left!" But in that quiet time with the Lord, He says, "No, I want you to deal kindly, deal gently. After all (and now He is reminding *us* of His Word), 'It is the goodness of the Lord that leads to repentance.'" Romans 2:4 And again, He chooses a weapon and ammunition for us that this world knows nothing about.

Let's look at some Biblical examples. Peter, in Acts 2:16, is given an audience of thousands of people. They have come from "every nation under the sun." They are in Jerusalem for the festival of Pentecost. Many of them are still here from Passover. Some are, no doubt, sightseeing—remembering when they were here two years before. "Oh, look!" someone says. "They've built a new taco stand!" OK! I don't know what they said. They were looking for excitement. And as they congregated around 120 followers of Christ, they found it! Somebody shouted, "Hey, they're all drunk with wine."

Peter hears that and capitalizes on it as he gets the crowd's attention. "These men are not drunk with wine as you suppose, after all, it is only nine o'clock in the morning." His audience, being Hebrew (or Jewish proselytes), knowing and loving God, know the Word. So Peter begins quoting Joel. He adds a few words of explanation. Then he's quoting Jesus. Then Joel again. Then David. A few words of his own. Then David again! Whew! This man Peter knows the Word. And the Holy Spirit is helping him, empowering him and guiding those words, for we read in verse 37: "Now when they heard this, they were pricked in their heart, and said, 'What must we do?'" Wow! 3,000 of them get saved!

The Sword of the Spirit with these God-fearing non-Christians has done its work. The work has taken place in their *heart*, not in their emotions. No one says, "Hey, man, that Peter is a right-on dude. A great speaker. I like that guy. He's got such a smooth way with words." Talk like that would indicate that they had been tantalized in their emotions. No one says, "Oh, this is a studied man; he certainly is well-versed in the Scriptures. I wonder what degrees he has." No, they haven't been affected in their minds. The Word of God has touched their *hearts*, causing them to ask, "What must we do?"

Stephen in Acts 7 finds a listening audience of non-Christians in the gathered Sanhedrin. Stephen, as opposed to Saul (who is also in the room), has not been trained at the feet of Gameliel. Yet he has so hidden God's Word in his heart that he just starts quoting passage after passage of Jewish history. Then verse 54 tells us the result: "They were cut to the *heart!*" Their consciences have been sensitized. The truth of his words, "You have betrayed and murdered the Just One" has hit the mark.

Now unfortunately, they don't say, "What must we do to be saved?" Instead, they stone him! So it isn't always going to happen when you rightly use God's Sword of the Spirit with non-Christians that you're going to have 3,000 trust in Christ as Savior. They might stone you—figuratively or literally! But it is still the Word of God—ammunition that the Holy Spirit chooses and guides to their hearts.

Without being too speculative, I believe that when Jesus appeared to Saul on the road to Damascus saying, "Isn't it hard to kick against the goads?" He was referring back to, and including all the struggles Saul had experienced since that day of Stephen's martyrdom. For on that day he had heard the message of salvation for Israel, but would not yield to it. It is interesting that in Acts 13, Paul gives an almost identical sermon as Stephen's. And the following Sabbath almost the whole city came out to hear the "eloquence of Paul?" No! That is not what Scripture says. That does not sound like God. Rather, "...they came to hear the *Word of God!*" Acts 13:44 When the Word of God is properly taught or preached, the focus will be on the Message, not on the messenger.

Paul instructs, "The keynote (the bottom line; the focus) of our conversation—our lifestyle—should not be nastiness or silliness or flippancy, but a sense of thanks to God." Ephesians 5:4

In Colossians 4:6, he says that in all our conversations we are to season our words with salt. Our very lifestyle, Jesus said, is to be salt that whets people's appetites for hearing more. Matthew 5:13 Then Peter says that once their appetites have been whetted, and they are coming to us with questions, we should have "a quiet and reverent answer for the reason of the hope that lies within us." I Peter 3:15

One day I was attending a backyard wedding reception. It had rained furiously for the previous several days, and rain was forecasted for this day. But the bride had so wanted the backyard reception, and we had been praying for a clear day.... Anyway, a non-Christian friend also came. In an attempt to whet his appetite for the things of the Lord, I told him we had prayed for this beautiful day. To my chagrin, in true New Age fashion, he turned to me and said, "Yes, *we* did bring this day into being, didn't we!" I realize that God isn't finished with him yet. But at the time it seemed to me that my words did nothing to whet his appetite for the things of the Lord! Rather, it gave him opportunity to espouse his current religion.

Let's look at two Biblical illustrations: We find that Jesus' dealings with those seriously seeking the Savior were very gentle. He didn't drop any "atomic bombs" on them. One is found in John 3: The seeker was a most highly respected teacher in Israel, a man named Nicodemus. For fear of the Jews, he asked Jesus for a midnight meeting. Jesus obliged. His very first words whetted Nic's appetite! And then came the questions. And couched in this discourse is the most-used salvation Scripture, "For God so loved the world...." Nicodemus remained a "secret" follower of Jesus (we presume) until His death. Then boldly, with Joseph of Arimathaea, he brought spices for the burial. See John 19:38-39.

A second illustration is found in John 4. We find Jesus in a whole different setting, for sure. He is among the Samaritans, the people Jews despised above all others. Yet, again, Jesus whets the woman's appetite by asking her for a drink of water. Even when she seeks answers to theological questions not germane to the issue (vs. 19-20), Jesus masterfully brings her back to her need for the Christ.

Model your dealings with those who are seriously seeking the Savior after the example of Christ. He spent more time talking with individuals than with crowds. (At least we have more Record of personal conversations.) Read and study these conversations. Let His Spirit guide you, giving you the "It is written's..." that will whet your friends' appetites so you can give them the "quiet and reverent answers" that will lead them to the Lord. See also II Timothy 2:24-26.

When you realize that your non-Christian friend doesn't know the Word or has decided to ignore or despise the Word, your words will have to be very well seasoned with "salt" to make him thirsty. Maybe you won't even quote Scripture to him, lest you "cast your pearls before swine." Matthew 7:6 Or, the Scripture God has given you may be couched in the vernacular, showing from current events how the Truth of the Word has always been there.

For example, the media declared with great hurrah that (at the government expense of several hundred thousand dollars) a study showed that when thieves were rehabilitated into jobs that required the constant use of their hands, they were less likely to go back to a life of robbery. You could say, "Yes, a fellow by the name of Paul knew that 2000 years ago. He wrote to some friends in the city of Ephesus and said, 'If you used to be a thief you must not only give up stealing, but you must learn to make an honest living with your hands.'" Ephesians 4:28

Or, if you're looking at a map showing the ocean currents—or in some way talking about ocean currents—you can say, "You know, the sea captain who discovered ocean currents got the idea when he was laying in a hospital bed. The nurse was reading to him some poetry of an ancient writer. The poet was talking about man's dominion over all the earth. He said, 'You have put all things under his feet: sheep, oxen...and everything which passes through *the paths of the sea.'* Psalm 8:7-8 The captain said, 'Read that again!' When he was well, he went out and discovered ocean currents."

No matter into what arena of conversation you venture (Government and taxes are a couple of good ones!), you can find a cultural bridge to draw your friend to the truth of the Word.

Use The Word With Christians
You are becoming familiar with your use of the Word against the enemy. You are using His "It is written..." as you try to lead your non-Christian friends to Christ. And now in your dealing with a Christian who is flirting with sin, you need God's wisdom. This friend may be

older in the Lord than you, yet blatantly "playing with fire." As you pray, you say, "Lord, this is my mentor, the one who brought me to You. How can I say anything to him?" And the Lord firmly assures you that you must rebuke him—in love, of course. You are to be His instrument of chastisement and He directs you to Scripture that clearly exposes his actions as sin. And He says, "Here is My 'It is written...' for you in this situation."

This same Sword of the Spirit, the Word of God now becomes a delicate surgical instrument. Solomon, in his wisdom wrote: "Open rebuke is better than secret love. Faithful are the wounds of a friend." Proverbs 27:5-6

James talks about the degeneration of sin in a Christian's life. Man's "flesh" gives a fertile womb for the alluring enticements of the world with which satan tempts him. When man's lusts (evil desires, passions) unite with the enticements of the world, sin is conceived. In those secret moments, hours, days or years of gestation, the "wicked imaginations" (Proverbs 6:18) grow and develop. And as suddenly as the birth pangs of labor hit, the evil passions and desires give birth to sin. And the degenerative spiral continues: When sin is fully matured, it ends in spiritual death. Just in case we did not take careful note of that, James adds, "Make no mistake about that, brothers of mine." James 1:14-16

We are dealing with "joint and marrow" stuff here. So any "open rebuke" we are going to use needs the careful choosing and guiding of the Holy Spirit. Paul instructed, "Brothers, if a man is overtaken in a fault, you who are spiritual, restore such a one in the spirit of meekness; considering yourself, *lest you also be tempted.*" Galatians 6:1

Again, let's go to the Master restorer of broken lives for our example. No one could have been in deeper agony of heart than Peter when the cock crowed! Here was

Peter, the big fisherman, with a personality equal to that hard profession. Considering earlier incidents in his life, we can see that he was not perfect. But Jesus was forming him and changing him into a fisher of men.

It is now the night of His betrayal. Peter has sworn that he will never deny the Lord. He has slept through three hours of Christ's agony. He has cut off the servant's ear. And now he is warming his hands in the courtyard. Once, twice, he denies association with his Master. The third time he curses and swears that he never even knew the Man! "Cock-a-doodle-doo!" And it's all over. His remorse is accompanied by bitter weeping.

Our first clue that Jesus is going to deal gently with him is in His words, "Go tell the disciples—*and Peter*—that I go before them into Galilee." Mark 16:7 And in that early morning light, along the shore of the Sea of Galilee, Jesus says, "Peter, do you love Me?"

"Yes, Lord you know that I am your friend." After such devastation, he couldn't bring himself to make so bold a statement of love.

A second time Jesus asks, "Peter, do you love Me?"

Again, "Yes Lord, You know that I am your friend."

And the third time Jesus asked, "Peter, are you My friend?"

Peter was grieved. "Yes Lord, you know everything. You know I am Your friend." John 21:15-17

I believe this trilogy of restoration (I am sure more words than just those recorded were spoken) parallels the triple denial. And we see that big fisherman go on in ministry unto the Lord.

You, too, can be His instruments of restoration for your Christian friends. A beautiful testimony I enjoy telling (It stills gives me "goose bumps" to tell it.) is of a young sailor:

A number of years ago I was one of twelve elders at

a church. On Sunday evening we would be at the altar to meet and minister among those who came forward. On one occasion, two Navy couples came to me. By their haircuts they were obviously new recruits. "What can we pray about?" I queried. One of the men said he would have to board ship the next morning, but he was scared to death of water. There was no way he was going to be able to walk up that gangplank. (Right at this point my "natural" inclination was to ask him, "Why in the world did you join the Navy?" Fortunately, it was also at this time that the Holy Spirit quickly brought to my memory His "It is written..." for the control of my tongue, Ephesians 4:29.) So, instead, I encouraged him to recall what might have caused such a fear of water. He readily began:

When I was ten years old, my extended family was at an outing at a lake. I had swum out alone, and too far. In trying to return to shore, I yelled out, but no one heard me. Panic and exhaustion overtook me. I sank. The bottom was a mucky mud that sucked on my feet rather than giving me some propulsion toward shore. I fought my way to the surface several times. Without an ounce of energy left, I went down again, thinking this is it—this is the last time. I have no more energy.

But this time my foot landed on a big rock. I kicked off that solid substance with just enough force to make it to shore. To seal the fear of this incident in my consciousness, the next month at the same lake, my cousin did drown.

How many times he had rehearsed that story in his mind, I do not know. But at this crisis moment, we went to prayer. The Lord brought to my mind a number of Scriptures referring to Himself as the Rock. I just quoted them in a prayer of thanksgiving. While we were still in prayer—the five of us holding hands in a circle—he began jumping up and down, up and down, shouting, "I'm free! I'm free!"

In yet another illustration, from the Word, we walk along with two disciples, returning to Emmaus. They had followed Jesus. They had been sure He was the Messiah. But now their hopes and dreams are shattered. Not only has He suffered the most brutal execution known to man, but someone has desecrated His grave and stolen His body.

Jesus comes alongside and walks with them. He doesn't strut around and say, "Hey, guys, look at me! Don't you know who I am?" He hides His identity from them. This is a point to be well-taken. Too often (once is too often), when we are going to share the Word with someone, it just comes out (in action or word): "Hey, you guys, notice me! I read through the Bible twice every year, and I've got a word from the Lord for you."

Not so our Lord. He does not reveal His identity to them. He encourages them to tell their whole story of sorrow and disappointment. Then He lets the Word of God do its work. Beginning with Moses, going the through the Psalms and continuing through the Prophets, He weaves the most phenomenal prophecy lesson ever taught! He stays for dinner. He breaks the bread.

After they realize Who He is and He disappears, what do they say to each other? "Didn't our *hearts* burn within us as He talked with us on the way?" Luke 24:13-35 That's what the Word of God, the Sword of the Spirit should do to your Christian friends after you leave. They should be able to say, "Wow! He shared the Word in such a way that my heart has come back alive. It is burning with the fire and power of the Holy Spirit."

The two disciples were alive! They ran the seven miles back to Jerusalem, shouting, "He's risen! He's risen! The Messiah is risen!" Now, the other disciples didn't believe them. But the witnesses had delivered the message of their hearts. As with Stephen (Acts 7) and these two disciples, your sharing may not always bring the positive results you desire. Yet, led by the Spirit, you still must share what He puts in your heart.

The Sword of the Spirit, the Word of God is the most powerful of weapons in our hands. We must recognize that it is His Sword. As we build a stockpile of ammunition, we will have specific, brief, quick, accurate "It is written's..." to use against the enemy at the Spirit's choosing and guidance. We will have words seasoned with salt for non-Christians who show no apparent interest in spiritual things. And quiet and reverent answers for non-Christians seriously seeking the Savior. For our dealings with Christians, we will have the most delicate of surgical instruments—aborting, if you will, that conceived sin. Or (to change the analogy), if it has spread like cancer, we must build up his immune system (help him build a stockpile of ammunition) to fight the sin at its root cause. Telling him to "stop lusting" is no more than trying to cut off a tumor. It doesn't give him victory over of the "disease" of sin.

Use The Word With Hypocrites
There is yet one category of people to consider—the hypocrite! Jesus was merciless with the hypocrites. He was obviously following the declaration of the Lord in Jeremiah 23:29, "Is not My Word as a fire? And like a hammer?" He certainly brought down His heavy, torch-like words on the fake—the play-actors. In Luke 13:32 He called Herod a fox! In Matthew 23, He blasted the scribes and Pharisees calling them, "Hypocrites, blind guides, fools, serpents, generation of vipers, whitewashed tombs, full of dead men's bones!" Matthew 23:13-33

Jesus made no apology. Nor should we—*if* we are sure we are speaking to a hypocrite! And there is the catch. It is not so easy to identify one. Many struggling Christians are wrongly labeled "hypocrite," but they are not. They are struggling Christians. So I am very hesitant to use the words of Jesus in Matthew 23—unless, of course, He clearly directs me to them.

Using the Sword of the Spirit, which is the Word of God, wisely in all situations is the number one goal for the Christian warrior.

*Praying Always With All Prayers And Supplications
In The Spirit*
The second of the two weapons Paul mentions in Ephesians 6 is prayer. Most of us are aware of the significance of prayer in God's global plan. We have powerful articles and books on the topic: *An Army of Intercessors; A Concert of Prayer; Seven Minutes with God; Mountain Movers; Praying the Four Ways Christ Taught; Power in Prayer; Destined for the Throne; Effective Prayer Life; Touch the World through Prayer; With Christ in the School of Prayer.*

What is the sum of their message? In the words of Augustine, "Without God, we cannot; but without us, God will not."

In His sovereignty, God has voluntarily linked Himself to human cooperation. He has inextricably bound Himself to the prayer of faith of His children. He merges His working with man's praying.

Though this is a deep mystery, it is clearly revealed in the Word and throughout history. Joshua's day in battle would have gone poorly without Moses' prayer. Exodus 17 Jacob's place in Israel's history would not have been the same without his wrestling with the angel of the Lord at Peniel. Genesis 32 The cross would have been intolerable without Gethsemane. Luke 22

The Spirit through James assures us that even today "the fervent prayers of a righteous person yield tre-
mendous power." James 5:16 Jesus taught us to go into
our closet, shut the door and pray to our Father in secret...." Matthew 6:6 Paul encourages us to "pray without
ceasing." I Thessalonians 5:17

And modern science is "researching" the efficacy of
prayer! In "double blind" tests, with the prayer warriors
in lead-lined rooms (so no "psychic energy" could escape), they are documenting decisive results of heal-
ings, leading them to conclude, "If comparable statisti-
cal results had been obtained through drugs, the news
would have made medical headlines." (It is exciting to
read news of this world's science "catching up" with the
Bible.)

As a missionary of the first century, Paul was continually calling on the churches for prayer support.
"Brethren, pray for us," he simply stated in I and II
Thessalonians and Hebrews. His appeal to the Christians in Rome seemed a bit more pressing, "I beseech
you, brethren...that you strive together with me in your
prayers to God for me." Romans 15:30 Paul assumed
Philemon was on his prayer support team. Philemon 22
To the church in Philippi, he stated his confidence that
what he was experiencing would turn out well because
of their prayers *and* the resources of the Spirit of Jesus
Christ (Philippians 1:19)—indicating again that insoluble
cooperation of God and man in prayer.

Paul Billheimer said, "In spite of all of her lamenta-
ble weaknesses, appalling failures and indefensible
shortcomings, the Church is the mightiest—the only—
force that is contesting satan's rule in human affairs!"
And that Church on her knees is the purifying and pre-
serving influence which has kept the fabric of all we call
civilization from total disintegration, decay and despair.

Samuel Chadwick said, "The one concern of the devil is to keep Christians from praying. He fears nothing from prayerless studies, prayerless work and prayerless religion. He laughs at our toil, mocks at our wisdom, but trembles when we pray!" Paul Billheimer, again: "Prayer is not begging God to do something He loathes to do. It is not overcoming God's reluctance to act. It is, rather, enforcing Christ's victory over satan." It is the effective, fervent communication with the Creator of the Universe—in line with His will—which controls the balance of power in this world.

Prayer transcends the dimensions of time and space and ushers us into the very throne room of God, worshipping, petitioning and interceding in that spiritual realm of His presence. The Psalmist says we are to approach His throne by entering into His gates with thanksgiving, by walking through His courts with praise, and by coming into His presence with singing. Psalm 100:4,2 The writer of Hebrews says we are (because of Christ our High Priest) "to come boldly to His throne of grace, that we may obtain mercy, and find grace to help in our time of need." Hebrews 4:16

Spiritual battles are won in prayer. The first and decisive battle in prayer is won when we decide *to* pray. Prayer is sometimes shouting *alleluia.* Psalm 150 It is sometimes telling God the details of our *needs.* Philippians 4:6 It is sometimes laboring in unutterable groans of *intercession.* Romans 8:26

Prayer is the weapon of our warfare that can be utilized no matter where we are or in what circumstances. It can be as quick and brief as "God!" when that out-of-control car is hitting us on the freeway. Or it can be a continual spirit-relationship that we enjoy with the Father. For though our lives are lived on a conscious level within this physical world, we also are alive spiritually and can be in union with our Father by the simple acknowledgement that God is.

A Model Prayer

Jo Shetler had completed the translation of the Balangao New Testament. A flourishing church had been established. She was now called back to the Philippines to be a speaker at the Balangao Bible Conference. Her subject was prayer.

She said that her prayer life had consisted of "...all we ask God to do, such as heal our sicknesses, provide money to put children through school, give the ability to learn a language, translate Scripture and interact well with people.

"Then I decided to pray the prayers of Paul, David, and others in the Bible. I copied them out and started in. Wow, did I ever get a surprise! Those people weren't asking God for the same things I was! These 'model prayers' from Scripture seemed to center more directly on God and His program, rather than on people and their plans."

Read all the articles on prayer, if you will. Read all the books about prayer, if you must, but when you are done, *read, study and pray* the prayers of the Bible!

For example, let's go back to the issue of the tongue! I have admitted I have a problem with mine! (James said we all do!) Do you remember the Ephesians 4:29 "It is written..." God has given me? Well, I also—often—pray the prayer of Psalm 39.

Now, Record has it that David did not always achieve this level of control as Psalm 41:5 would indicate. (He had trouble with his tongue, also!) Psalm 39, however, is clearly a model prayer. In this situation he did it right: The wicked were before him. We do not know what they were saying, but by David's reaction it must have been intense. "My sorrow was stirred; my heart was hot within me; while I was musing, the fire burned. But I had determined that I would not sin with my tongue; I will keep my mouth bridled. I was dumb with silence. I held my peace—even from saying good words. But after they were gone, I opened my mouth and spoke." At this point, a very human tendency would be to yell at somebody—spouse, friend, neighbor, roommate. Or, kick the cat, slam the door, dent the fender. But in this model prayer, David addresses the Lord. So he's going to pray. Does he then blast his enemies to the Lord? "Lord, you were there. Why didn't you strike them dead? Why didn't you confound their speech? Why did You keep me quiet?" (For verse 9 says it was the Lord who kept his mouth shut.) No! to all of this. Rather, he says, "Lord, teach *me* to know *my* end, the measure of *my* days and how weak *I* am." (v. 4) And the prayer goes on to the end of the chapter. There is a powerful lesson for us in this prayer on the control of our tongue. Read it. Study it. Pray it.

We find in David's prayer of penitence in Psalm 51 a beautiful restoration. Though adultery and murder might not be the sins that have broken our relationship with God and man, when we find ourself caught in sin and we need to be forgiven that the joy of His salvation may be full in our lives again, this prayer might provide a model for us.

The Psalms are full of prayers of adoration and praise and thanksgiving and exultation. They form excellent models for us, living in a world with so little good news.

Prayers of confession are critical to all other prayer, for, the Lord's "ear is not heavy, that He cannot hear. But it is your iniquities that have caused the separation between you and your God, and your sins have made Him hide His face from you, that He will not hear." Isaiah 59:1-2 A prayer of confession may be as brief and simple as, "God, be merciful to me—a sinner." Luke 18:13 Or, it may be modeled after Nehemiah's prayer of confession for Israel. See Nehemiah 1:4-11.

An excellent model prayer of intercession is Paul's prayer in Colossians 1:9-13. He is praying for a group of Christians whom he had never even met. He had only heard of them from Epaphras who is now in prison with him, but who is "always striving fervently for you in his prayers as well." Colossians 4:12 When you study this prayer, look for the eight points of intercession. And use them as a model when praying for your friends. You may be amazed at how they focus on God and how we fit into His plans rather than "me and what my God can do for me!"

Solomon's prayer of personal petition in I Kings 3 is a "mind-blower." His prayer definitely "pleased the Lord." He could have asked for anything in all the world. But he asks for an understanding heart. And God answers him, "Because you didn't ask for a long life, nor personal riches, nor death to your enemies, but for a wise and understanding heart, I am going to do according to your word. And I will also give you what you didn't ask for—both riches and honor!" I Kings 3:10-12 James emphasizes this principle in the negative: "You ask and don't receive because you ask amiss, that you may consume it on your lusts." James 4:3

In our prayers of petition, do we ask for the communion and fellowship expressed in Psalm 42:1: "As the heart pants for the water brook so my soul longs for You, O God?" Or do we ask Him for the glittering trinkets of life? Do we ask Him to search our hearts as in Psalm 139:23-24? "Search me, O God, and know my heart: try me, and know my thoughts. And see if there be any wicked way in me." Or do we ask Him to look the other way when we take a break today. When we come boldly into His throne room of grace, do we ask for "mercy and grace in our time of need." Hebrews 4:16 Or do we ask Him to keep problems away from us?

Prayer is easy to talk about. Like motherhood, everybody believes in it. Books and articles and seminars abound on the subject. And there can be a lot learned by such studies. There is value in coming to understand to a greater measure the breadth and depth of our communication with God.

However, for all of our learning—whether our words are "right," our physical position is "right," our tone of voice is "right," what all we include in our prayer is "right"—the irreducible element is, "Is our heart 'right' with God?" Scripture says, "If I regard iniquity in my heart, the Lord will not hear me." Psalm 66:18

Our hearts being "right," then, before the Lord, we have even this promise: "The Spirit...helps us in our present limitations. For example, we do not know how to pray as we should, but His Spirit within us is actually making intercession for us in those agonizing groanings which cannot find words. And God who knows the heart's secrets understands, of course, the Spirit's intention, for He intercedes according to the will of God." Romans 8:26-27

Therefore, prayer is not theory; prayer is action. It may seem like a mere play on words, but when the disciples asked, "Lord, teach us *to* pray," Jesus did not answer with a discourse on prayer theory, but said, "After this manner, therefore *pray...*" Luke 11:2 And He gave us a model prayer.

Though the Lord's Prayer (really the disciple's prayer) is often prayed or sung verbatim, my encouragement is for us to use this prayer, and *all* the prayers of the Bible as patterns of prayer rather than rote, word-for-word recitations.

When we say, "Our Father...," we can relish in the awesome family plan He established: That out of every kindred, tongue, tribe and people we have brothers and sisters. We can meditate on the mind-boggling concept that God in Christ Jesus became (and is) our Elder Brother. We can appreciate the fact that our Father is perfect in wisdom and understanding—that God is love. We can marvel at the creativity of our Father's universe.

We might even find ourselves spending a whole hour in fellowship with Him without ever getting beyond that first phrase. You can see, I trust, that this is an activity far beyond the scope of printed prayers to read. Prayer is the dynamic communication link with God!

In this brief study we have considered a number of types of prayers: Praise, personal petition, confession, intercession, worship, thanksgiving, and penitence. I would like us to look at two more thoughts which speak of an intensity in prayer: Wrestling with God and In-the-Gap Praying.

Wrestling with God
Many of the model prayers of the Bible indicate a fervor that would suggest that the people really meant business with God. This level of prayer can give way to much theological debate. However, I intend to stick to the Word with illustrations from the lives of four people.

Jacob: His very name betrays him. Supplanter, cheat, conniver. And he had certainly lived up to it! And now he has devised another plot, this time to appease his brother from whom he has stolen the birthright. All of his servants and livestock and wives and children have been sent ahead with their instructions. Jacob is alone. And he wrestles in prayer with a Man until daybreak. He ends up with a hip joint out of place. But victory in prayer is his. His name is now Israel: Prince of God. See Genesis 32.

Hannah: Childless. Not a good thing for a wife in those days. And the adversary also provoked her mercilessly. She fretted, she was in bitterness of soul and she wept uncontrollably. She went to the temple to pray. So intense was her prayer that her lips moved but no sounds came. To Eli she confessed, "I am a woman of a sorrowful spirit. I have poured out my soul to the Lord." But victory in prayer was hers. She gave birth to Samuel. See I Samuel 1.

Elijah: Quite a story! Under King Ahab and Queen Jezebel the nation of Israel had forsaken the commandments of the Lord and is now following Baalim. At this point Elijah says to Ahab, "Let's have a showdown!" Thus, all of Israel climbs Mount Carmel. Elijah throws down the gauntlet: "How long will you halt between two opinions? If the Lord be God, follow Him; but if Baal, then follow him." You know the story: Two altars. The 450 prophets of Baal pray first—from morning til noon. At noon Elijah mocks them. "Cry louder! Maybe he's meditating or going to the bathroom. Or maybe he's on a journey. Or sleeping!" They cry until evening, cutting themselves. No answer.

The altar of the Lord is repaired. The sacrifice is laid on it. Water drenches the bullock and the wood and fills the trench around the altar. And at the time of the evening sacrifice, Elijah prays: "Lord, God of Abraham, Isaac and of Israel, let it be known this day that You are God...Hear me, O Lord, hear me...." Then victory in prayer is his. The fire of the Lord falls. See I Kings 18:17-40.

What a powerful answer to prayer. Yet it is interesting that the next day God did not answer Elijah's prayer after the manner of his request, "Lord, let me die," he requested, "for I am no better than my fathers." See I Kings 19:4.

Jesus: His hour had come and He knew it. "My soul is exceedingly sorrowful, even unto death." And in those terrifying three hours, the most critical battle of the ages raged as all of Jesus' humanness rose up to

shout, "No! Father, there's got to be another way to re-
deem man back to You. I can't drink this cup. It is too
bitter." We don't know all that was said in that time. We
do know that after one hour He had wrestled His will
into submission to the Father. Yet, it rose up in a second, and third hour. So great was the physical, emotional, mental and spiritual trauma that He suffered
hematidrosis, also called the bloody sweat. Under such
duress as Jesus experienced in His time of prayer, the
capillaries in His forehead burst. And the blood came
out through the sweat glands. But victory in prayer was
His. He paid the price for our salvation on Calvary. See
Luke 22:39-46.

In each of these four illustrations from Scripture, it
is obvious that a level of intensity was expressed that
communicated to God (and should communicate to us)
a seriousness of purpose unparalleled in normal conversation. May our fervor for righteousness be so expressed as we wrestle in prayer with God.

In-the-Gap Praying
In-the-gap praying also speaks of an intensity of prayer
that is awesome to consider. "And I sought for a man
among them that should make up the hedge, and stand
in the gap before me for the land, that I should not destroy it: but I found none." Ezekiel 22:30

The "gap" mentioned in Ezekiel has been used to express a number of concepts. Prophetically, Jesus came
to bridge the chasm between God and man. As an appeal for people to go to the mission fields of the world,
filling in the "gap" with front-line workers is critical.
There are cultural "gaps" between the missionary and
the people group he is trying to reach. And training is
good to help fill in the gaps.

But in the context of Ezekiel, standing "in the gap"
speaks directly of the role of an intercessor—one who

forms a barrier (a hedge) between God (who is speaking) and "the land that I should not destroy it." Stop! Back up! Run that through again. Is that really what God is saying? Yes! He is angry. In His justice, He is saying, "I have had enough! I am going to destroy the land (the people of the land). But "I am a God who is longsuffering and kind, patient and easy to be entreated." Psalm 103:8 I am looking for someone to hold Me back—to slow Me down—to give the people a little more time to repent. But I have found none!

"I looked for a man..." Abraham became that man: "God, will you not spare the city for fifty righteous men? Forty-five? Forty? Thirty? Twenty? Ten? Far be it from Thee to slay the righteous with the wicked...Shall not the Judge of all the earth do right?" See Genesis 18. Those are powerful words for one who had "taken upon himself to speak to the Lord, seeing he was but dust and ashes!" He stood in the gap.

"I looked for a man..." Moses became that man: "And Moses besought the face of the Lord his God, and said, 'Lord, why does Your wrath wax hot against Your people?" Just four verses earlier, in His anger God had called them *Moses'* people! After two more verses of intercession, "the Lord repented of the evil which He thought to do unto *His* people." Exodus 32:11-14

Another time Moses even more boldly said: "Yet now, if you will forgive their sin...; and if not, blot me, I pray Thee, out of Your book which You have written!" Exodus 32:32 Read Deuteronomy Chapter 9 for a review of the many times Moses stood in the gap for God's people. The Psalmist also remembered Moses as a man who "stood before Him in the breach to turn away His wrath, lest He should destroy them." Psalm 106:23 Moses was definitely an "in-the-gap" intercessor!

"I looked for a man..." Aaron became that man. Numbers 16 Nehemiah became that man. Nehemiah (The whole

book!) Jesus became that Man. John 17 Paul became that man. Romans 9 Others through the generations of time have become that man, that woman who stood in the gap.

And today Scripture still declares the voice of God— which perhaps is speaking to us, "I am looking for *you* to make up the hedge, to stand in the gap!"

Two excellent novels, *This Present Darkness* and *Piercing the Darkness* by Frank Peretti, give thought-provoking possibilities to the subtleties of this war. They give a glimpse of what might be going on behind the scenes.

But let's look into the book of Job. Here we have been given some Scriptural insight into the spiritual realm from which this war emanates and the hedge of protection we are talking about. Job had arrived! He was rich. He was famous. He was perfect and upright. He feared God and hated evil. This is what the world could see.

But behind the scenes of this visible world is the invisible, yet real world. And satan sees the hedge complete—not only around Job, but "about his house, and about all that he has on every side." See Job 1:1-10.

The "accuser of the brethren, day and night" (Revelation 12:10) is "going to and fro in the earth, and is walking up and down in it seeking whom he may devour." I Peter 5:8 When he sees the breach in the hedge, the broken-down walls, the secret thoughts of sin, he enters the minds of men with ease. When he sees the hedge complete, he presents himself before God and taunts, "Does 'Job' (Put your name in here.) reverently fear You for nothing?"

A battle is raging for the souls of mankind. Many are on the fields of battle, warning men and women of impending doom. The anger of the Lord is kindled against the filthy unrighteousness in every avenue of life: "I must destroy the earth." But He "is not willing that any perish, but that all come to repentance." II Peter 3:9 Will we step forward? Will we with lifted hands hold back His anger and intercede for the lost of the world, saying, "God, be patient a little longer."

Yes, the prayers spoken of in the Word of God are a bit more rigorous than "Now I lay me down to sleep...!" Indeed, God has said that nothing lies beyond the potential of prayer. See John 14:13-14.

Lord, teach us *to* pray!

This has not been an exhaustive study on the two main weapons of our warfare. But it has "covered some ground." In summary, therefore, I would say:

1) The Sword of the Spirit, which is the Word of God, is a powerful weapon, not to be reckoned with lightly. Read it. Study it. Meditate on it. Let all of the spiritual nutrition of its life-giving words strengthen you for battle. And then let it be in your hand the mighty Weapon it is as you go out to fight for right, allowing the Holy Spirit to be the ammunition chooser and the guidance system.

2) Prayer, for all that can be written about it, is simply communication with God. Because the dialogues we have with people are so often tainted with our human limitations, reading, studying and using the prayers of the Bible as models for our communication with God will more readily put us in touch with His world. Whether we use a one-word cry for help or enjoy a continual spirit-dialogue with our Maker, His lines are never busy or out of service. And there is never a charge.

| PRACTICAL INSIGHTS |

WHEN SATAN HASSLES CHRISTIANS

I have observed that many of satan's strongest attacks come at particular times. As we look at these experiences you will recognize that they are times when we are especially vulnerable. Think of the times when you are especially vulnerable.

Problem The enemy tries to hassle me in the days or hours preceding any kind of ministry, such as teaching or counseling. And most likely the attack will be on the very point on which I am planning to minister.

Maybe you have been asked to organize an outreach, or you are going to lead a group study, or you are planning to share your testimony with your new neighbor. In each of these situations, it is the enemy's determined purpose to stop you. He will do whatever is necessary to: 1) bring feelings of condemnation on you; 2) to cause you to feel like a failure; 3) to believe you are inadequate for the task; or 4) just plain get you upset! How about an unjustified speeding ticket as you are on your way to teach about "all civil authority is established by God?" Or, you are "yelling" at the kids just as your new neighbor is at your door? You *had* planned to share with her about the peace Jesus brings.

Solution Be prepared. Pray ahead of time for the protection needed to prevent you from falling prey to his attacks. Learn to recognize what is happening at the very starting point of a situation going wrong, and that will diffuse the power of what is happening. Refuse to get caught in such a snare.

This type of attack was so consistent with me when I started teaching. Whatever the subject I was preparing to teach, I would be attacked in that very area the preceding week. And I fell for it week after week after week! I would be so disgusted with myself for blindly falling for it again and again. Finally, after it had happened enough times and I had experienced enough pain, I began to recognize what was going on. Then I would try to remember to pray for protection and awareness at the beginning of the preparation time and to be on my spiritual guard, so I would not fall for his tricks.

Allow time to be quiet before the Lord as a critical part of your preparation to minister. Find that quiet time early in your preparation.

Problem The enemy attempts to "rob" me after a spiritual "high"; a personal victory over a temptation; a valuable lesson learned; a refreshing weekend retreat; a particularly meaningful time with my husband; after leading a person to the Lord; having taught a challenging class or seminar—a time when I am feeling real good within myself!

(Are you recognizing yourself in any of these situations?)

Solution Be on guard. After any kind of victory it is our natural tendency to relax because everything is so good. After all, we have just reached a spiritual mountain top. But the enemy is relentless in his attacks, and we are particularly vulnerable at those times of victory.

Jesus is our example: It must have been a real spiritual high for Him. He had lived in relative obscurity for 30 years. Then, John's strong declaration, "Behold the Lamb of God Who takes away the sins of the world.... I saw the Spirit descending from heaven like a dove, and He remained on Him." And His Father's voice from Heaven, "This is My beloved Son in Whom I am well pleased."

Then Jesus is driven into the desert by the Holy

Spirit to be tempted by the devil. He did not let His guard down. Using the Word, He drove off every attack of satan. See Matthew 3-4. Use the Word—be in the Word!

As you think about those times of victory—they are often a result of taking extra time in fellowship, prayer and the Word—take time to be quiet. Rather than concentrating on "Let your light so shine before men that they may see your good works...," focus on "...and glorify your Father Who is in heaven." Matthew 5:16

Problem The enemy takes advantage of me when I am sick or tired or pressured—under too much stress, over-committed, sleep-deprived or when I've left everything to the last minute!

Solution We need to take responsibility for ourselves. It is not spiritual to "burn out"—even to burn out for God! We must learn how to say "no" to everything that is not His will so we have enough of what it takes to do His will!

There are people who believe it is not spiritual to think about their own well-being. They may equate their body with the *flesh* of the Bible. For most of us, the weaker the condition we are in physically, the more vulnerable we are to attack and the less we can accomplish for God. We must take the responsibility to get enough sleep, enough exercise, to eat right—to live a balanced lifestyle. (Do you hear me talking to myself?)

Prevention is better than cure. It is quicker and easier to stay healthy than to regain health. But, if you get to that "burn out" stage—too tired, too run down, too..., then take the cure! Take a break; take a rest; get away. It is not selfish; it is necessary! "And Jesus said to them, 'Come away to the solitude of a quiet place and rest a while,' for there were so many people coming and going they had no time to even eat a meal." Mark 6:31

Problem The enemy preys on me when I am "alone." This aloneness could mean physically alone. An extreme case would be the example of a Bible translator out in a tribal village where there are no Christians—no one with whom to fellowship, no church to attend—really alone in a physical setting.

But we can also be "alone" in a crowd—alone emotionally, or spiritually withdrawn from the Body of Christ. Like the little lamb, a straggler always hanging out on the edge of the flock is easy prey for the wild animals. When we allow ourselves to be isolated, we are easy targets for the enemy's attack.

Solution To be alone in a physical setting where there is no opportunity for fellowship is very unusual. If we find ourselves in such a unique situation, we must think of creative ways to communicate with the outside world: Letters, short wave radio, music and Bible study tapes, e-mail! If those means are not available, God will sustain us, as we depend on Him, alone. See Philippians 4:19. Be sure to read it carefully in its context!

However, most of us have many opportunities for fellowship. Maybe it is not your personality to reach out to people or to initiate friendships. Maybe you are a very private person, or it is your nature to prefer to be alone a great deal of the time. But being without fellowship, is like being the straggling lamb on the edge of the flock. It is a very vulnerable position.

If you don't have anyone you can share with on a heart level, or pray with, ask God to bring someone into your life with whom you can have spiritual fellowship. At the same time take the initiative of reaching out to people and also be approachable yourself. Don't expect God to plop someone into your path who says, "I'm here to share with you." We need to work at relationships. Whether we like it or not, whether we are comfortable with it or not, whether it comes naturally or not—it is necessary. Solomon said, "A person who wants friends needs to be friendly." Proverbs 18:24

Building a relationship takes time and work. Patience in communication over a period of time will give you a strong friend with whom to relate. "Counsel in the heart of man is like deep waters, but a man of understanding will draw it out." Proverbs 20:5

Also, we need to be willing to take risks. Deep, accountable relationships always carry with them the risk of getting hurt. But it is worth the risk to have an open, honest relationship with a person who can admonish you—in love—as you listen to them. Equally, then, they can listen and receive admonishment from you—in love. "Faithful are the wounds of a friend." Proverbs 27:6

Another part of this solution is group fellowship. To be a participant in a group for social activities, mutual sharing, Bible study and prayer, protects you from that unsafe, vulnerable position of "straggler." It's called being part of His Body, and being part of the family of God.

Problem The enemy subtly attacks when I think I am "strong." Paul warned, "Take heed, you who think you stand, lest you fall." I Corinthians 10:12 Sometimes we think we are strong. Maybe we are even proud of being strong. So we think we can skip a few days of reading the Word or praying. "I can stand by myself! I don't need to be accountable to anybody! I can handle this situation on my own!" To have that attitude is to walk into a ready made trap!

Solution Humility must replace pride. Paul told the Christians at Ephesus (5:4) that the whole focus of their lifestyle should be with a sense of thanksgiving to God! When we realize that even our breath is under His control, there is no room for pride. A disciplined, reasonable, interesting, enjoyable, regular reading and studying of His Word will keep us spiritually fed. Regular two-way communication with God (prayer) will keep our spiritual fellowship with Him open and accountable.

But there is another area I want to mention here: sex. Many good men and women—strong, committed Christians—have been drawn into immoral relationships because they thought they were so strong that they just couldn't fall.

It takes very little time to cross from spiritual oneness to emotional oneness. And then just a bit longer to go from emotional oneness to a physical relationship. It can happen in a counseling session or even when two people are just praying alone together. And don't think this happens only in heterosexual situations.

The misuse of sex is one of satan's primary traps, and though he has used it generation after generation, many people remain naive and think they don't need to be on guard. We must realize that satan can drop an idea into anyone's head— anytime! There is no one above that trick of his. No one! We need to recognize the source of the idea when it comes, and rebuke him. Refuse to walk into his setup.

The solutions are so simple they are often overlooked: Don't counsel in a private place, such as your house or theirs. Get together where you can be "alone" in a crowd—a coffee shop or sitting in the back of a church after service. Pray in three's. As a general rule, men should counsel men, women counsel women. Don't make a practice of working and/or traveling in two's with the opposite sex unless, of course, you are married to that person!

Beyond these practical safeguards there may be a need to deal with issues on a heart level. We can probe the underlying causes for moral failure in this area—emotional deprivation, unhealed areas of childhood trauma, or maybe it just happened because they found themselves in a lonely isolated location when they were in need of affection. The point is, they never thought it could happen to them. They were not aware and thus were not on guard.

In the final analysis, it comes back to Scripture. Jesus said, "Blessed are the *meek....*" Matthew 5:5 Meekness is defined as "strength of character under control." Nehemiah encouraged the people, "The joy of the Lord is your strength." Nehemiah 8:10 There is only good when we deal with our strength in terms of meekness and the joy of the Lord. There is only bad when we think we stand (strong in our own strength), because then we are setup for a fall!

3

OUR ATTITUDE TOWARDS WAR

"...that we may please Him
who has chosen us to be soldiers."
II Timothy 2:4

The Bible is a marvelous book of figurative language. Analogies, metaphors and similes fill its pages. There are analogies of relationship: We are the Body of Christ; He is the Head. We are the Family of God; He is our Father and Christ is our Elder Brother. Individually, our body is the temple of the Holy Spirit. Collectively, we are the "living stones" in the Building of God; Jesus is the Chief Cornerstone. When we first come to Christ, we are babies needing the "milk" of the Word. As we mature, we eat the "meat" of the Word. But we will always remain the children of God. We are the Bride of Christ; He is the Bridegroom! (Now—as a man—I do have a bit of a problem with that analogy. I just can't picture myself as a "bride" to anyone! But I have confidence that He will work that whole thing out as we enjoy the marriage supper of the Lamb.) I am sure you can find more such analogies of relationship.

There are analogies of God's care for us: We are the sheep of His pasture. He makes us lie down by still waters. We are safe and secure in the palm of His hand. The Name of the Lord is a strong tower. We are as little chicks safe under His wings. Certainly you can think of others.

There are analogies of our service for Him: We are ambassadors for Christ, representing the Kingdom of God to those who are held captive in the kingdom of darkness. We are to go out among them as wise as serpents, as harmless as doves, and as sheep among wolves. We are harvesters in His fields. We are fishers of men. We are to be servants who after a long day in the fields come in and fix the master's meal, eat the left overs (if there are any) and then say, "I am your unprofitable servant; I have only done what I was supposed to." (I better give you the Scripture reference for that one! We don't hear it often. Luke 17:7-10) Then we are also to be a servant-leader, seeing things from God's perspective and then ministering unto people from that perspective. John 13:1-17 The analogies of our work for the Lord are wildly creative!

But there is another analogy yet to be mentioned. There is a theme that marches through the pages of Scripture that many wish to avoid. The hymns of the Church of past generations that spoke of this parallel are today selectively ignored. The new Scripture choruses do not often sing of this theme.

This issue does not make most Christians "feel" good; it does not fit within their "comfort zones." It does not allow them to pamper themselves. Some organizations lead young people out for a "summer of service" camouflaging this theme as a "bandwagon," painted in competitively bright colors. They might even encourage, "Oh, yes, we're going to have fun in the sun this summer. Be sure to bring your tanning cream along."

The theme is *war!* The analogy is that we are *Soldiers of the Cross.* The figurative language is "Put on the whole armor of God. Fight the good fight of faith. Through God we will do valiantly!" Instead of using gaudily decorated "bandwagons" our teams should be going out to fight the enemy in well-camouflaged tanks—in armored cars. Instead of tanning cream, they should be sure they are taking with them the Sword of the Spirit which is the Word of God.

As we pointed out in Chapter 2, Jude was wanting to write a "nice" letter—just talking about our common salvation (nothing inherently wrong with that, by the way). But the Spirit compelled him to exhort us to "earnestly contend (fight, grapple in hand-to-hand combat) for the faith." Jude 3

Within the Church of Jesus Christ at large, it often happens this way: A person comes to seek the ways of the Lord. You have whetted his appetite with the seasoning salt of your lifestyle. He has read you as a living epistle. Yes, he has seen that you have your problems. But somehow you also seem to have the answers to life's questions—or are content to not know everything. As he begins asking the questions, you use all the "warm fuzzy" analogies. You withhold anything to do with spiritual warfare. You don't tell him that as a Christian he might face greater conflict—experience more difficult struggles—than before he trusted in Christ as Savior. You don't tell him that when he believes in Christ as Savior, he is conscripted into the Army of God!

And you don't share these thoughts of war because you are afraid you might "lose" him. He might get scared and stay in the world. The whole business of spiritual warfare has become a very unpopular subject in the Church. Its unpopularity helps to form and perpetrate our attitudes of aversion to the subject. Our fear of turning them away prevents us from proposing so daring a prospect as going to war!

Further, our culture teaches us that we are a peace-loving people. We want to avoid war whenever possible.

If we are forced into secular war, we are there to *defend* the rights of this group or that nation. Even the excuse, "He started it; not me!" was formed in us at a very early age. You see, we just don't like war.

How does this, then, affect our attitude towards ourselves as soldiers? We will look at a number of categories that display a wrong attitude. Some may appear to be harmless; others will be seen as obviously destructive. Allow the Holy Spirit to question you on each to make sure satan is not messing with your mind.

The Volunteer

Scripture after Scripture tumbles through my mind that refutes the ever-popular concept of volunteer. But so strong is our cultural belief in "I am in charge of my life; I know my rights; don't mess with me!" that—cultural being that I am—I am struggling to write this section. I would rather not!

We are proud of our all-volunteer army in peacetime. But when the threat of war looms, "individual rights" might be violated. And we have the potential of a worse threat—that of an army going on strike or overthrowing the government!

The church has fallen into this pattern: "We need five 'volunteers' to work in the Sunday school." And week after week the leadership has to "beg" people to fill those positions. "It is interesting that when my church was suffering under Communistic persecution," a Slovakian pastor recently told me, "we had a commitment among the people that found every responsibility cared for. But now that we are free, we can't get anyone to work unless we pay them!"

The Body of Christ was not made to be supported by volunteers but by conscripted members. God intricately wove the Body of Christ together to function just like He made our physical body. See I Corinthians 12. When my body "decides" it is time to get up and move around, the control center in my brain doesn't ask for a "volunteer" sentry to check that all the "volunteer" nerves and muscles are present and ready for action. No! They are instantly and automatically ready to respond to the head's command. And if that body movement is a jog in the park, a swim in the pool or a particularly grueling tennis match, those nerves and muscles and sinews and sweat glands and heart will strain themselves to their maximum endurance. Other body systems will cooperate by slowing down (e.g. digestive system) during this time of vigorous activity.

Paul told the Christians at Ephesus that they "are His most finely crafted work of art, created in Christ Jesus, 'to sit back and wait for the rapture.'" No! That just doesn't sound like God! Still many "living epistles" read that way by their lifestyle. What did God, the Holy Spirit say? "...created in Christ Jesus to walk in those good deeds that He beforehand determined for us to do." Ephesians 2:10 We are to actively, automatically respond to the Head's commands to us.

This sounds more like God's Plan of the Ages and how I fit into it. It is much more Christ-like than the me-centered distortion of the Gospel that many walk in today. Fitting into His Plan is like Esther's answer to Morticai's question, "Who knows but for an hour such as this you have been called to the kingdom?" Her response was, "If I perish, I perish!" And she went in to the king. See Esther 4.

We are called to be servants, not called to offer service. A servant looks to His master's hand for direction and obeys it. Psalm 123:2 One who offers his services reserves the "right" to choose what, when, where and for how long he will engage in that activity. "Do you love Me?" Jesus asks. "Then feed My sheep." John 21:16 Again He said, "If you love Me you will keep My com-

mandments." John 14:15 Wherever we read of Jesus calling His true disciples (not just those looking for a sign),
it is assumed that they will follow. The tone of response
seems to center on the degree of willing obedience, not,
"Should I or shouldn't I 'volunteer!'" See Matthew 4:19-22;
8:19-22; 9:9; 16:24; 19:16-22 for starters! And Paul appealed
that the only reasonable response to the mercies of God
was to give our entire being to Him as a living sacrifice.
See Romans 12:1.

The Mercenary

"What's in it for me?" In a culture wallowing in self-
indulgence, it is not surprising to find those with this
attitude towards war and themselves as a soldier. "Are
we having fun yet?" "Try it, you might like it!" "If it feels
good, do it!"

Why do I pamper myself? Because I'm worth it! Why
do I deserve a break today? Because I believe in me!
And there is the automobile ad that tells us, "It just
feels right!" Subtle and not-so-subtle media input has
our culture focused on "*me!*" And the occult religious
influences permeating our society dawn and brighten
and explode into the "brilliance" of "I am god!"

"What's in it for me?" is the guiding question. A
good number of years ago when I was principal of a
Christian school, I interviewed a woman for a teaching
position. How she had gotten through all the prelimi-
nary steps, I don't know. But within minutes of our introduction, I could see that this lady wasn't even a
Christian. In trying to kindly ease ourselves out of this
interview, I said that we had a very thorough Bible cur-
riculum. "Oh, that's okay. Just tell me what you want
me to teach. I'll do it!" My response had to become a bit
more firm as I saw in front of me a person who would
teach anything—whether she believed it or not—just to
have the job.

Mercenaries hire on to war for the wages or excitement or the thrill of it. The drama, the intrigue, the danger, the adrenalin rush...! What's in it for me? In our fun-crazed culture, we might even get involved in the Lord's work just for the fun we will have. "Everybody's doing it. Yeah, let's go to the beach today. Pass out tracts. The whole gang is going. It'll be a lot of fun!" Is this a new tactic of the enemy? A new attitude towards war? No. At least two thousand years ago, a pair of brothers with their ambitious mother devised a plan. It was a plan to secure position of high honor in Christ's Kingdom. It was obvious they were not going to make it as fishermen—spending all their time following this Nazarene. There was never going to be the sign, "Zebedee & Sons" over her husband's fish market. Therefore, they came to Jesus with their request, "Let us sit one on either side of You in your Kingdom! We were some of your first followers, Jesus. Surely, we are deserving of these places of honor. This 'little thing' is all we want out of following You."

Jesus displayed such love as He chided them, "Can you drink the cup of which I must drink?"

Whatever their growing feelings of embarrassment might have been under the gaze of not only Jesus, but the other disciples who were listening to this discourse, they pushed ahead, "Sure we can!"

"Yes, you will," Jesus prophesied, "but it is still not for Me to assign those seats—they are reserved for whom they are intended." See Mark 10:35-41.

There is no room for mercenaries in the Army of God!

The Ill-Prepared

If ever there was a group of guys ill-prepared for battle, it must have been the seven sons of Sceva! From a Jewish high-priestly family, exorcists they were—no doubt with some measure of success. But when they heard of this Jew named Paul, they perhaps thought to improve on their method, for "evil spirits went out of all who were possessed" when Paul prayed. The magical name is "Jesus," they discovered. But obviously not knowing Him personally, the best they could say was, "We command you evil spirits to come out in the Name of Jesus whom Paul preaches!"

They're ready to try it; sounds good. It works for Paul. They enter the house of one possessed of an evil spirit. Whether they laid hands on the man or not is not known, but here it is: "We adjure you in the Name of Jesus whom Paul preaches!" The evil spirit looks at them quizzically and answers them, "Jesus I know, and Paul I know; but who in the world are you?" ("Whoops! Brothers, this doesn't look like it is working!") The man in whom the evil spirit was leaped on them and overpowered them... (Some manuscripts say "two of them;" some say "all of them." But don't let this "flesh and blood" battle deter you from the point of the story!) ...and treated them with such violence that they fled out of the house wounded and naked."

"Hey, guys! What did he say? 'Jesus I know! Paul I know! But who are you?' Doesn't he know we are the seven sons of a Jewish Chief Priest?" As they bound up their wounds, they wondered what they had done wrong!

In the heat of battle we cannot minister in the Name of Jesus whom somebody else preaches. All who enter the arena of spiritual warfare must have a personal relationship with Jesus Christ. We cannot minister in the name of our pastor. We cannot minister in the name of our church. We cannot minister in the name of this or that organization. We cannot minister in the name of this or that evangelistic tool or teaching method. We minister only in the Name of our Lord Jesus Christ because of our personal, intimate relationship with Him. Anything less will have us running "naked and wounded" from the battle. See Acts 19:13-16.

Whatever message—however simple or extensive— that we take to the battlefield must first be worked deep into our own heart. There is no room for the ill-prepared in the Army of God! As has been said before, "No! We do not need to be theological geniuses before we go to battle." But that which we plan to share must be real in our own personal life.

The Unfaithful Servant
Jesus illustrates a fourth category of warrior with an attitude problem. Using another analogy, He calls him an unfaithful servant. Luke 12:47 tells us that this person knew the master's will. That's great. He was a third of the way home! A lot of people get lost in the morose of not ever being able to know their master's will. They act as if there is some cosmic hide 'n' seek game going on. And, of course, since God is a much better "hider" than we are a "seeker," we will never be sure of His will. They just don't know what God wants them to do. So, as they flounder around, they fall back on a Christian cliche: "Well, I'm just waiting on the Lord!" Or these people might jump from one ministry opportunity to another just hoping they will hit on the service to which their Master has called them.

But this unfaithful servant knew the master's will. At least he had come that far. It is, however, in the next step that he crashed. He didn't "prepare himself to do that ministry." Today's life is a busy life. "Why, after all, I work 123 days a year just to pay my taxes," one could defend. For all of our time-saving conveniences, the world still seems to have less disposable time to even prepare for ministry and much less time to actually minister.

Or, others may fall into another dilemma: To know His will, yet never feel quite ready to do His will. They are sure they need one more class, one more area of study, a little more maturity. (And I am not saying any of those things might not be necessary.) But when these reasons become an excuse—when the soldier of the cross becomes a professional student, then he is in trouble.

The Scripture continues: "Neither did he the master's will." Today, lounging in a thousand "country club" churches, there are troops who know the Master's will, "Go into all the world and preach the Gospel to every person. Then, when they have positively trusted in Me, teach them how to live by My commandments." See Mark 16:15; Matthew 28:19. And while the ice clinks on the crystal of their beverage glasses, they look at the illuminated map of Acts 1:8 which tells them where to do that will. "Do it in Jerusalem—bloom where you're planted. Go! Preach! Go! Teach! in Judea (your state, providence, district, country or whatever geographic area encompasses your Jerusalem). Do it in Samaria—a district next to Judea, but a "special" one to the Jews.

Samaria represented to the Jews the most hated, despised people in the world—the unlovables. I believe Jesus wants us to take this Gospel and the teachings of Christ to the *unlovables* of the world today. And while some are fighting the good fight of faith in these areas, He also directs some to the uttermost parts of the earth. We *know* the Master's will. Its clarity is written in His Word.

The Church is well-prepared to do that will. We have the personnel, the economics, the logistics, the resources—we have everything needed—to give the whole world the Good News. But through rose-tinted glasses those same "country club" loungers can so easily say, "Our God has everything under control!" And they ask the waiter (pastor) for another drink.

In 1793, a young, zealous Christian, filled with a passion for the lost, was given an opportunity to share his vision with a congregation of his country's pastors. When he was halfway through his appeal for a unified thrust to the unreached of India, the moderator said, "Young man, sit down! If God wants to save the heathen, He'll do it without your help or ours!" Fortunately for his generation and ours, he was not dissuaded.

I have not heard those words spoken from any modern day pulpit. However, this distorted theology is being shouted by the lifestyle of thousands in the Church! Because they are lounging around or hiding out in the busyness of "churchianity," these unfaithful servants will be beaten with many stripes for their failure to prepare for and to do their Master's will. See Luke 12:36-48 for a fuller understanding of this most difficult subject.

The Uncommitted

Bumper stickers abound: "I'd rather be sailing! I'd rather be...." (You fill in your own desire.) "When the going gets tough, the tough go fishing." (Or, again, whatever it might be that would make you "feel good.") The uncommitted. Today, commitment seems to be measured in micro-seconds! Someone might promise,"Yes, I will...." But before he gets the full expression of commitment out of his mouth, he is reconsidering, "How will this benefit me?"

Jesus' reputation had spread throughout the whole region. Quite a number of people—several thousand, they believe—were following Him here and there. They were following His stories and His miracles. He had become quite popular. Then He preached a sermon: He said, "Unless you eat My body and drink My blood..." and what happened? They split. They all left Him. So dramatic was the exodus that Jesus turned to the twelve disciples and said, "Are you going to leave Me, too?" See John 6:22-71.

Uncommitted people are those who see a good thing and jump on the bandwagon. "Let's go for it!" they shout! But then, when it gets to be a little work, they say, "Well, uh, I'm not so sure that that was the Lord's will for me." And they fall back on the "cosmic hide 'n' seek" excuse, "I think I'll wait for the Lord's direction."

Or they might say, "The Lord closed that door." In the Lord's message to the church of brotherly love, He clarified that He holds the keys of David. What He opens no man can shut and what He shuts no man can open. Then He says, "Before *you* I have set an open door and no man can shut it." Revelation 3:8 Even as Paul acknowledged in I Corinthians 16:9, "A great door that offers wide and effective ministry has been opened for me...." Then, as if he had come to expect it, he adds, "...*and* with many adversaries."

Paul had come to understand that behind every door of opportunity, the enemy was standing with his foot out, trying to trip him up. On another occasion he said that the Spirit had warned him that he could expect persecution and imprisonment in every city he visited. Acts 20:23

When we are walking in His will and things start getting tough, it could be the "big toe" of the adversary trying to trip us up—*not* the Lord "closing doors." It takes commitment to persist through difficulties, instead of saying, "Oh well, I guess God closed that door."

Wow! This is becoming quite a lengthy list of those with wrong attitudes. Hold on. There are just a few more to consider. And may we continue to allow the Holy Spirit to help us sort through them, making sure that these wrong attitudes are not "tripping around" in our mind. Later we will look at three simple words that describe the attitude God *is* looking for.

The Doubtful

Beware when doubtful thoughts enter that secret place of your mind. Poor Thomas. His name will ever be associated with doubting. But let's look at Barnabas. A lot of good things are said about Barnabas. He came from Cyprus. He moved to Jerusalem. He sold his farm. He laid the proceeds at the Apostles' feet. He had become so well-known at Jerusalem as a peacemaker that they changed his name from Joseph (meaning increaser) to Barnabas, which means, son of consolation. A guy who could bring reconciliation between people who are not getting along; he was prominent in the church at Jerusalem. Remember, he brought Saul (Paul) to the Apostles when they were afraid of him. See Acts 9:27.

They hear about a revival going on in Antioch, so they send him up to check it out. He stays there. The revival continues. He realizes that it is growing. He goes over to Tarsus to get Saul and says, "Come work with us." They go on that first missionary journey. So many things happen, and Barnabas is right there in the middle of them. They return and get back into the Antioch ministry.

And then, Peter comes up from Jerusalem to Antioch. Having had his "sheet of unclean animals" vision—three times—in Acts 10, he eats with the uncircumcised Gentile Christians. But when certain others of the circumcision "denomination" came from "General Superintendent" James in Jerusalem, Peter would no longer eat (have fellowship) with the Gentiles. So great was the confrontation over this ongoing controversy that Barnabas was "carried away" by it. It caused him to wonder, to doubt. See Galatians 2:11-14. Even veteran warriors are susceptible to doubts.

Another Biblical situation: The events of the past few weeks have been mind-boggling. The triumphal entry. The mock trial. The brutal crucifixion. The "robbed tomb." The risen Lord. "No, I'm not going to overthrow Rome now. But you will receive power after the Holy Spirit has come upon you...." And when they saw Him, they worshipped Him but some *doubted!*" Matthew 28:17 The doubtful: "I think so... Maybe... I'm not so sure... How can I be sure...?" The doubtful greatly impede victory in battle.

Again, lest we think (or satan plants the seed thought in our minds) that we cannot do any work for the Lord unless all things are perfect, let's look at a good Biblical attitude: A father has brought his son to Jesus' disciples, believing that he can be cured of a demonic possession. They can't drive it out. Jesus comes down the mountain. The story is told. Jesus asks the father, "Do you believe...?" And his answer is classic: "Lord, I believe! *Help my unbelief!*" Mark 9:24 I must admit that I have been in that position—too often! The son was delivered of a demon! And can we can be delivered of unbelief. There is victory over doubt!

The Draft Dodger

Poor Jonah! His story makes for a whale of a tale! And he illustrates another category of "soldiers of the cross" that our Commander-in-Chief is *not* looking for. Draft dodgers do not even show up on the battlefield.

"Nineveh, Jonah!" God commands.

"Not me! Lord! I'm going to Tarsus." Now, let's give poor Jonah a break. It was not without reason that he wanted to avoid Nineveh. It wasn't just that they might not like his message and ask him kindly to leave. You have probably said or heard the phrase, "I'm going to skin you alive!" That's what they did in Nineveh— literally! That's how they took care of their enemies! I believe it is God's humor, then, that puts Jonah in the belly of a great fish for three days and nights? For, when one survives such an ordeal, he comes out completely hairless with his skin bleached white! So Jonah had to go around the rest of his life not being "skinned alive," but with skin bleached by God! Anyway, the fish has had his belly full and spits Jonah up on the shore. And now in God's plan, He again says, "Jonah, I want you to go to Nineveh."

"Uh! yes, Lord, You still talking to me? I think I'll obey this time."

My father died when I was eight. My mother never remarried, so an adult male role model was not easy to find. My church had many different pastors over the years. Several with whom I tried to get close held me at arm's length, but I had a cousin who lived in a nearby town. When I was eight, he already was an adult and in business. He had come up through the ranks in a bank and was at that time bank president. So he sort of became my role model—from a distance. He was a good man, a family man. He attended church and was a Sunday school superintendent—all the good things expected of a Christian.

A number of years ago, he retired and was coming to California on a vacation. But he became deathly ill, and was flown back to Wisconsin. I am told that on his deathbed he was screaming and crying. Here was a man who had lived his whole life as an exemplary Christian. My role model—right! But on his deathbed—and I don't want to get too theological here, I'm just saying this is how he perceived it—on his deathbed, he was screaming and crying:

"I can't face God! I don't want to see my Maker!"

His family couldn't understand why he was saying that until he finally told them something he had never even told his wife:

When I was a young man, God called me to be a pastor. I have refused and resisted that call of God all of my life. Yes, you have seen me live

an exemplary Christian life. Yet way down deep inside, I know that I have not done His will.
He had ignored and run away from God's call on his life. And though I'm sure he went to heaven, and I'm sure there were rewards that were given him that he was able to lay at Jesus' feet, at that moment in time, he realized that he had been a draft-dodger.

Allow the Holy Spirit to question your (possible) attempts to dodge His draft. Go ahead. He's very gentle. But firm!

AWOL (Absent Without Leave)

John Mark went AWOL at a very crucial time. Barnabas and Saul were going out to battle. John Mark accompanied them as their minister (servant). When the battle got tough, Scripture says that John Mark left them and went back to Jerusalem. See Acts 13:13. It wasn't until many, many years later that he was ready for the battle. Paul said to Timothy, "Bring Mark with you when you come, for he can be of great help to the ministry." II Timothy 4:11

David went AWOL, for the Scripture says, "At a time when the *kings* went out to battle, David *sent* Joab." II Samuel 11:1 It wasn't until Nathan confronted him with the "little lamb" story that David repented of this great evil. See II Samuel 12:1-7 and Psalm 51.

We read of Peter's strong declaration: "God forbid, Lord! This (His imminent suffering and death) shall never happen to You!" Matthew 16:22 Just before his betrayal, when Jesus assured him that He was going to die, Peter said, "I will die with You." Matthew 26:35 However, just hours later...AWOL time...for he is cursing and swearing that he never knew the Man!" Matthew 26:74

Paul wrote a warning to Timothy: There are two men, Hymenaeus and Alexander, who have suffered shipwreck as far as their faith is concerned. They had gone AWOL, and left the faith. "Watch out for them," Paul advised. "They are trying to do us evil now." See I Timothy 1:19-20.

In Paul's second letter to Timothy, another warning is given against Hymenaeus who is now disrupting the church with false doctrine. See II Timothy 2:16-18. If the Alexander in II Timothy 4:14 is the same one, no good is being said of him, either. Those who once put their hand to the plow and then turn (even *look*) back are not useful to God as warriors. See Luke 9:62.

In each of the foregoing illustrations, even with an attitude problem revealed, the warrior could be considered a soldier. However, there is one more category to consider. One who has fallen to such depths cannot be even remotely regarded as a Soldier of the Cross.

The Traitor

Judas! That very name communicates traitor! It has become synonymous with the most despicable deeds of war: To turn your back on your allies and join the enemy. In Luke 22:3 we read, "Then satan entered into Judas..."—an awful, awful, awful thought...and he became that traitorous betrayer of Jesus. Of him, Jesus said, "It would have been good for him if he had not been born." Matthew 26:24

Lucifer himself—the Luminous One—became a traitor. "Wherefore art thou fallen, O Lucifer, Star of the Morning!" But, in pride, he lifted himself up and said, "I will be like the Most High!" See Isaiah 14:12-14. And in his rebellion, he took a third of the angels of heaven with him. A traitorous lot they became, as well. They still "believe in one God and tremble in fear at such knowledge." James 2:9 But for their deeds "they are bound in chains of everlasting darkness until the great judgment." Jude 6

In Hebrews 6:4-6, the writer talks about those "who

have been enlightened, who have experienced salvation and received the Holy Spirit, who have known the wholesome nourishment of the Word of God and touched the spiritual resources of the eternal world and have then fallen away. It is impossible to bring them again into repentance." Whatever theological stance you wish to take on that one, the state of those people is not enviable, in the least!

Lastly, the whole tenor of the New Age Movement is the age-old lie of satan: "You shall be as gods." Genesis 3:5 No more traitorous attitude can fill a person's mind than to "know all the time that there is a God, yet refuse to acknowledge Him as such..." (Romans 1:21) ...and try to fill that role, himself.

Heavy stuff! All of it! At this transition point, we need to review each attitude. And allow the Holy Spirit to "...search me and test me and know my thoughts; and see if there is any wicked way in me and lead me in the way of everlasting life." Psalm 139:23-24 May His Word delicately divide between our soul and spirit; between the thoughts (of our mind) and the intent (motivation) of our hearts. See Hebrews 4:12. These attitudes of the world must be put behind us as we look forward to consider His design for our attitude towards war.

Called, Commanded, Commissioned
Yes, He has called us into the Family of God. Yes, He has called us the Body of Christ. Yes, He has called us the Bride of Christ. Yes, He has called us to be the "living stones" in the building of God. And, *yes*, He has called, commanded and commissioned us to be Soldiers of the Cross. Paul's strong admonition to Timothy, "Endure hardness as a good soldier of Jesus Christ...that (we) may please the One who has *chosen* (us) to be a soldier." II Timothy 2:3-4 As clearly as the Word declares that it is His good pleasure for us to be His children, it

unquestionably states that we are Soldiers of the Cross. The men and women that God is looking for to serve in His army are called, commanded and commissioned. In Luke 10:1, Jesus appointed 70. He didn't say, "Okay, I'm looking for some volunteers. Who will raise their hands?" He said: You! you! and you! And He appointed 35 teams of 2. He *appointed* 70 to go out.

In Matthew 9, He tells the disciples to pray. He laments that the harvest is plentiful, but the laborers are few. "Pray, therefore, to the Lord of the harvest to send out laborers." In Chapter 10, just a few verses later, He says, "Okay, guys, get going!" He didn't say, "Oh, did you fellows pray about it? Did you discern that it was the Lord's will for you to go?" He said, "Get going! I *send* you!"

In Matthew 10:16, He says, "I *send* you forth as sheep in the midst of wolves." In the calling of the disciples, it was a *command.* He simply said, "Follow Me, and I will make you fishers of men." Matthew 4:19 And on the Mount of Ascension, in His final commissioning, He simply said, "Go! Preach! Go! Teach!" See Mark 16:15; Matthew 28:19.

At this point some might reason, "See—He has put out a challenge to us. We must rise to the occasion—and volunteer!"

No! A thousand times—No! A challenge is one of the ways of the world—even in a Christian context. Pictures of great needs are painted in vivid, living color. The opportunities for ministering to those needs are presented with glowing expressions of reward *if* we will accept the challenge and say—Yes! (The most extreme "reward" I have heard of is "We will bring back the Kingdom!")

As we think about the challenge, the tenor of our musings will likely begin to focus—on *me!* And how *my* decision will affect *me* and *my* plans. Or even how *my* decision will impact His Plan! (We would never say, "I wonder how *my* decisions will help God out!" Or would we?)

On the other hand, God does not challenge us. In our dealings with the Lord, He simply says, "This is the way, walk ye in it...." Isaiah 30:21 Or even more simply, "Follow Me!" Matthew 9:9

The choice is still ours. But the focus has changed. We are now centered in God and His Plan. We ponder the privilege to walk in those good deeds that He beforehand ordained for us. For we are His most finely crafted work of art, created in Christ Jesus. Ephesians 2:10

The difference is subtle—so subtle. But it is a difference of great consequence. Simply said, the contrast is: We *accept* a challenge; we *obey* a command. Our acceptance becomes the focal point in the former. Our friends will say, "Wow! That's quite a challenge you have taken on!" Conversely, the One we obey becomes the focal point in the latter. The Word of God says, "You belong to the power you choose to obey...." Romans 6:16 When we respond to fulfill His calling on our lives, *He* becomes glorified by our obedience.

As we look at the "vast cloud of witnesses"—those who have walked in His ways before us—we see that the choices they made are always shown in the light of the degree of obedience.

Jonah had a choice. At first he didn't obey. Then he did. Esther had a choice. At first she didn't obey. Then she did. Note with keen perception what persuaded her to obey. "Esther, Esther, my dear cousin," Mort reasons. "Salvation will come. God will save His people. God's Plan is not contingent upon you. Somebody will come along to be His instrument of deliverance. Of course, do consider that you and your father's house will be destroyed. So, Esther, in light of that perspective, let's talk a bit more. Remember when we were wondering if you should try out for the Miss Universe contest? The doubts; the excitement! And you won! Who knows whether you have been brought to the kingdom for a time such as this? God's Plan moves forward. Will you be a part of it?" Her response: "I will go in to the king. If I perish, I perish!" See Esther 4 for a less paraphrased version of this story!

As we look at characters in the Bible, we do see varying degrees of availability and willingness to obey His commands. To help us think about where we fit on the continuum of obedience, it might be good to examine two extremes:

1) Once we look beyond the Hollywood image of Moses and read Scripture as Scripture, we see that he was an ordinary human being.

In fact, as we look at him fitting into God's Plan of the Ages for his generation, we find a very reluctant soldier in God's army. First of all, he tries it on his own, and having killed the Egyptian, he flees to the back side of the desert for 40 years. But as we read in Exodus 3 and 4, God starts talking to him from the burning bush. "I've seen the sorrow and anguish of My people. It is now My time and I will show you My way for you to go and deliver them from the hand of the oppressor."

Moses is not tripping over himself to get going. He comes up with five excuses! He says, "Who me? I'm not good enough!" God answers that excuse. He comes up with a second excuse. "By whose authority do I speak?" God answers that excuse. The third excuse: "They won't believe me." God answers that excuse. He comes up with a fourth excuse, which, by the way, is an outright lie. He said, "I am slow of speech," whereas Stephen rehearsed that he was "learned in all the ways of Egypt and was *eloquent* in speech." Acts 7:22 But God still answers that excuse.

(It might be more than just curious here to note that

God's answer to each of Moses' excuses centered in God, not in Moses. In each case God said, "I'll be with you." How different are the ways of the world—even the Christian world!)

Having failed to sidestep God's call with reason, Moses now sidesteps all reason and comes up with his fifth excuse. It is an excuse that every one of us has used at one time or another; it is common to all. In modern English, he said, "Let George do it!"

And then what? The anger of the Lord is kindled against him. God gets angry with Moses! Now, finally he gives a positive response, "Okay, okay; I'll go!"

As God's anger and the fire of the burning bush cooled, Moses might have even said, "Now why did I promise that?" At the least we see a very reluctant called, commanded and commissioned leader. In the final analysis it was his obedience—however reluctant—that put Moses into the Hall of Faith as he became one of the greats in God's Kingdom.

2) Way to the other extreme, we have an example of what I believe was the most willing obedience to God's calling. I am speaking of Mary, the mother of Jesus. Now, it is a little bit difficult for us in this generation to picture her situation, but in those days, unmarried girls just didn't get pregnant. Or if they did, they got stoned. And by stoned, I don't mean "high on drugs." I mean, literally, stoned to death. See Deuteronomy 22:13-21.

When Joseph was pondering in his heart how to put Mary away "privately," he wasn't just thinking about, "Well, if I have her go live with Aunt Elizabeth until the baby comes and then we can give the baby up for adoption and then Mary can come back and we can get married and nobody will know...." No! He was pondering in his heart how to have a private stoning instead of a public one, which was the way it was supposed to be done. Mary knew all of this, too. I am sure this was only one of many things that Mary was "pondering in her heart" the night the angel came into her bedroom. Another thing to consider is that Mary was waiting for Joseph to come. It would be any day or night now, she was sure. The tradition of those days was being followed. The betrothal had taken place about a year before. Joseph was building a house. (Usually it was just a room addition on his father's house.) The father would test his son's patience by saying, "I think you need to redo this trim. The miter is not neat enough." So both the bride and bridegroom are waiting for the him to say, "OK! Now you may go get your bride!"

Further, it was the custom for the men to play a little trick on the women. They would come at the most unexpected time to see if the bride and the bridesmaids would be ready. The bridegroom and his troop of men would come running down the streets of the bride's village. His men would come first, shouting, "The bridegroom cometh!" And of course, the bride would be caught up by the groom, they would have their seven days of festivities, and they would be married.

Okay, Mary is waiting for that. Night and day she wonders, "When is Joseph going to come?" And then this angel shows up in her bedroom and messes up all of her wedding plans. I mean, face it, here's a little Jewish girl wanting to get married, and the angel comes and says, "Mary, the Spirit of the Lord is going to hover over you and you're going to get pregnant."

"How can this be, since no man has been with me?"

"It's going to be unique, I assure you."

And this young girl in her willing obedience to the call, command and commission of God in her life simply says, "Be it unto me as you have spoken." No more pure words of obedience could be spoken! Luke 1:26-38

I believe everybody else in the Bible (and all of us) fit

somewhere in between these two illustrations. It is our willingness, it is our availability to fit into God's Plan of the Ages for our life that becomes the issue. We could do biographical sketches of many other Soldiers of the Cross. And God can speak to us through the experiences of others, whether they are Bible characters, men and women down through the ages of time or people who are currently out on the battlefield for the Lord.

But far more important than how my cousin responded to God's call on his life, far more important than how Moses or even Mary responded, is how *I* respond to God's call on my life.

This very real analogy marches through the pages of Scripture: A war was declared in heaven. From the day Lucifer lifted himself up in prideful rebellion against God until today a war rages for the souls of all people. It is a war in which our Commander-in-Chief, Jehovah-Sabaoth calls, commands and commissions His Church to active duty.

Thus, all Christians are Soldiers of the Cross. Whether or not we knew it at the time of our conversion, part of the "package deal" was our conscription into the Army of God.

Every human being is a target of the enemy. Toward Christians—at the least—he will attempt to rob us of the joy of our salvation. At the most, he would "deceive the elect if it were possible." Matthew 24:24 Towards non-Christians, "the god of this age has blinded their minds." II Corinthians 4:4

Though we are not expected to love war, our hatred for the enemy compels us to examine our attitudes toward war and ourselves as soldiers. For our attitude will to a large part determine our effectiveness.

Volunteers, mercenaries, draft-dodgers, the ill-prepared and unfaithful do not have what it takes to overcome the enemy. Neither can the uncommitted and doubtful soldiers fight victoriously. Those warriors who have gone AWOL are no longer a useful part of the army! And traitors have joined the enemy's camp. As willing as Mary or as reluctant as Moses, in the final analysis, yielding to His will is the important factor. May we allow the Holy Spirit to work in us. Each one of us needs to say, "He has called *me*, He has commanded *me*, He has commissioned *me*. May we willingly declare, "I am a Soldier of the Cross!"

PRACTICAL INSIGHTS

WHEN SATAN HASSLES CHRISTIANS

As we continue to unravel the subtle attempts of satan to hassle us in our daily walk, let's be sure to allow the Holy Spirit to ask this question in each of these problem areas: Is this a problem in my life?

Problem The enemy tries to hassle me when I am not in the Word and prayer. When we haven't eaten for five or six hours, our "stomachs" are screaming, "I'm starving to death!" When we neglect spiritual food we become weak spiritually. Often the cause of this neglect is that we have become so busy working *for* the Lord that we neglect our fellowship *with* the Lord. Or, we become malnourished because we are not eating a balanced diet of the Word—maybe we are just reading the promises of the Word. Or, always focusing on His judgements, or just reading about end times, or some other theme.

Solution The solution is not: "OK, January first I will make a new resolution. I will. I will. I will!" Or, "Well, tomorrow I'll get started. Yes!" Or... (Name your put-off-the-decision-until-later excuse here!) The solution lies first in asking God to help you, then in a self-discipline which involves making concrete plans which will include the Whole Counsel of God. Answer the questions: What am I going to do differently? When am I going to do it? What method of Bible reading and study am I going to use? And, maybe—With whom am I going to do it? Be creative. If you are having a hard time reading your Bible, if your mind wanders and you can't concentrate, try listening to the Bible being read on tapes as you follow it in your own Bible. Hearing it and seeing it at the same time might help your concentration.

Record the key points of your daily Bible reading in a log book. Read aloud to yourself. Study inductively, keeping a notebook. Covenant with another person in an accountability agreement to encourage and check up on each other. You can agree to read the same passage and share what God has shown you and how you applied it to your life.

Maybe you have a hard time praying. Again—ask God for help in this area of discipline. Ask God to block distractions and to help you to concentrate on Him. Sing—pick out a worship tape or CD that says what you want to say to God and sing your prayers. There might be occasions when you can concentrate better if you write a letter to God.

Do you fall asleep while you're praying? Don't pray in bed; don't lie down; don't close your eyes! One of the best times for me to pray is while I am walking. I can't see projects waiting to be worked on or hear the phone ringing when I'm walking! Another idea is to keep a notebook of what God is saying to you during your prayer time.

I am sure you can also find other creative ways to make Bible reading and prayer an important part of your life.

Problem The enemy tries to hassle me when unhealed emotional areas in my life are touched. Everyone gets hurt while growing up. As surely as children get skinned knees, emotions get "skinned." Sometimes the "scars" are so minor, they are not remembered. On the other hand, there may be deeper hurts that never were healed. Some people go through their whole life without dealing with those hurts. Those unhealed places are weak spots that are open to repeated attacks from the enemy.

Solution Make a plan to deal with them. Now! I know these areas in our lives are usually very painful, and we would rather just bury them. We don't even want to think about them. But we need to work through them—now—because as long as we have unhealed areas, we are particularly vulnerable in those places.

I had a friend who was constantly getting attacked in a particular area in her life. To me, it was obviously connected with a situation in her past. When I would try to help her to face it, she would say, "Oh, that's past. Anyway it's just a spiritual attack."

And I would say, "That may be, but where does the enemy attack? He isn't going to attack us where we are strong. No, he attacks in our weak spots, because that is where we are vulnerable."

We need to take care of damaged areas so they are no longer weak spots where the enemy can easily get at us. Allow God to give us victorious insights through His Word. In our hearts forgive ourselves or another who has caused this deep pain. If a resolve cannot be found on your own, talk with someone—a friend, or a godly counselor. Get someone to pray for you and with you.

I am not saying that every issue of your past life has to go through some "healing process." But if it is an issue that regularly comes to your mind or negatively affects your life, deal with it! Now! It can't be ignored, or you will continue to be vulnerable to the enemy's attack in that area of your life.

Problem   The enemy tries to hassle me when I feel badly about myself. I know the subject of "self-acceptance" is a hot issue. I don't want to get into that controversy, but neither do I want to ignore the fact that when people do not see themselves as accepted and complete in Christ, there can often be major problems. It is easy to feel rejected, worthless, and just no good, and that creates a need to have the approval of someone—anyone! When we don't have a realistically good self-image and we believe that certainly God sees us the same way, it leads to a miserable life of being discontent, often coupled with people-pleasing instead of God-pleasing.

Solution Develop concrete plans to deal with this now! There is a reason I keep repeating "deal with it now." If you finish reading this section and just say, "Yes, that is exactly what I need to work on," and then go on to read the next section with the same, "Yes, that is just what I need to see," you will get to the end of the book and be no closer to a solution than when you started reading. You may have more knowledge about the subject, but you will be no closer to victorious living.

If your response is, "Yes, I'm going to cooperate with the Holy Spirit in working on that issue," but you don't have a specific plan that spells out the what, when, where, how and with whom, it is very unlikely to just happen. So, for example, if there is something you don't like about yourself—something that makes it hard for you to be content and at peace with yourself, find out what it takes to bring about the desired change. If it is worth it to you—make a plan of how to do it. If it is not worth it—accept yourself as you are. For, "Godliness with contentment is great gain." I Timothy 6:6

With the deeper, far more significant things that bother us, we need to determine what steps to take to bring about the change and start walking in those steps now! An example might be—knowing in your head that God loves and accepts you, but you are not experiencing this Truth on a daily basis; times of doubt often come. Saturate your mind with the Truth of His Word. One good Scripture to read and pray (several times a day) would be Ephesians 3:16-19. Do it until the Word changes you! Do it so the enemy can no longer easily attack you with the feeling that God does not really love and accept you.

If you don't know how to handle any particular problem, "...tell God the details of your *needs* in earnest and thankful prayer." Philippians 4:6 He is faithful to His Word; He will bring the solution.

Problem The enemy tries to hassle me in situations where I lack confidence. I am looking at myself alone, instead of looking at the facts: The Holy Spirit is in me; the Lord is my strength! We can become paralyzed and unable to do what God wants us to. The thoughts of "I'm not good enough," "Somebody else can do it better," "I'll just quit, anyway," or "I won't even try that," can prevent us from feeling able to make commitments or walk into the opportunities that God has for us.

Solution To stop the enemy at this point of attack, our confidence must be in the One Who said, "Without Me you can do nothing." John 15:5 Paul came to that place of true confidence, "I can do all things *through Christ* Who is my strength." Philippians 4:13

There was a time when I could not talk in front of a group of people—any size group. Now when my husband and I are planning to do a seminar together, I say, "I need *more* time!"—in good humor, of course. But that didn't happen in a day. Small step by small step, God put within me the confidence to walk in the ways He had for me. He enabled me to realize I am just a normal human being, like anyone else, but with the huge advantage of being accepted in Christ and loved by God and empowered by the Holy Spirit!

4

TACTICS OF SATAN

---

*"...lest satan should get an advantage over us;
for we are not ignorant of his devices."*
II Corinthians 2:11

Paul, the Apostle, now on his third missionary journey, writes to the Christians in Corinth, "I'm going to
stay in Ephesus until Pentecost, for God has opened a
great and effective door of ministry to me...*and* there
are many adversaries." I Corinthians 16:9

By this time in Paul's ministry, he had come to recognize that with every door of opportunity there would
be adversaries. Later, to the elders of Ephesus, he
would say, "I don't know what may happen to me there
(in Jerusalem), except that the Holy Spirit has warned
me that imprisonment and persecution await me in every city that I visit." Acts 20:22-23

Since there is a war, there is an enemy! Since there
is an enemy, we need to know about him. For as we
walk through the "doors flung wide open" (Rev. 3:8) for
us, we don't want to let "the enemy have the advantage
over us; we do not want to be ignorant of his devices." II
Corinthians 2:11 We need to understand his character.
We need to know his methods "so that we may stand
against the *wiles* of the devil; so that we can successfully resist the devil's methods of attack." Ephesians 6:11

HIS TACTICS OF DEFENSE

In Ephesians 6:12, Paul continues: "For we wrestle not against flesh and blood...." Included in this phrase alone are two of the devil's most effective tactics—two defensive distractions by which he protects himself from battle. Paul is merely making the statement as an assumption that, of course, we know 1) that there is a war and 2) that our warfare isn't against any physical enemy. But the enemy has so cleverly glossed over these two issues that many Christians are not even aware of the battle that rages. Or, if they do see beyond that smoke screen, they expend their energy in "flesh and blood" battles.

There is No War

"For we wrestle *not....*" And satan has stopped a large segment of the church right at that point. "There's no war," he slyly chides. "Peace, brother!" "Detente!" "Live and let live!" "That's beautiful! That's your reality." And with those lies, he camouflages the most basic reality of all: We are at war!

Many—too many—Christians (regardless of what they may say they believe about war) live their lives as if there is no war. Granted, war is not the most pleasant of subjects. It is a lot more fun to appreciate the "warm cuddly" analogies of the Word: We're the Children of the King, the Body of Christ, the Bride of Christ, etc. As these Christians settle into the deep leather comfort of their country club church atmosphere, they say, "There now, let's just sit back and praise the Lord."

Or, as J. I. Packer observed of this modern church, "The ultimate step, of course, would be to clear the church auditorium of seats and install hot tubs...what people want is total tickling relaxation, the sense of being at once soothed, supported and effortlessly invigorated." *Hot Tub Religion*, (Tyndale House, Wheaton, 1993), p. 61.

It would only happen by mistake, but suppose a true warrior were given an opportunity to speak in such a church. As he raises the heart-stirring battle cry— "We are Soldiers of the Cross!" the people become nervous. The service would probably end with the song leader coming to the pulpit and saying, "Well, now, Brother Jones really does have quite a ministry. And in closing, let us turn our thoughts toward God and sing our favorite hymn, 'I'm a Child of the King.'"

And, in so doing, the song leader actually proves to be an adversary of God, one who has fallen prey to the philosophy of satan: "Come on, you do your thing and I'll do mine. Okay, so you want to be a Soldier of the Cross? Great! I just want to be a Child of the King!"

Whether these words accurately express the tone being used in your situation or not, the philosophy of the world screaming at us from every quarter today is, "Detente! Let's live and let live!" And satan has successfully silenced the majority of the church by this tactic.

"Flesh and Blood" Battles

Paul, by the Holy Spirit, wrote that there is a battle. It is wrestling; it is fighting; it is hand-to-hand combating with the enemy. But it is not against any physical foe; it is not a "flesh and blood" battle.

Yet, herein lies the enemy's second most successful line of defense. If he cannot convince us that there is no war, he will divert our attention toward physical battles. Christians are caught up in hundreds of "flesh and blood" conflicts. Energy spent in each dissipates the force of battle that could be waged against satan. Let's look at four categories of "Christians against...." There may be more.

Christians Against Christians

Christians are battling against Christians. Why else

would there be 20,800 (or more) different denominations? And many will "spill blood" more quickly defending their doctrinal distinctives than in defending the Name of Jesus Christ.

In Proverbs 6:19, as Solomon is listing seven actions that God regards as abominations, he includes "those who sow discord among the brethren." And yet, tragically, Christians are daily caught up in this battle. Whether the scandal involves nationally-known personalities or if it is a bad report about a brother or sister in your home fellowship group, there is no place for name-calling or finger-pointing among believers.

As Melody Green wrote following a scandal involving some TV evangelists, "I believe God is testing us to see how we respond to those who have fallen.... How do we reach out to those who are hurting because of their own sin or wrong choices? We need God's pursuing love if we are really going to help people struggling with personal failure. Recently, my spirit has been grieved as I've seen Christians pointing the finger at other Christians. My spirit has also been grieved as I have seen myself starting to point a finger at those who are pointing theirs." *The LAST DAYS Magazine*, Vol. 10, No. 2, 1987.

How did Jesus handle a finger-pointing session in His day? The Pharisees had caught a woman in the very act of adultery and brought her to Him. (Hmm! Why didn't they bring the man, also? He was as guilty as she, and deserving of the same punishment. See Leviticus 20:10.) But when Jesus told them that the one without sin should throw the first stone, everyone walked away. When he finally spoke to the woman, He spoke with forgiveness and acceptance saying, "Where are your accusers? Neither do I condemn you. Go, and sin no more." John 8: 3-11 To hate evil—to be sure; but to destroy the wounded—never!

Yet the "flesh and blood" battles of Christians

against Christians continue. Another scenario: We have high expectations of Christians—and rightly so. Our spirits have been made alive in God through Christ. Our feasting on the Word has sensitized our consciences to the clear-cut right and wrong of our actions. The full brightness of His Light has eliminated the shadows of gray that used to hide our sinful deeds. We are living by the Law of Christ. And we expect other Christians to do so as well.

Unfortunately, though, we have selectively ignored the host of Scriptures on forgiveness, thus exhibiting a lower tolerance level when a Christian does sin. When a fellow Christian sins, recognizes his sin and with a repentant spirit asks for forgiveness, our attitude too often is, "I'm not sure. After all, you're a Christian. You should have known better!"

Sometimes, if we are willing to forgive, we may get hung up on Peter's horn of dilemma: "Lord, how often should we forgive our brother? Seven times?"

"No, Peter, but an infinite number." For in their culture seventy times seven did not mean 490. Seven times seventy equalled 490. But when the larger number was spoken first it meant a number without end. See Matthew 18:21-22 and Luke 17:3-4.

Other times, fear of lawsuits keeps us from exercising church discipline on those who "hold aught against their brother." See Matthew 18. And the battle rages on...but not against the enemy! Energy to fight the enemy is dissipated on Christians fighting against Christians.

Christians Against Non-Christians
There are zealous Christians who would suppose getting non-Christians out of places of authority and decision-making is the solution to what ails us. But Scripture says the solution rests with Christians: "If My

people who are called by My name will humble themselves and pray, and seek My face and turn from their
wicked ways; then will I hear from Heaven and forgive
their sins and *heal their land.*" II Chronicles 7:14

Christians in politics—no problem! But it is not necessary to make a difference. If Christians had responded to a former president's request for each church to
take on the responsibility of one welfare family, he
would have been able to shut down that whole government program! And Christians could have dealt with
the real enemy of the souls of those on the welfare
treadmill. (There are now some localities and states doing this with a good measure of success.)

As if arguing over Bible trivia could lead our co-
worker to Christ, other zealous Christians scan the
Scriptures for just the right words to "nail him to the
wall" or debate with him whether five or five thousand
angels can dance on the head of a pin! Our words
should be "seasoned with salt" (Colossians 4:6) to make
them thirsty for the Living Water. Our attitude should
reflect Christ's love rather than an adversarial antago-
nism.

Christians Against World Religions

A first-term missionary friend of mine was going to a
country where Roman Catholicism is the state religion.
His purpose was to establish a church. He showed me
his prize shoe box of anti-Catholic tapes! Patting it, he
said this was his sermon material for the first several
years! After hearing the following stories, he agreed not
to take the tapes.

There was an evangelist by the name of Paul. He
had a zeal for the Gospel—a simple message. In fact,
though he was a very learned man, he often said, "I am
determined to know nothing before you except Christ
and Him crucified." I Corinthians 2:2

Contrary to his normal strategy of continually moving on to unharvested fields, one time he settled down in a major commercial and idolatrous center. He began teaching in the hall of a local Christian. People came from the surrounding cities to hear Paul preach and teach. More and more people were trusting in Christ and laying aside their idols.

Things got better and better for the Christians and worse and worse for the silversmiths who were making the idols. One day a very upset silversmith named Demetrius created a riot. Almost the whole city rushed into the arena. Most didn't even know why they were there. Finally, after two hours of constant praise to their idolized deity, the city manager got them quieted down. He said, "We are in trouble, for this is an unlawful assembly." Then, testifying to his own belief in Diana, he added, "These men have neither robbed our temples nor *blasphemed our goddess*." Acts 19:10-37   A revival so great that it adversely affected the economy was accomplished without stealing the temple's money nor talking against Diana.

On another occasion, Paul was waiting in Athens for Silas and Timothy to join him. While he waited, his spirit was stirred, for he saw a city totally given over to idolatry. Not being able to hold himself back any longer, he went into the synagogue and into the marketplace doing street evangelism. Certain philosophers heard him and invited him to speak with them some more in the highest court in Athens, the Areopagus.

Lining both sides of the road leading up Mars Hill were hundreds of altars to their gods. When Paul was given permission to speak, not only did he not rail against these many gods, but he used one—the altar to The Unknown God—as a cultural bridge: "This God whom you ignorantly worship, Him declare I unto you." Acts 17:16-23

Other religions are not the enemy, and their adherents are all potential Christians! We must deal kindly and gently with those whose eyes are blinded. Our goal is to "open their eyes." Acts 26:18

Christians Against Social Injustice
I have read the statistics: 4,000 babies aborted every day; 30,000 children dying of malnutrition and water-related diseases every day. I have visited the museums meant to keep alive the memories of the atrocities of man against man. Calling Christian efforts against social injustice "flesh and blood" battles is by no means saying these atrocities are right or should be ignored. But I do believe that most Christian *action* in these issues is *reaction.* Whereas, had Christian action been proactive—taken before the fact of such unthinkable atrocities—much more good would have been accomplished.

For example, if the Christian community had taken up the battle cry for "moral purity" in the '60's instead of being overwhelmed by the flower power and free love, we may not have experienced Roe vs. Wade. Further, if the time, money and energy (and now prison terms for murder!) that is being spent by Christians at the doors of abortion clinics were spent in providing alternative counseling and care, I venture to say the desired results—saving babies—would increase. And the testimony of a Christian lifestyle would be more clearly seen by the world.

Or, how about *now* dealing with the abortion issue—proactively—at that more basic level—moral purity?

Christians Against...
It is my strong belief that Christians in their fight for right don't have to be against any group or course of ac-

tion. We believe the Truth. We have the real thing; we know the only true God. And when we are promoting the best, we don't have to put anything else down. It is only if there is a flaw in our own "product" that we have to point out the bigger flaw in theirs. Yet, in the world, our distorted thinking believes that if I make you look bad, it somehow makes me look good (or, at least, better).

When we are dwelling in the Light, we don't have to try to drive the darkness out. When we go out into the world where it's really dark, the Light of His countenance will shine brightly. And the darker it gets, the more brightly will appear the Light of Life. But watch out! It's the mosquitos and bugs that are attracted to the light on a dark night! But then again, Jesus came to save the ungodly, not the "righteous." See Matthew 9:13.

Paul continues by pointing out our very real foes: "But we do fight (wage war, battle, combat) against principalities and powers, against the rulers of the darkness of this world and against spiritual wickedness in high places." Ephesians 6:12

And would you believe that there are those who have gotten into "flesh and blood" battles trying to identify what these categories of spiritual enemies represent! I am not saying that a little digging into the theological import of these entities is wrong. But really! To fight with another Christian over it is dissipating the strength of both Christians to fight the real enemy.

THE CHARACTER OF SATAN

The world was shocked to hear a general admit (thirty years too late) that his country's defeat in Vietnam was a result of not understanding the nature of the enemy. Knowledge of the enemy's character gives us insight into his world view, his frame of reference—where he's coming from. Character determines methods. And the methods of the enemy are what we face day by day.

Without wanting to give undue attention to the enemy (for some have fallen prey to that and have become enamored with evil), we must now look at his character.

He is a liar
"He does not stand for the truth, because there is no truth in him. When he speaks a falsehood he speaks what is natural to him; for he is a liar and the father of all lies." John 8:44 The very nature of this characteristic makes it the most difficult of his tricks to withstand. Though unnatural to him, he can speak the truth. But even as he speaks, we have to wonder, "Is this the truth or is it a lie?" Yet, unfortunately, we listen! And as he speaks the truth, we begin to nod our heads in agreement; Yes! Yes! Yes! Then he slips in a lie. But our heads are nodding in such agreement, when the lie comes, before we know it, we have said "Yes" to that, as well. "Give no foothold to the devil." Ephesians 4:27 Remember, the best way to recognize a lie is to be totally familiar with the Truth!

He is a deceiver
Jesus warned in Matthew 24:24 that there would come in satan's name those who would show signs and wonders to deceive even the elect if it were possible. See also II Thessalonians 2:9. There are many stories in the Bible pointing to the deceptive nature of satan. But there is one that boggles my mind above all others. It has not happened yet. Only because it is written in the Word can I possibly believe that it will occur. And it gives me a healthy respect for the ferocity of our enemy:

There is One whose name is King of Kings and Lord of Lords who, with the sharp Sword of His mouth, will smite the nations and for 1,000 years will rule them with a rod of iron. During this time, satan will be bound in chains and sealed in the bottomless pit so that he cannot deceive the nations.

For us who have not seen justice among the nations in our lifetime—or in the history of the world—it is an awesome consideration that there will be perfect justice for 1,000 years! Christ will rule the earth! And then (and here I shudder at the deceptive nature of satan), "satan will be let loose from his prison and shall go out to *deceive* the nations; to gather them together to battle against the beloved city. And their number was as the sands of the sea!" Revelation 19:11-20:9 Even after a millennium of justice under Christ's rule, a sea of people will again be deceived by the evil one.

Lest in our delineating the awful power of our enemy *we* become enamored with him, let us here be reminded of Job's wisdom and understanding of the deceiver. "The deceived and the deceiver are God's." Job 12:16

And again, Isaiah, inspired by the Holy Spirit, gives us insight to the fall of Lucifer, son of the morning. We read: "They that see you will look narrowly, and consider you, saying 'Is this the one that made the earth to tremble, that did shake kingdoms?'" Isaiah 14:16

The day will come, evidently, when some will actually see satan. What he will look like I am not sure. But those who see him will squint their eyes in unbelief, "Is this the one that deceived the nations?" The picture I get is characterized in the movie, "The Wizard of Oz." When the curtain is pulled back and the one who had exercised such power and control is revealed for who he is—a wizened old man—we are amazed at his ability to deceive! Likewise, we will be amazed at the puniness of the master deceiver!

And yet, while we fight against him—while we are doing battle against powers and principalities under the

136 *Prepare for Battle!*

control of this wicked one—let us not be deceived into believing that his deception is not to be reckoned with. It is no small thing to engage the enemy in battle!

He is subtle

"...as satan beguiled Eve through subtlety." II Corinthians 11:3 The enemy is subtle. He has to be subtle. Can you imagine him coming up to us and saying, "Hi! I'm satan. If you follow me, I can promise you an eternity in hell!" The dullest of us could see right through that. He has to make us think that the here and now is all there is to live for.

Or, if we believe in a future life, his craftiness says that we will be as gods. But you see, there is even the necessity for subtlety there. For, few of us would admit (out loud) that we want to be god. "Yes, I would like to be my own boss. Yes, I would like the freedom to make my own decisions. Yes, I..." and what have we said? "I want to be in charge; I want to be god!"

"Now the serpent was more subtle and crafty than any living creature of the field.... And he said, 'You shall not die, for God knows that in the day you eat of it your eyes will be opened, *and you will be as gods!*'" Genesis 3:1,4 It was his first temptation. And it has been a successful ploy through the ages of time.

He is slanderous

Slander is part truth and part lie. Job was slandered when satan asked God, "Does Job fear God for no reason? You have put a hedge around him and all that he has...." Job 1:9-10 The truth was that, yes, God had put a hedge around Job and all that he had. The lie was that Job's fear of God was contingent on everything going his way. We know this is a lie, for Job said, "Though He slay me, yet will I trust Him." Job 13:15

I believe we can slander God. When things are going

well, we praise Him. "God is so good to me!" we sing. Yet, when things are not going well, we grumble, "I don't know where God is!" (Of course, we would never sing, "God is so bad to me!") When things are out of sorts, we have mixed truth with lie—that is slander. God does not change! To counter the slanderer's temptation in this regard, you will find me deliberately saying, "God is good!" more often when things are going *not so good* in my life than when things are going well.

He is an Accuser
Evidently, satan is still able to present himself before God. Revelation 12:10 seems to indicate that it is not until some future time that he is finally cast out of heaven. And in that passage, we are told that he accuses us before God day and night.

What he does in the heavens is not too great a concern to me. Or even whether his accusations are true or false. For I have the assurance of a Perfect High Priest, my advocate before the Father, saying, "I covered that at Calvary." What does affect me is when the enemy's agents on earth hurl accusations at me. I wonder if there is a parallel between his accusations in heaven and those on earth. I wonder!

He is Fierce
"When all kinds of trials and temptations *crowd* into your life...." James 1:2 He *is* fierce! We will never be approached by satan with a gentle tap on the shoulder and hear him say, "Well, you've been living a pretty easy life. Do you mind if I throw a temptation your way—just one; just a little one?" No! He doesn't do it that way. All kinds of trials and temptations assail us. We find ourselves inundated with the slanderous accusations of the enemy. Experiencing media overload, our minds are bombarded with a thousand voices, demand-

ing our attention. For he is fierce.

Now, if you are looking up all Scriptures to read them in their context, you will note that the verse just quoted is clearly a "half-scripture." I deliberately did that to show the fierceness of the enemy.

But to live in the abundance of the Whole Counsel of God, we must read on. We do not face the forces of the enemy on our own. When all kinds of trials and temptations crowd into your life, "...don't resent them as intruders, but welcome them as friends. Realize that they come to test your faith and produce in you the quality of endurance." A Christian can take those trials and temptations and turn them around for good.

Nonetheless, the nature of his character is that he is a fierce enemy.

He is Powerful
"We wrestle...against powers and principalities...." Ephesians 6:12 The forces of evil at work in our world are powerful. Hardly a day goes by but that we don't see another bastion of righteousness toppled from our Christian cultural heritage. If it isn't depreciating the sanctity of life, it is barring a plaque of the Ten Commandments from a courtroom. Even during periods of time when various segments of society are shouting "Reform!" the foundations of sound principle and judgment are crumbling under the power of the enemy. II Thessalonians 2:9 tells us that the lawless man will come through the working of satan, "...and with great power...!"

I BELIEVE IN SATAN! And I hope you do! I hope you believe that he is exactly what the Bible says he is. *HE IS THE ENEMY!*

If you thought that was a somewhat emotional outburst in the middle of this study, it was! I get very emotional about this issue. The spiritual forces of evil are saying, "This is no war—no enemy." Society is saying, "Man is inherently good. It was your poor environment (or your parents, or your teachers, or the overdose of sugar) that made you do it! You aren't responsible!" And a large segment of the Christian church—if not in word, at least by their lifestyle, is saying, "Detente! Let's live at peace together. You do your thing; we'll do ours."

Yes, I get emotional. For this proud, powerful, fierce, subtle, slanderous accusing liar would even deceive the elect if it were possible! See Mark 13:22.

He is Proud
The five "I wills" of Isaiah 14:13-14 are the words of one lifted up in pride. What audacity for one to declare, "I will be like the Most High!" Did not his first temptation, "You will be as gods" (Genesis 3:5), dangle that very prize before Eve? Yet, how many earthlings would follow Shirley MacLane—lifted up in pride—to shout at the setting sun, "I am god!"

Yet, He is a Cowardly Imitator
Because he does not have the courage to show himself for who he really is, he puts on his neon-lighted costume, trying to be the Light of Life. He was Lucifer, the luminous one—the light-bearer. But no longer does he hold that position. He only "masquerades *as* an angel of light." II Corinthians 11:14

I Peter 5:8 tells us that he "roars *like* a lion." No, he is not the Lion of the Tribe of Judah. In his roaring he goes about seeking whom he may devour. In cowardly disguise, he tries to make us think he is Jesus, the Christ.

And, today, as the world awaits their coming messiah, 2000 or more self-proclaimed christs—all shams and imitators—stand in the wings, planning their debut.

He is Wicked

In I John 3:12 we are admonished to "not be like Cain who was of that wicked one...." In the King James Version of the Bible, satan is referred to as the wicked one 454 times. Ingrained in the character of a wicked one is the determination to think and do evil. "They (wicked persons) cannot sleep unless they have caused trouble...or caused someone to fall." See Proverbs 4:14-17.

We have been warned! The devil, satan, the old serpent, the prince of this world, the ruler of darkness, the dragon (and there are about thirty other names and titles given to him) is *wicked!*

He is the Adversary

"Give no occasion to the adversary to speak reproachfully...." I Timothy 5:14 Satan is a created being. He is against God; he is not the equal opposite of God. It is easy in our rapid delineation of contrasts between God and satan to go too far: God is good; satan is evil. God is love; satan is hateful. God is truthful; satan is a liar. Then, recognizing satan as a spirit-being, as we move into some of the characteristics reserved for Creator God alone, we may fall prey to think satan also has those powers. Rather, God is omnipotent (all-powerful); satan is not. God is omniscient (all-knowing); satan is not. God is omnipresent (everywhere present at the same time); satan is not. God is eternal (without beginning or end); satan is not.

The foregoing character sketch, I trust has been lengthy enough to give us a sane estimate of the deadly enemy we face. Yet I hope it has not been so long as to discourage us. We have given more time to the enemy in this brief section than I care to think about him in a lifetime. Yet, trying to ignore the nature of our enemy is playing the deadly game of ostrich. With our head in the sand, our posterior is fully exposed for destruction!

THE METHODS OF SATAN

Having inquired a bit into the character and nature of this foe, we'll now look into the Word for instruction about the methods of attack he uses. We will find it is not a limitless list, for satan is not that creative. Yet, we will find that because of his deceitful subtlety, generation after generation has fallen prey to his same tricks.

As we study the following methods of satan, it would be well for us to overlay them with an understanding of this basic strategy of secular war: "A wounded soldier will be more morale-sapping for his comrades than a dead one, and a burden to his own side's medical and logistical services." *Ammunition for the Land Battle*, Lt.Col. P.R. Courtney-Green.

From this cruel truth, understood by the diabolical mind of satan, were born the following maiming tactics of the enemy.

Misdirection of Priorities

Once the enemy finds that we are committed to the battle, he will try to diminish our effectiveness by distorting the focus of our priorities. Fighting the wrong enemy—getting caught up in "flesh and blood" battles—is one way our priorities get messed up. Emotions run hotter and hotter as we get involved in these battles, thus consuming more and more of our time and energy. And the more energy we expend in that arena, the less energy we have to fight the real enemy, satan!

Varsity Press published a little book titled, *Tyranny of the Urgent*. It clearly describes this dastardly tactic of the enemy. So consumed do we become with "putting out the brush fires," that we have no time to establish a fire-prevention program. Those of us in the grip of linear logic fall prey to this more readily than those given to conceptual logic. I find myself too often just doing what's in front of my nose instead of looking at the bigger picture and drawing on God's wisdom for His priorities.

Corollary to this is the dilemma of getting so busy doing good things that we are robbed of the more excellent part. Poor Martha! She was very busy doing good. And she was not rebuked for that. The aroma of her home-cooked meal must have been tantalizing to the taste buds of even our Master. Yet, when her doing good distorted her perception of Mary's action, she received His rebuke: "Martha, Martha, you are worried and bothered about providing so many things. Only a few things are really needed, perhaps only one. Mary has chosen the best part and you must not tear it away from her." Luke 10:41-42

How can we keep our priorities in line with those "good deeds that He beforehand determined for us to walk in?" Ephesians 2:10 The illustration in Luke 12:47 is in the negative, but I believe the three points can just as accurately advise us in the positive. (We looked at it briefly in Chapter 3, but let's review it here.)

1) Know the Lord's will. Yes, this takes some time— some slowing down. First, take time to read His Word. It is said that direction for 90-95% of our decisions of life are written in the Bible. A second activity to help us know the Lord's will is praying according to the model in Colossians 1:9: "That (we) may be filled with the knowledge of Your will in all wisdom and spiritual understanding." And third, we need some quiet time in His presence to hear the voice of His Spirit behind us saying, "This is the way. Walk ye in it, when we would turn to the left or the right." Isaiah 30:21

2) Prepare to do God's will. We must take the necessary steps to prepare ourselves to do a good job. Whether we are seeking His priorities for a long-term commitment to ministry, or just establishing the priority of getting a good night's rest to be alert for a driver's li-

cense test, the time of preparation is vital.

I work with a lot of churches and cross-cultural teams who have heard the Lord's will. But in their zeal to "be about the Father's business," they go off without the basic preparation for living and ministering in a second culture. Too many of them return (or, more tragically, stay on the field) as casualties of war.

On the other hand, unfortunately, others are always "learning, but never coming to the knowledge of the truth." II Timothy 3:7 Therefore, they lament that they are never quite ready to go. Zeal without knowledge is dangerous; knowledge without zeal is merely cerebral!— a cranial pursuit! Zeal with knowledge, however, yields a servant ready to do his Master's will.

3) Do it! Yes! As scary as it may seem, the time must come when we must just—*do it!* I had graduated from a college which was to have prepared me to be a school teacher. "You are ready," *they* said. The first day was great. The superintendent told us how wonderful the district was. The second day was great. The principal told us how wonderful our school was. But on the third day, when it got down to writing my lesson plans for that first week, after several attempts, I had to go next door to my teaching partner (who had taught more years than I had been alive) and say, "Mrs. Curry, I don't know how to do this!" Kindly, she summarized my four years of college and her twenty-five years of experience in twenty minutes, and as I walked out her door, she said, "Just do it!"

Burnout
Daniel prophesied that in the last days a king (who derives his power from satan) "...shall wear out the saints of the Most High." Daniel 7:25 Wearing out (or in modern vernacular, burnout) is the gradual breaking down of a person's stamina—his resistance—until one day, in to-

tal exhaustion, he reaches crash and burn!

Obviously, burnout is a tactic satan has not reserved exclusively for use by the lawless one, for statistics abound to verify mankind has fallen prey to it through the years. Two out of every three American hospital beds are occupied by psychiatric patients. More than 250,000 are admitted each day into psychiatric facilities for treatment. Depression, a corollary ailment to burnout, is noted by the United Nations World Health Organization as the world's single greatest health problem.

This process of wearing down the saints involves many tactics. The effect of each may appear insignificant. But the sum of them takes its toll.

1) *Sleeplessness:* Many Christians cannot go to sleep without taking a pill. This is not of God. The Psalmist assures us that "He (God) gives His beloved sleep." Psalm 127:2 And if, like David, we find ourselves awake in the night watches, (like David) let's talk with the Shepherd rather than counting sheep! Or popping pills! We must learn to "cast all our cares upon Him for we are His personal concern." I Peter 5:7

2) *Constant Accusation:* Exhaustion, burnout, total mental or emotional breakdown are also brought about through the enemy's constant accusations. The accuser of the brethren relentlessly tries to charge sin to our account. Some Christians live in a continual flood of accusations about the failures of their past life—the wrong choices, the broken relationships, the laments of "...could have, should have, it might have been, if only...." Others are so burdened with (false) guilt that they become a part of every altar call, trying to pray away the condemnation of satan.

Rather, we must wield the Sword of the Spirit in a death blow to satan's accusations, "It is written, 'There is therefore now no condemnation to those who are in

Christ...."' Romans 8:1 Or, "If we confess our sins, He is faithful and just to forgive us our sins, and to cleanse us from all unrighteousness." I John 1:9 We insult the grace of God by not living in His Promises of redemption.

3) *Denial of Food:* Who doesn't enjoy a good meal? The savory smell of spices. The tantalizing taste of tripe—or turnips! Too often our discomfort is from too much food rather than from too little. Yet, denial of food—a *real* starvation diet—will produce a loss of strength, a lack of energy, even mental disorientation. It was in this faint condition that Esau, regarding it lightly already, sold his birthright. See Genesis 25:29-34. It was in this state of literal starving to death that Jesus was approached by satan in the wilderness and was tempted to turn the stone into bread. See Luke 4:1-13.

Fasting, commanded by our Lord, is denial of food. But when it is a fast that God has chosen, it has both physical and spiritual benefits. See Isaiah 58 1-7. This is not the same as satan's denial of food. The enemy's method creates a religion allowing rats and cows to be gods. Because they eat the grain of India, thousands of people suffer malnutrition and starvation. The enemy's method creates a slender-conscious society that has girls' health deteriorating from anorexia. The enemy's method creates a god of materialism, so milk and wheat are dumped into the ocean (to keep the price "stable") rather than letting it be used to feed the hungry. The enemy's method creates a fast food, junk food craze that denies the body of its proper nutrition. The *enemy* does this!

The Bible is replete with feasts and festivals with plenty to eat and drink. See John 2 and Matthew 14:15-21. It seems like one of our first activities in heaven will be a marriage supper. See Revelation 19:9. We are to take no anxious thought for what we should eat. See Matthew

6:31. But we are to eat with thankfulness of heart. See I Timothy 4:3. Food is meant for the body. See Mark 7:19.

Paul had been tossed about the Mediterranean Sea for some fourteen days by a tempestuous wind called Euroclydon. Everything that could be thrown overboard had been jettisoned to help lighten the ship. They didn't know where they were, but by the soundings, they knew they were coming close to land. They threw out four anchors, and wished for the day. In this setting, Paul said, "'Let's eat!' ...and when he had thus spoken, he took bread and gave thanks to God in the presence of them all; and when he had broken it, he began to eat." Acts 27:14-35

4) *Confusion:* When all truth becomes relative, there is confusion. If Dr. Goldstein's Hopeful Monster Mechanism was not confusing enough, evolutionists next foisted on us the Chaos and Complexity Theory. Confusion! Worldwide deficit spending. Confusion! Doctor-assisted suicides. Confusion! Turning the baby around to come out feet-first, thus leaving the head in the birth canal while the doctor slits the baby's neck to harvest the brain cells. Confusion! It is not the Hippocratic Oath; it is a hypocritical oath! Truly, "behind a façade of wisdom they became fools." Romans 1:22

Confusion is brought about by planting doubt. In the Garden, satan asked Eve: "*Hath* God said...." In the Wilderness, satan taunted Jesus: "*If* you are the Son of God...." Demons were often the first to confess that Jesus was the Christ, yet how many of them have planted doubts about hell, sin, holiness, baptism, the virgin birth, heaven—even about life itself? From more than one confused mind I have heard, "Life is but an illusion."

The apostle Paul marveled that the Galatian Christians were so soon removed to "another gospel." Galatians 1:6 He chided the Christians at Corinth for the confusion of denominationalism. See I Corinthians 1:12-13. And, yes, Paul even rebuked Peter for the confusion he caused by first eating with the Gentile Christians in Antioch; then, when others came from Jerusalem, separating himself—so much confusion that even Barnabas was "carried away" by his actions. See Galatians 2:11-14. Yes, satan wants the saints of God to be confused. Confusion yields chaos. And chaos ends in burnout! The opposite of confusion is order. So Luke assures his friend Theophilus that he, "having investigated the course of all things from the very beginning, determined to write an orderly account for you that you might know with certainty the truth concerning the things in which you have been instructed." Luke 1:1-4 John gives us confidence that "these things are written that you might believe that Jesus is the Christ." John 20:31 Jesus is sure that "whoever does not receive the Kingdom of God (with the simplicity and trust) as a little child, shall not enter." Mark 10:15 Paul boldly declares that "that which has been hid for ages and generations is now as clear as daylight to those who love God.... The message is 'Christ in you, the hope of glory!'" Colossians 1:26, 27 Do we now see all things clearly? No! But we have the confidence of His Word that the day will come when "we will know, even as we are known." I Corinthians 13:12

Although from every facet of life (from the world's perspective) there seems to emanate confusion, God's Word declares order.

5) *Continuous physical pain:* The most inevitable fact of life is death. The body cells begin dying even before birth. Add to the natural decay of our body the lack of exercise, poor diet, abusive substances, accidents and numerous other causes and you have the sick state of modern man. Though death is as sure as life, I plan to fight it to my dying day!

Isaiah 53:4 (Amplified) says: "Surely He has borne our griefs—sicknesses, weaknesses and distress—and carried our sorrow and pain." Peter said, "By His stripes you were healed." I Peter 2:24, quoting Isaiah 53:5 And God said, "If you will diligently obey the voice of the Lord your God, and will do that which is right in His sight, and will listen to His commandments, and keep all His statutes, I will put none of these diseases upon you, which I have brought upon the Egyptians: for I am the Lord that heals you." Exodus 15:26

Am I saying that no Christian will ever be sick? No! But there are practices of safety and nutrition that we can employ to lessen the possibility of our falling prey to this tactic of the enemy.

6) *Emotional fear and tension:* We live in a world gone mad. What more can be or needs to be said? Almost every headline points to the bizarre. Murder has become a child's pastime. Terrorists release poison gas in subway tunnels, use commercial jets as lethal rockets or blow themselves up as suicide bombers. Christ prophesied, "In the last days men's hearts would be failing them for fear." Luke 21:26 Yet, again, it is Scripture—God's Word, the Sword of the Spirit—that leads us out of the world's dilemma: "Let not your heart be troubled...." John 14:1 "God did not give us the spirit of fear...." II Timothy 1:7 "Don't worry over anything whatsoever; tell God every detail of your needs in earnest and thankful prayer, and the peace of God, which transcends human understanding, will keep constant guard over your hearts and minds as you rest in Christ Jesus." Philippians 4:6

In short, to combat this insidious burnout tactic of the enemy, we must be a Bible-reading, Bible-hearing, Bible-believing, and Bible-living Christian. Then all hell cannot wear us out. However, "Let him who thinks he stands take heed, lest he falls!" I Corinthians 10:12

Isolation of Thought

"Shhh! You're the only one doing that. Don't tell anyone. No one will understand. You must keep this a secret—from everybody!" satan whispers in our ear. "You can't share that with another Christian. He'll have you kicked out of the church. Keep it quiet." Thus, in our inward struggle, he brings us to that isolation of thought. It is a method of the enemy whereby we can get enmeshed in those secret sins, those "besetting sins which so easily trip us up" that Paul talks about in Hebrews 12:1. Secret sins send thoughts racing helter-skelter through our brain, bombarding our good intentions with evil interruptions. But we dare not tell a soul. No one could have as wicked thoughts as I! Or could they?

Our only way out of this trap is to expose the sinful thoughts to the Light of His Word. "Men love darkness rather than light for their deeds are evil," Jesus said. "For everyone that does evil hates the light, neither comes to the light, lest his deeds should be exposed to the light. But the one who does the truth comes to the light." John 3:19-21

Oftentimes the weight of these secret thoughts to sin are so heavy that it is impossible for us alone to carry them to Calvary, there reckoning ourselves dead to sin and alive unto God through Jesus Christ our Lord. Romans 6:11 Even as Jesus needed Simon of Cyrene to help Him carry His cross to Golgatha, we, at times, need to call on the accountability counsel of two or three intimate friends. In the security of that trust relationship (developed through prayer and sharing), we can "confess our faults one to another and pray for one another so that we may be healed." James 5:16

Majority Rules

Because of the character of satan, he doesn't have to be

logical or reasonable. So, for his purposes, he can now yell, "Hey, you guys. Everybody's doin' it! Join the fun! Come on—try it! You'll like it!" If "isolation of thought" does not trip us up, he will try "majority rules." And we (too often) fall for it.

Yes, I am glad we are free from the "guilt" of "cultural, church-determined sins" of past generations. (And that is not to say that there are not some such "cultural sins" still around.) But I wonder if all the "liberty" we are now "enjoying" in the church is truly Christian liberty? Or is it the whitewashed sin of satan who is saying, "Join the party. See, even your pastor is doing it!"

It is a difficult concept for us to understand, but God is not running a democracy. We did not vote Him in for a four-year term, and if He does well, we will give Him another four. It is a theocracy! A benevolent dictatorship! A Kingdom! And in a kingdom there is one king. And all others—no matter to what place of honor that king might call us—are subjects. "Don't you realize that to whom you yield yourself to obey, his servant you are...." Romans 6:16 It doesn't matter if six billion people may be doing it, if my Master says, "No!" that must settle it. "For now, having been made free from the bondage of sin, we have become servants of God...." Romans 6:22 All things might be lawful, but all things are not expedient! See I Corinthians 6:12; 10:23.

Prosperity, Physical Well-Being, Security
Whoa! Have the winds of doctrine blown this tactic of the enemy around. And yet, it "kinda' hit the fan" when a vocal espouser of the doctrine: "Prosperity—Your divine right!" went bankrupt! But is it such a new method? No! It is at least as old as Job. His response to the news of his prosperity and family's being destroyed in a day is classic: "The Lord gives and the Lord takes away. Blessed be the name of the Lord." Job 1:21

Next we see his physical well-being taken away. His wife says, "Curse God, and die!" Job replies, "You speak as a foolish woman. Shall we receive good at the hand of God and not evil?" See Job 2:9-10. Along come his "comforters"—the men who held him in high esteem. But any security he may have hoped for in their companionship is gone as they begin railing at him. Though more was to come, at one point he stopped them to say, "Hold your peace!...Though He slay me yet will I trust in him." Job 13:15

Hear the three Hebrew children's last words before being thrown into the fiery furnace, "Our God is able to deliver us...but if He doesn't...." Daniel 3:17-18 Or Esther's, just before going in to the king: "If I perish, I perish!" Esther 4:16 And then good old Peter, urging the Lord to avoid Calvary, "...took Him aside and began to rebuke Him, saying, 'Nothing like this must happen to You!' But Jesus turned His back to Peter and rebuked him, 'Get behind me, satan! You stand right in My path, Peter, when you look at things from man's point of view instead of from God's.'" Matthew 16:22-23

May we take our rightful position, "seated in heavenly places in Christ Jesus." Ephesians 2:6 From that vantage point, we can more easily see things from God's perspective. Seated with Him, it is easier to look down upon our circumstances instead of saying, "Well, under the circumstances...."

Pride, Sex, Money
Here is another trilogy of satan's methods in his attempt to destroy the servants of God. The warning about this tactic was first written in Deuteronomy 17:16-17 in reference to choosing a king: "He shall neither multiply horses to himself (pride that accompanies the ownership of horses continues today), neither shall he multiply wives to himself, neither shall he greatly

multiply to himself silver and gold." It is of interest to note (and should be a warning to us) that the wisest man who ever lived fell for all three of these! Solomon had 40,000 horses (I Kings 4:26); he had 700 wives, princesses and 300 concubines (I Kings 11:3); he had 666 (an interesting number!) talents of gold coming to him each year, and silver was as pebbles in the streets of Jerusalem. See I Kings 10:14, 27.

Again, the enemy's tactics are not new, nor that clever. Yet we fall prey to them generation after generation. It is interesting to note that this trilogy of methods is still tripping up the leadership of our world, whether Christian or secular, whether male or female.

Scriptural admonitions (our "It is written's...") to avoid these temptations abound. Let these three suffice for this study. (Can you guess that these are mine? Of course, you have to allow the Holy Spirit to be *your* ammunition chooser.)

1) "Humble yourself under the mighty hand of God, and He will lift you up and make your life significant." James 4:10

2) "The will of God for your life is holiness, and that entails first of all abstaining from sexual immorality. Every one of you should learn to control his body, keeping it pure and treating it with respect, and never regarding it as an instrument of self-gratification.... It is not for nothing that the Spirit God gives is called the *Holy* Spirit." I Thessalonians 4:3-5, 8

3) "Don't lay in store for yourselves treasures on earth, where they may be destroyed by bugs and weather and where thieves can steal them: But keep on storing up for yourself treasures in Heaven where there is no moth or rust to consume them and where thieves cannot break in and steal them: For wherever your treasure is, you may be certain that your heart will be there too!" Matthew 6:19-21

Temptation, Condemnation, Stronghold
Yet a third devilish trilogy is the sequence of temptation, condemnation and stronghold. James assures us
that "when we are tempted, we are not tempted by God,
for He can neither be tempted nor does He tempt anyone." James 1:13 But when man is tempted an unholy
trinity is at work in the degenerative spiral that follows.
The world, the flesh (our sinful nature) and the devil in
diabolical harmony provide the means for this slippery
slide. Here is how James describes it:
> "But every man is tempted..." (by the devil)
> "when he is enticed..." (by the worldly pleasures)
> "and drawn away of his own lust..." (his sinful
> nature, minding the things of the flesh)
> "when that lust is conceived..." (the sinful nature
> begins indulging in the worldly pleasures)
> "it brings forth sin..." (sin is the child born of
> this unholy union)
> "and sin..." (the monster we have produced)
> "when it is finished..." (as it plays itself out to
> the limit of its potential for evil)
> "brings forth death!" James 1:14-15

And that's just the first third of the trilogy! Once we
have fallen to the enemy on that battlefront of temptation, is he content to leave us there? No! He continues
to fight us—with condemnation. Even as our screams
are echoing down that slippery slide, he follows us in
hot pursuit with his taunts of condemnation: "You? A
Christian? A really good Christian doesn't act like that!
Don't you dare pray. You are regarding iniquity in your
heart. God will never hear you. You've done that once
too often. You have committed the unpardonable sin...!"
And you can probably add other revilings he has used
against you.
    But he goes on. As a boxer is trained to keep punch-
ing at the injury he has already inflicted, so satan

keeps pounding on the weaknesses he has discovered in our flesh. And the wound goes deeper with each jab. Time and again he incessantly leads us into temptation and condemns us when we fall.

He continues. As a spider slowly encases its prey in silken thread, satan weaves a case against us. We come to believe his lies. And we are caught in the snare of bondage to sin—a stronghold. "O wretched man that I am! Who shall deliver me from the clutches of my own sinful nature?" Romans 7:24

Even as I write this, I shudder at the dismal prospects of people trying to find a solution without the Word. But here is where the Sword of the Spirit enters to cut a swath through the tangled mass of satan's web: "No temptation has come your way that is not experienced by all men. But God can be trusted not to allow you to suffer any temptation beyond your powers of endurance. He will see to it that every temptation has a way out, so that it will never be impossible for you to bear it." I Corinthians 10:13

And "We don't have a High Priest who is out of touch with the feelings of our infirmities—for He Himself has shared fully in all our experiences of temptation, except that He never sinned. For this very reason, therefore, we can approach the throne of grace boldly and with full assurance that we may receive mercy, and find grace in our time of need." Hebrews 4:15-16 And again the Sword slashes: "The servant of the Lord must correct in meekness, in the hope that they will repent and come to know the Truth, and that they may come to their senses and escape out of the snare of the devil, having been held captive by him, henceforth to do God's will." II Timothy 2:25-26

Curiosity, Experimentation, Addiction
Yet another trilogy that has ensnared untold numbers

of unsuspecting people. "I would never actually *do* it. There's no harm in watching others do it," they deceive themselves. "I'm just curious—maybe I'll learn something," they defend their action. But sooner or later, the desire to 'try it, you might like it' overpowers any compunction of restraint. "See, now that wasn't so hard," the enemy encourages. Then again. And again and again. As the poor frog in the slowly heating pot of water does not realize he is about to lose his life, so the one who has *just* experimented becomes addicted.

The initial thought of addiction might be to that of alcohol or drugs. But anything can become an addiction. A friend of mine was addicted to shopping. Pornography, gluttony, movies—anything that has come to control your behavior is an addiction. Paul said, "All things are lawful unto me, but I will not be brought under the power of any." I Corinthians 6:12

Questioning God's Word, Half-Scriptures, Selectively Ignoring Scripture
Though, no doubt, there are other tactics the enemy has used and is using, I will conclude this subject with one last trilogy of methods. The enemy knows the Word. Yet he has been questioning it and sowing doubt in the minds of people since he asked Eve, "Did God *really* say...?" A classic of this generation (and probably of others) is the question: "Do you really believe that a God of love will send all those people to hell?"

The answer, of course, is "No!" God is not going to send anyone to hell. Hell was made for the devil and his angels. Matthew 25:41 Each individual who ends up there will have done so by his own free will and choice. "God is not willing that any perish, but that all come to repentance." II Peter 3:9 "And He (Jesus Christ) is the personal atonement for our sins; and not for ours only, but also for the sins of the whole world." I John 2:2

We don't have to leave the church to illustrate half-scriptures. I was raised on them! "Nuggets of truth" lifted out of context from the Holy Pages of God's Word that sounded too good to be true or sounded so bad that they struck fear into our young minds. And we weren't encouraged to read the Bible on our own. "Bring your Bible to church. What? Don't you trust the preacher?" was jokingly directed at me when I began to carry my Bible and really study the Word.

It wasn't until I was an adult (even after four years of Bible college) that I began to realize that the other half of the thought of Philippians 2:12 was Philippians 2:13! Yes! "We *are* to work out our own salvation with fear and trembling...." Why tremble? Because it is awesome to consider that "...it is God who is working in us both to will and to do of His good pleasure" (Refer again to the section on half-scriptures in Chapter 2.)

Another culprit of "half-scriptures" is the "Promise Card Box." They are Precious Truths of God's Word taken out of context. Most of the promises of the Word are tied to some action on our part. But without seeing the promise in context, it is too easy to forget our part and only "claim the promises of God!"

We want "...and it shall be given unto you, good measure, pressed down and shaken together, and running over, shall men give to you." Wow! That is a mouthful of promise. Oops! In "claiming" that promise, we left out one word, the first word of that verse: "*Give...*"! And the last part of the verse which says, "For with the same measure you use to *give* will it be given back to you." Luke 6:38

It was the religious leaders of Israel who selectively ignored all of the prophetic Scriptures of a suffering Messiah. The Scriptures were all there. Jesus went through them with the two disciples on the Emmaus Road. See Luke 24:13-35.

It was the religious leaders of England who selectively ignored the Scriptures which spoke of their part in the fulfillment of the Great Commission when they shouted down a youthful William Carey with the words, "If God wants to save the heathen, He will do it without your help or ours!"

And it is the Laodicean church of today—"rich and increased with goods and having need of nothing" (Revelation 3:17)—that selectively ignores the cries of the poor and needy. Yet, the Word still shouts: "Open your mouth, judge righteously, and plead the cause of the poor and needy." Proverbs 31:9 And again, "But whoever has this world's goods, and sees his brother in need, and closes off his heart of compassion from him, how can the love of God dwell in him?" I John 3:17 See also Proverbs 24:11-12.

The solution to this trilogy of error is in a lifestyle equal to Paul's passionate statement to the elders of Ephesus, "I never held back from declaring to you the Whole Counsel of God." Acts 20:27 It is the "Whole Counsel of God" that will keep us from error. As you study the Word, consider the following:

1) When a passage of Scripture doesn't seem to line up with our lifestyle, it is our lifestyle that should be put in question, not the Scripture;

2) Always read, study and understand a Scripture in its context, allowing Scripture to interpret Scripture; and

3) Develop a study of the Word that gets us from Genesis to Revelation and all that is in between.

What more can be said? What more needs to be said? Only this: "And when he had exhausted every kind of temptation, the devil withdrew until his next opportunity!" Luke 4:13

BEWARE! BE AWARE!

PRACTICAL INSIGHTS

WHEN SATAN HASSLES CHRISTIANS

I trust you are reading through these problems and solutions very slowly. Give yourself enough time to think about whether or not you are vulnerable at each point. Ask yourself, "Is there a weak spot in my defenses here?"

Problem   The enemy tries to hassle us when we have expectations that are unrealistically high. When that situation exists, we are in a vulnerable place for attack. Those unrealistic expectations could be of ourselves, or of other people, or of a particular circumstance or situation. This sets us up for disillusionment and disappointment, which can then lead to anger and ultimately bitterness. All because we expected too much, and it just didn't happen. We have opened ourselves up for the enemy's attack.

Solution   Learn what is realistic by getting feedback. In Romans 12:3 Paul tells us to "...have a sane estimate of our capabilities." (And, I might add, we need a sane estimate of other people's capabilities, also). We need to be realistic. But that's too easy to just say. Maybe we think we *are* being realistic. But we find ourselves angry and disappointed—disillusioned and bitter because time after time things just don't happen the way they *should*.

Find a qualified third person who can and will be objective with you. Discuss your expectations with them, and be open to their perspectives on what is realistic. Get their feedback and listen to what they have to say, and then be open to revising you expectations.

Write your expectations down on a piece of paper. Look at them at different times of the day, week, and month. Maybe your goals are too high. Or, too low! Rewrite them. Modify your expectations and goals to a challenging level which realistically allows you to reach them.

Problem The enemy tries to hassle me through "accidents." I put the word "accidents" in quotes because we know that from God's perspective there is no such thing as an accident. Sometimes we go through things that seem totally unexplainable.

In the two years we were in Brazil every family member experienced serious "accidents" or strange physical problems. Our youngest son drowned in the university pool. When my husband arrived at the emergency room, the attending physician was filling out his death certificate because he was too far gone. He didn't know what else to do! But, by a miracle of God, our son was completely restored within 24 hours. He was healed.

Another time Neal sustained a fractured skull and severe brain concussion. That occurred while he was watching another son undergoing a serious hernia surgery. Our daughter's adenoid surgery resulted in her almost hemorrhaging to death. A basketball standard crashing down resulted in "only" a broken nose, and a bruised foot. Fire ant stings resulted in parts of my husband's body swelling to twice his size. Another son had a serious relapse of hepatitis with "permanent" liver damage. I was suspected of having leprosy. I didn't have it, but the tests took two months to eliminate that possibility. Do you think that waiting caused a "little" stress?! So, through weird things—accidents and strange sicknesses—the enemy can get to you.

Solution Allow yourself to feel; talk things out; and choose to trust God. There are some Christians who believe we are not to have feelings. We are to be stoic. It is not holy or righteous to be stoic—to be out of touch with our feelings and deny them. We all have feelings; it is just that some of us (and maybe all of us some of the time) bury them. We try to ignore them. Whereas others not only feel them, but freely express them—sometimes too freely!

If you are upset, you might as well admit it and talk about it with a wise and trusted friend. It is therapeutic to talk it out instead of holding it in.

Choose with your will to trust God. Realize that He knew that the "accident" was going to happen. He didn't lose control; He is still God. Talk to Him about your feelings. Look for the good that God wants to bring out of this situation, and be confident that He uses all things for His purposes. "And we know that all things work together for good to them that love God...to be conformed to the image of His Son." Romans 8:28-29 James 1 is a good chapter to study to help us understand and accept the trials and temptations that come our way. They can build our faith, develop patience and endurance or teach us some new lesson. The "refining fires" of I Peter 1 bring our faith "to the praise and honor and glory on that day when Jesus Christ reveals Himself."

Unfortunately, if we do not choose to trust God, "accidents" can cause anger and deep bitterness. But know that He is still in control. He is still God. We can know that there was a good reason and a positive lesson that could have been learned.

Problem   The enemy tries to hassle me through depression. Oppression—which we will look at next—is supernatural in nature. Depression, however, is from natural causes. It may come from a physical condition, or from an emotional state of being, or from circumstances. Unfortunately, considering the world we live in, there are a lot of natural reasons to be depressed. And satan will take advantage of every possible situation to sink us deeper into depression. **Solution** Find the reason behind the depression. As soon as you are aware that a "slump" is beginning, you need to ask why? Why am I feeling depressed? Am I too tired? Have I been eating right? Have I been getting enough sleep? Is it a physical condition? Do I need a check-up? Am I drained emotionally or spiritually? Have I been giving out more than I have taken in? Am I too isolated?

A "yes" to any of those questions—especially if it is a recurring problem—is a pretty good clue to the source of the problem. Those situations that you can change—change! If you cannot change the circumstances (newborn baby keeping you up all night, night after night after night), talk with someone about it. It is true that sometimes just admitting something out loud can help to ease its pain. Have a friend pray with you for God's strength and wisdom. The worst thing to do is sit down alone and think about how bad the situation is that is depressing you! You will only sink deeper and deeper and wallow in it, until it seems nearly impossible to get out.

Sometimes you need to break the depression by changing your activity. Many years ago I was on a treatment for a physical condition. There were times when all of a sudden I would feel depressed. There seemed to be no apparent reason. (And it wasn't oppression.) I learned to immediately stop whatever I was doing, and do something else. I would turn on the radio or read a book or call a friend—anything different from what I was doing when the feeling of depression hit. It would avert the descending gloom.

Problem The enemy tries to hassle me through

oppression. As I mentioned in the last section, whereas depression has a natural cause, oppression is supernatural. Again, to illustrate, let me tell you about one place we stayed on the mission field. Every time a new person came to our area, within a week they would be saying that they felt depressed. But they couldn't understand why. Well, it wasn't depression. We who had been there awhile knew it was oppression. It was like a heavy blanket that hung over the area all the time. Logic says it was because we were surrounded by spirit worshippers who often made sacrifices at the entrance of the area where we lived and tried to put curses on us. That is a reasonable explanation for oppression!

Solution Learn to recognize the oppressing spirits; take authority over them; resist them! Draw near to God. The key thing here is recognizing who the oppression is coming from. One of the major problems in overcoming this atmosphere was that some did not acknowledge the oppressive atmosphere was demonic. They would kick the broken pottery bowl (with votive candle still burning) into the ditch and mutter, "Mere superstition."

The second action step is to take authority over the enemy in Jesus' Name and resist him. Realize that "greater is He that is in you than he that is in the world." I John 4:4 Oppression was a recurring problem for me in that place. It easily took the first six months to get a handle on what was happening and not be knocked down day after day! The real key came one evening at the dinner table. The devotions were being read from Isaiah. It was a verse that was very familiar to all of us, but all of a sudden it just clicked. He will give "...a garment of praise for a spirit of heaviness." Isaiah 61:3

I got mad! I got really mad at the deception of

the evil one. "You know," I said to him, "you have had me fooled and deceived all this time. I'm not going to put up with it any longer!" Well, it was not "roses" from then on. But now I recognized the source and the solution. I took authority, resisted him, and then focused my attention on God with praise!

Sometimes it took as long as fifteen minutes. Because we lived in a group housing situation, I couldn't be assured of much privacy at home, so I often went for a walk to be alone. I would tell the enemy he was a liar and to leave—in Jesus' Name! I would then begin talking with God: "I'm glad I'm Your child. Thank You for sending Your Son to die for me. Thank You for loving me. Thank You that You are all-powerful and that nothing is too hard for You." I would just keep thanking Him for everything that would come to my mind.

All that I would say would be directly from Scripture so the enemy couldn't argue with it. I would not voice my opinions or feelings on anything—only Scripture. Then, after I would run out of things to say (all of this was out loud), I would start singing praise and worship songs in the spirit, and I would sing until my mind was back in the right perspective. Then I would walk back home. Sometimes I would have to do this several times a week because it was such a constant battle. But I won! Rather, God won! I accepted His provision.

5

SPIRITUAL AUTHORITY

"In My Name you will cast out evil spirits..." Mark 16:17
"Resist the devil and he will flee from you." James 4:7

Never would I want to do such an exhaustive study on the character and methods of satan (as in the previous chapter) without immediately following it with the powerful, victorious message of spiritual authority. The dynamics of spiritual authority over satan and evil spirits have been vested in every believer in Jesus. Satan is a vanquished foe; he lost at Calvary. The power and authority of Jesus' Name can be invoked by every Soldier of the Cross. The devil is a defeated enemy; he lost at Calvary. Victorious living can be the norm for every child of God. For the wicked one is a conquered adversary; he lost at Calvary!

We will consider two significant dimensions of spiritual authority that we are able to exercise over the enemy: to Cast Out and to Resist. They are equal in power and scope and importance, though they are generally applied in different arenas of battle.

Peter stood on the Mount of Ascension with Jesus, still hoping that He would then establish His earthly Kingdom. Instead, he heard Jesus say, "You must go out into the whole world and proclaim the Gospel to every creature.... These signs will follow those who do

believe: They will drive out evil spirits in My Name...."
Mark 16:15,17

Though the former level of authority, "casting out," has the mystique and suspense of drama (and gets more attention—positive and negative), it is practiced less often than the latter. The more common authority that we are to exercise over the enemy can be summarized in one word: Resist! This is a daily—hourly—moment-by-moment aggressive, offensive action of repelling the always-encroaching forces of evil.

Both phrases—*cast out* and *resist*—are fighting words. Both embody the full authority of Jesus Christ. Neither should be exercised apart from His authority. Neither should be engaged in without full battle preparation. It is important that we strongly depend on Scripture and upon the Spirit of God (Who will lead us into all Truth) as we consider our authority over the enemy.

CAST OUT
As riots of a few hundred angry people are more "exciting" than peaceful demonstrations of thousands of law-abiding citizens, so the spiritual authority of exorcism—the casting out of demonic beings—is more intriguing than resisting the devil. At the outset of this study we need to be very careful with our use of terminology, because in this area of authority, satan has successfully side-tracked Christians into an intensely heated "flesh and blood" battle.

As we watch the Christians fight with each other, we can so clearly see this as a tactic of the enemy to divert us from casting him out in Jesus' Name. While the poor bedeviled sufferer looks on—still in the anguish of his pain, Christians go to war with each other. If we could see behind the scene into the spiritual arena, I think we would see satan smiling in sick satisfaction at having diverted the battle away from himself—again!

With Swords in hand, the warriors begin their battle: "Can a Christian be *demon-possessed?*" one queries. "Well, no, he can't be demon-possessed, but he can be *demonized!*" another states. "Well, no, he can't be demonized but he can *have a demon!*" yet another counters. "Well, no, he can't have a demon in his spirit but he can *have one in his flesh!*" argues a fourth. "Well, no, he can't have one in his flesh but *it can be attached to his body!*" surmises a fifth person. Well, no.... Exactly—no! For the suffering soul is still suffering. And the Christians who battle Christians over this issue have to retreat, suffering from their own wounds, still not having resolved the issue.

(In the original draft of this chapter, I had to scratch out several paragraphs of argument, for, in reading back over them, I realized that satan had drawn me into a "flesh and blood" battle over this "flesh and blood" battle!)

To avoid the semantics of the location of evil presence, I simply use the word: *hassled!* Satan hassles people—Christians and non-Christians. The word, hassled, doesn't say where he is or how he got there or even if it is actually satan who is there. (Remember, he is not omnipresent.) However, "hassled" acknowledges the presence of evil (evil forces, evil beings, demons, evil spirits, powers and principalities of evil) which, in Jesus' Name, must leave.

Was this not Jesus' approach when He loosed a woman from a spirit of infirmity? She was a daughter of Abraham. Yet she had been bound by satan for eighteen years. Should she not be freed even on the Sabbath? See Luke 13:11-17.

My wife's uncle, a theologian of distinguished recognition, taught in a seminary in West Africa for some 52 years. In reference to the location of an evil power, he would say, "When someone walked into my classroom or office and I sensed in my spirit the presence of evil, I never pulled out my theological texts to try to analyze the situation. I simply said, 'In the Name of Jesus, be gone!' And it had to leave!"

As we prepare for battle, we open ourselves up to the spirit world. We become more sensitive to the presence of demonic power. We also need to believe there *is* authority in Jesus' Name. And we need to believe *in* that Authority in order to allow the "signs to follow."

Some Biblical Examples
We don't have to look far into Jesus' ministry before we see Him busy casting out demons. In Mark 1:23-27, Jesus "rebuked him (an unclean spirit), saying, 'Hold your peace, and come out of him!' And when the unclean spirit had torn him, and cried with a loud voice, he came out of him."

In Mark 3:22, in an attempt to discredit the fame that surrounded Jesus for His authoritative actions (Mark 1:28), the scribes from Jerusalem said He was possessed by Beelzebub, and that He drove out devils because He was in league with the prince of devils.

Mark 5:2-20 records the story of one who lived among the tombs, for he was a man with an unclean spirit. Jesus said, "Come out of him, you unclean spirit." And they cried with a loud voice, "What have I to do with you, Jesus, Son of the Most High God? I adjure You by God not to torment me!" Jesus asked him, "What is your name?" "My name is Legion, for we are many."

Mark 7:25-30 tells the story of a young daughter of a Greek woman who had an unclean spirit. After a very interesting cultural discussion, Jesus said to the mother, "For this saying, go your way; the devil is gone out of your daughter."

In verse 17 of Chapter 9 of Mark, it is called a dumb

spirit. The disciples could not cast it out. Jesus asked the father when this spirit came into his son. "Since he was a child," was his reply. In verse 25, Jesus rebuked the foul spirit, commanding the deaf and dumb spirit to come out of him.

Only a few verses later (v. 38), John said, "Master, we saw one casting out devils in Your Name, and because he was not part of our group, we told him to stop." But Jesus said not to stop him, "...for he who is not against us is for us!" Mark 9:40

Demonic activity, for sure! But you never heard Jesus debating where the spirit was. And you will never catch me in a debate as to where that spirit is. It is evil. It is of the devil. It is hassling the lives of people created to worship the Living God. In the Name of Jesus, and on the authority and power of His Name, we as His believers, can see victory in these battles.

Demonic Activity Today

America was founded by godly men on godly principles. The restraining powers of our heritage have held at bay the full force of demonic activity in our country. However, in recent decades as more and more of what we regard sacred is stripped away, headlines become more frequent of witches and warlocks and of animal sacrifices. And—tragically—many of America's missing children are now known to have been involved in satanic sacrifice. "Snuff" movies, where the actors are literally murdered, are being filmed in America! But most of this activity is still under the cloak of secrecy—or denial.

In other countries, however, where the demonic dimensions of the spirit world have had free reign for centuries, these activities are believed and practiced more openly. F. Kefa Sempangi, in his book, *A Distant Grief,* tells of his mother sending him off (as a young boy) to learn to read the Bible. Evidently there was no school in his village, so his mother arranged for him to live with some people in another town. And as she told him good-bye, she said, "Do not come home until you can read the Bible to me."

The following account graphically portrays the power of demonic forces in Kefa's life in Africa:

> It was then, at the age of 12, that I (Kefa) said good-bye to Banga and to my childhood. My mother took me to Nantule herself, and we traveled on foot. It was my first time away from home. As we walked on small winding paths through heavy trees and tangled climbing plants, my mother explained to me about the gods. The god of the forest was not the same as the god of the grasslands; the god of the grasslands was not the same as the god of the lake. There were many other gods as well. There were gods of planting, of harvesting, of prosperity. There were gods of the earth and gods of the heavens. When I was older I would learn their names. For now it was enough that I learn to serve the living God; I was going to Nantule to learn about Jesus.
>
> We came to a river and, where the water narrowed, we crossed over a small wooden bridge. I stared curiously at someone bathing below. "Be careful," my mother warned, pushing me along. "It might be Omusambwa. She is the river goddess and she will strike you blind!" For the rest of our journey I was quiet in fear. I had not known the world was so full of gods.
>
> When we arrived in Nantule my mother placed me in the hands of a guardian family and left me with this stern warning: "Son, until you are able to read do not come back to me." As she walked away, I began to cry. She did not stop or turn her head, and it was then that I knew she too was

shedding tears.

The home my mother left me in was the home of a shrine priestess and only a few hours after my arrival I was taken to the shrine to meet my hostess and pay respect to the gods, "the elders" of the home. The shrine was a round, thatched-roof hut in back of the main house. It was surrounded by an elephant grass fence and as I walked towards it I could hear singing and the sounds of rattling gourds and beating drums. Behind the shrine was a small grove of shrunken coffee trees and their bare, neglected branches made me wish I was home again in Banga.

"Ingira. Tukulamusiza! Come in, my child. We welcome you to our home!" A deep male voice greeted me from the interior of the shrine as I peered nervously through its doorway. I stood hesitating on the threshold until I heard the command repeated and then, taking a deep breath, I stepped inside. For a moment I was surrounded by darkness. When my eyes grew accustomed to the dim half-light of the room, I found myself standing among a small group of people who were sitting on a floor of lemon grass. They stared at me curiously as I looked nervously around the room.

In the center of the shrine were four roof poles embroidered with colored reeds and backcloths, and through the poles I saw a log hearth covered with goat skins. The hearth was protected by a barrier of raised spears and shields, and behind the barrier was a burning fire. In the hot coals of the fire sat a woman!

I stared at her in astonishment, and she welcomed me in the same deep male voice I had heard from the doorway. "Come here, my child.

*Do not be afraid. I am glad to see you and you
will be happy in your new home."*

My heart was beating furiously as I knelt and
returned her greeting in the manner my mother
had taught me. The woman smiled at me, pleased
at my politeness, but my own face was frozen in
fear. Who was this woman who could sit in the
middle of a scorching hot fire and not be burned?
Why did she speak like a man? I stared at the
flames licking around her clothes but I could see
nothing unusual in her dress. She wore a simple
cloth garment, like the women of my own village,
and her hair was well-trimmed. There were no tribal scars on her face. Her one exceptional feature
was her kindness to me, a small child and a
stranger in her home.

"While you are a guest here," she said, still
speaking in a male voice, "it is your duty to tend
the fires of the shrine."

Looking back, I do not know why I answered
the shrine priestess as I did. I knew nothing
about Jesus except the chorus my mother had
taught me, but somehow I felt that I was already
in His service and that it would be wrong to serve
in the shrine of another god.

"I cannot tend your fires," I said, hoping not to
offend the priestess. "My mother has sent me
here to learn to read the Book." The words were
barely out of my mouth when my hostess was
overcome with a shaking rage. She thundered,
and the devotees sitting closest to her covered
their heads. I stared at the convulsed woman in
terror. Seconds later a young girl grabbed my arm
and pulled me away from the hearth.

"That is not my mother's voice speaking to
you," she said, whispering in fear. "It is the god

of thunder. You must do whatever he tells you!"

Just then the god repeated his command and my legs trembled. I had never spoken with a god before and I did not understand why he would be so angry. But I was more certain than ever that I could not tend the fires of his shrine. My mother had sent me to Nantule to learn to read about Jesus.

Almost against my will, I refused a second time. The god thundered again and when he spoke the deep male voice was no longer kind. "If you continue in your stubbornness," he said, "you will die in the first drizzling rain. Lightning will strike you dead."

With this promise, the thundering came to an end. The woman moved from the fire and sat down near the hearth on a leopard skin. She spread a black goatskin in front of her feet and with both hands picked up an ivory horn filled with cowrie shells and coffee beans. She was ready to begin her divination, but first, without looking up, she ordered me from the shrine.

—*A Distant Grief*, F. Kefa Sempangi,
GL Regal Books, Glendale, CA. Used by permission.

This is not a "make-believe" story. It happened in our generation. These forces are at work in our world today. And they are being given more and more freedom to operate in America—in your town and mine.

A Personal Experience

To my knowledge, I have participated in only one exorcism. It was powerfully dramatic. The following day, I wrote down as many details as I could recall. I wanted to keep the account as accurate as possible. I share the story here so that we will "not be ignorant of his devices," so that we will not be caught off guard by the enemy. And to give personal testimony of the spiritual authority we have in Jesus' Name:

Susan and Bill were friends of ours. Sometimes we enjoyed a close relationship, and then through time and distance, we often lost contact. We had been back from Peru for a year and were seeing them more frequently now.

Susan called me in the middle of the night. "Praise God! It's over! It's over! They're all gone. Pray for Bill. I just cast demons out of him." I knew she could not have cast demons out of Bill. Just a few days before, I had had a good talk with him. I knew that he was not demon-possessed. And I knew that she was the one who had been involved in demonic activity, especially trying to contact her father's spirit on several occasions.

I called John, a good friend of mine who had had some experience with exorcism. After several phone calls back and forth, we decided to go over to Bill & Susan's house. Al, another friend, agreed to meet us there.

When we knocked on the door at 2:00 a.m., Susan answered. She was trembling. She greeted us by saying, "Praise God! They're gone!" As we stood in the entry, Bill came out of the bedroom, hesitantly agreeing that "something" might have come out of him. *This couldn't be true*, I thought. She was the one acting weird, not him. He seemed afraid, but not weird.

We sat in the living room, strewn with junk. A lot of paper bags were sitting in the archway between the living room and the front hall. Needless to say, this turn of events baffled John. I was saying she was the problem; now Bill and Susan were saying Bill had just been delivered from demons. John took Susan slowly through the steps of being a Christian. She answered "yes" to all his questions, even when he mentioned the "blood of Christ," which no demon is supposed to be able to acknowledge. (We'll talk more about that later.) "Well, why does it seem so eerie in here?" we asked.

Susan replied "Oh, it must be some more things in the house we need to get rid of." All of the bags in the hallway were ready to be thrown out. First she had decided the picture of a friend was possessed of a demon—and then a statue. And more items were added to the stack as she roamed through the house trying to rid it of the "demons" she had "cast out" of Bill. The three of us—no, all five of us—were perplexed!

Suddenly it dawned on me that all of this, including that pseudo-exorcism, was satan's attempt at throwing us off the real issue.

By now it was 3:00 a.m. We had earlier asked her about an experience she had told to my wife on a previous occasion. It had happened when she was in college. She had passed if off lightly. Now it came clear to me that this experience was the key issue. So we pressed in on it. She began confidently relating, "Yes, we were in the room." (It was in the dorm of a Christian college.) "Several other girls were there with me. When the room got cold they decided to leave. I knelt down. They warned me not to do it. I told them I knew what I was doing."

"What did you do?" we asked her. At this point she struggled and cried about not remembering. Then in an awful lament she wailed, "I didn't really do that! No, I couldn't have!"

"What did you do?" we insisted.

Finally, she pitifully groaned, "I told satan I wanted to help him with his work if he let me speak with my father." Upon this confession, the demons in her began showing themselves by speaking with strange voices through her lips.

Immediately, Al stepped forward and took such authority over the demons and the whole situation, that later he admitted that the power of God that had come upon him even surprised him. He commanded the demons to identify themselves as they came out. And they were going to come out! John and I stepped back and began praying.

Al: "What is your name? I command you to tell me your name, and then you are coming out!"

In a most gruesome tone of voice, we heard a demon say, "Envy; yes, envy!"

Al: "Yes, your name is envy, and there are six other demons in there with you. Now come out in Jesus' Name. I command you to come out and never enter this body again." And with a scream, saying its name, envy came out, leaving Susan weak and crying softly.

Suddenly, the contortion of evil reappeared. "I'm back! See, you didn't get rid of me."

Al, still displaying that mighty power of God said, "No, you are not envy. Envy is gone and will never come back, but you are another demon and you will soon be gone. What is your name?"

"Murder!"

"No, your name is not murder. There is no murder in Susan."

"Death!"

"No, your name is not death. What is your

name? I demand you to tell us."

"Fear! Fear! Fear!" The demon repeatedly shouted this word in an attempt to induce fear in Al. We realized this word was coming out in a different tone of voice than had just been speaking. The very utterance displayed the whole gamut of the feeling of fear, both within herself, and intending to affect us.

Al: "Yes, your name is fear. You have bound this poor girl in fear for 13 years. Now you yourself are fearful about where you are going. You are afraid of being disembodied. Okay, you can go into an animal. You are coming out of Susan right now. As you come out, you will make the sound of the animal you are going into."

The demon during this time was displaying total fear—recoiling from the forcefulness of Al's voice. It was wanting to argue with him and object to what he was saying, but could not. It had made attempts to speak, but fear itself stood silent in fear in the presence of the authority of the powerful Spirit of God. And in obedience to God's authority through Al, it began oinking like a pig—three or four oinks and it was gone, again leaving Susan limp and weak and crying.

Shortly, another demon identified itself by beginning to cause Susan's lips to babble and blubber. Susan—rather the demon—began speaking incoherently in a tone of voice yet different than those previously.

Al: "What is your name?"

"Confusion."

Al: "Yes, you have done so much to destroy this girl, and now in the Name of Jesus you are leaving her and going to the abyss—the pit from where you came!" It screamed an objection, but then was gone. (I did not take out my theology book at this point to determine whether a Christian has the authority to send a demon to the pit. We did discuss it later and decided since it left, it was gone and there was no value in debating where it had gone.) It was gone! By now it was 5:30 a.m. Surprisingly, we felt no fatigue. We had clarity of thought and such presence of mind that it amazed us. Also, at the times when the demons were not identifying themselves and having direct conversation with Al, we could talk to Susan or get her a kleenex. At this time, she was drinking a cup of coffee. Al would retire to the other side of the room. John and I continued in prayer and observation most of the time. When Al would step forward again, she would recoil, vividly showing the power of the unseen world. The powers and principalities of darkness were falling in defeat to the power of God.

Al: "Okay, envy, fear and confusion are gone. There are four more of you in there. In Jesus' Name, identify yourself."

A voice with a southern drawl spoke. (I have nothing against our friends in the South, but the voice did have a very clear southern drawl.) It had spoken on several previous occasions, I now remembered. "There aren't any others here. Only me, and Susan wants me to stay. She doesn't want me to leave."

Al: "No, there are four of you in there, and you are all coming out." There was more conversation with this voice. It kept denying the presence of others. Al insisted, "In Jesus' Name, identify yourself and come out.

A different voice snarled with fierce contempt. "Hate! Hate! Hate! I hate you!" And with that it had identified itself.

"Be gone in Jesus' Name!" Al said. It was gone. It was amazing to see the authentic demonstration of the power of God and the clear-cut results.

Al: "Okay, who is coming out next? Identify yourself."

From this point on the only voice we heard was that casual southern drawl. "Oh, go on, I'm not leaving. In fact, Susan is going to have many others joining me soon." About 45 minutes of continual, "Come out! in Jesus' Name" were opposed by that casual voice. *Why couldn't Al (by the power of God) exorcise this one?* I wondered. It just would not come out!

By now it was 7:30 a.m. We called a prayer chain in the church, gave brief information and asked that they spread the word to pray. We also called several other elders of the church to come over and help in prayer and in spiritual insight.

There was more demanding for this demon to identify itself and come out. A crucifix, from which the yet unidentified demon shrieked in fear, was used to keep the demon from talking.

As I was sitting back, trying to put it all together, it was suddenly revealed to me by the Lord that the demon was a lying spirit. It was this lying spirit then that had confessed the power of the blood of Christ. It had told innumerable lies: Susan wants me; others will be back; there aren't any others here.... I shared this with Al.

Al: "You are a lying spirit!" It gave a shriek!

Strangely, this demon, though now identified, would never openly admit its name. It would no more than give an assenting grunt with a sick, sly smile. It began patting Susan, rubbing admiringly up and down her arm, paying close attention to her hands and fingers. (Though it was Susan's hand that was making the motion, it was obvious that her movements were directed by this demonic being). "You like Susan, don't you? You don't want to leave her, do you? You are going to come out, in Jesus' Name!" Al's voice crescendoed.

There was a lot of shouting and demanding. But it was to no avail. Needless to say, we were dumbfounded. As other elders arrived, timeouts were taken to tell them what was going on. This one was quite talkative, which fact was very frustrating. At last, we realized that although it seemed we could not exorcise this demon, we could command it not to talk: "In the name of Jesus, be silent!" It would try to talk. Deep efforts at sounds came and would form and gurgle in her throat, but no words would come out of her mouth. This would last for 10 to 15 minutes, when Al would again command it to silence.

Our desire to have it silent was so that we could talk to Susan. We tried to reason with her to release this demon. When we were able to get through to her, telling her what control this demon had over her, how he was lying to her, she acted surprised. "Did I really say that? What does he want me to do?" she would reply.

Through much effort, we first received the understanding then shared with her that it had convinced her that it had given her her poetic and artistic talents. We assured her that those talents were God-given, that she had them before the spirits had been invited in.

On several occasions the spirit reached out to stroke Mark's arm, or one of the other elders nearby. Mark said, "You like my body, don't you? You want to enter me, but you can't. The Holy Spirit lives in me and you can't have this body." It would shrink away as if acknowledging that it knew that. At one point Mark retired to the other side of the room to pray for insight.

Mike (another elder) and John picked up the crucifix and again, shouting, tried to cast the spirit out. It screamed in fear of the cross, but it would not leave. The two men restrained Susan, trying to keep the cross on her mouth, but they realized that this was not working. Al, in exasperation from the struggle and all the yelling and the tenacity of this demon, prophetically said, "I don't know when you are coming out, but you are; and you are coming out silently and the other two are coming out silently with you. They will not utter a word."

As God had given me spiritual insight as to its name, now Mark, in prayer, received understanding as to the block in communication. The lying spirit had full control of Susan's tongue, but her body was still free to move of her own will. The insight God gave him was that she needed to renounce this demon, but it controlled her tongue. She could not verbalize its name or a renunciation.

Mark stepped forward, again binding the demon and talked to Susan about her need to give assent to wanting the demon out. And here was the plan: "Susan, look at my hands. They are outstretched to you. Let them represent to you the tender hands of Jesus reaching out to you. They want to give you peace. They want to hold you securely. They want to heal you of this nightmare. But, Susan, you need to reach out to me. Show us all that you want to be rid of this demon by reaching out and touching my hands. Let them represent to you the hands of Jesus." He continued his gentle coaxing for about 10 minutes, but in a moment of impatience he leaned forward and grabbed her hands. "Take my hands, Susan!" She recoiled and another scene of fear, shrieking, shouting and commanding ensued.

Realizing the error and remembering Al's prophesy about it coming out quietly, we all became silent before the Lord. The demon was commanded again not to speak. Mark explained to her her need to renounce the demon. "Susan, this demon is telling us that you want it to stay. We know it is lying to us, and you must know it is lying to you, also. But you need to take a step towards Jesus. Again, look at these hands as the hands of Jesus. Reach out to them."

The very room held its breath. All of us were praying silently—praying and watching and waiting to see Susan extend her hands to Mark. And she did! Immediately a hushed weeping was heard as full release was found. Susan was free! Repentance flowed and the blood of Christ cleansed her heart. Another two hours passed as we read Scripture, sang, cried and praised the Lord.

If we have authority over the enemy at all, we have authority over the enemy in this area. "These signs will follow those who believe: In the Name of Jesus, you will cast out demons." Mark 16:17 It is not something to be entered into lightly. It is not something to be entered into without prayer. It is not something to be entered into alone. But it is an arena of spiritual warfare in which we have the full authority of Christ in us, the One who sets the captives free.

Instruction From The Acts Of The Apostles
As has already been stated, the "signs and wonders" that Jesus promised would follow those who believed, did follow, as recorded throughout the New Testament. I would like us now to look at a few passages in the Book of Acts from which we might gain specific instruction in exercising this authority.

In Acts 19:13-16, we look at the story of a man named Sceva, a Jew, and chief of the priests. He had seven sons who were vagabonds and exorcists. What their success had been we are not told. But they had evidently heard of Paul's method of driving out demons. For, in their pursuit of those who had evil spirits, they tried to invoke the name of the Lord Jesus by saying, "We command you in the Name of Jesus whom Paul preaches."

On one such occasion, the evil spirit answered, "Jesus I know and I am acquainted with Paul, but who on earth are you?" And the man in whom the evil spirit was living sprang at them and over-powered them all with such violence that they fled out of the house, wounded and naked.

Let this one point be re-emphasized: We are never to approach the enemy "In the Name of Jesus that my pastor preaches!" or "In the Name of Jesus that my denomination teaches!" When you, by the power of the Holy Spirit, determine to stand up against the forces of evil in Biblical exorcism, be sure of your personal, direct relationship with Christ. And invoke the authority of the only True Power to deliver, the Name of Jesus!

Recorded in Acts 13:8-12, shortly into Barnabas

and Saul's first missionary journey, we find them coming across a certain sorcerer, a false prophet, a Jew whose name was Elymas. Sergius Paulus, the proconsul of the country of Cyprus, was anxious to hear the message of God that Barnabas and Saul had brought. But Elymas opposed them, doing his best to dissuade Sergius from accepting the faith. Then Saul (who is also called Paul), filled with the Holy Spirit—it is certainly a good thing to be filled with the Holy Spirit when doing battle against the enemy—eyed him closely and said, "You son of the devil, you monster of trickery and evil, you enemy of all righteousness, will you not stop perverting the right ways of the Lord? Now listen, the Lord Himself will touch you—you will be blind for a season."

You may say, "Wait a minute, I didn't hear any demon being exorcised." You are right! And that is my point. Every enemy of God is not possessed of a devil! Jesus, in explaining the parable of the wheat and tares, told His disciples: "...but the tares are the children of the wicked one." Matthew 13:38 John instructs us by the Holy Spirit that the way to tell who are the children of the devil is this: "Those who do not do righteousness and those who do not love their brother!" I John 3:10 But that does not mean they are possessed of a devil.

When Jesus rebuked Peter, He identified the source of Peter's wrong perspective—satan. But Jesus did not have to "exorcise a demon!" See Matthew 16:22-23.

We must be cautious in this area of spiritual authority. We don't want to be "vagabond demon hunters!" There is not a demon behind every bush or in every hiccup! There are times when it is possible to rebuke in the name of the Lord. But every situation of evil does not necessarily warrant an exorcism.

On another occasion, in Acts 16, during Paul's second missionary journey, he and his companions were going to the place of prayer by the riverside. They were met by a young girl who had a spirit of clairvoyance (divination) and who brought her owners a good deal of profit by fortune telling. After several days of being grieved by her action, Paul turned to her and spoke to the spirit, "I command you in the Name of Jesus Christ to come out of her!" and it came out immediately.

We don't know whether Paul did not know during those several days that she had an evil spirit, or if he sensed it was not the time to exorcise the demonic presence, or if he feared the repercussions of her owners, or if there was some other reason. But when the time was right, he spoke with the authority and power of Jesus' Name. And it was gone! Acts 16:16-18

And we can be assured of the same. Whether by word of knowledge, a deep sensitivity in our spirit, or by some other means, when we know there is demonic presence, we can act at His direction and on His authority and in His timing.

And in Acts 19:11-12, we see yet another demonstration of the power of God through Paul. Handkerchiefs and aprons that had been in contact with Paul's body were taken to the sick and those with evil spirits, and the diseases and evil spirits left them. Paul wasn't even present when the evil spirits were exorcised!

The humility of Jesus must be our protection if the Lord is going to use us in the ministry of exorcism. People are idol-worshippers. And one who can "display" such power of God will be "rewarded." Resist the limelight. Remember, it is the power of God that delivers. He is everywhere present; we might not have to even show up!

RESIST

The other dimension or focus of spiritual authority that we want to consider is mentioned a number of times in the Word and from many different perspectives. *Resist-*

ing relates to the day-to-day combat. Though it does not carry the same euphoria as an exorcism, it is constant battle we must face as the enemy is seeking to rob us of the joy of our salvation. It is on this level of authority that we must be keenly sensitive. Let's look at it closely.

Take The Offensive
Looking again in Ephesians 6, we are instructed by Paul "to fight, to combat, to war against the enemy." Then, in verse 13, "having put on the whole armor of God we are able to withstand evil in its day of power, and having done all *to stand.*" This is a strong military term referring to the turning point in a battle. It is the time when we are no longer defending, but we take our final stand against the enemy by launching an offensive. As Paul says in Romans 12:21, "Don't be overcome by evil, (take the offensive), overpower evil with good."

Resisting is not accomplished from a defensive posture. It is a powerful offensive against the enemy. (More will be said about this in the next chapter.)

Praise
Praise is a positive, proactive practice in resisting the devil. In Isaiah 61:3, we are assured that the Lord will give us a "garment of praise for a spirit of heaviness." In the daily hassles of life, when things look hopeless and glum, when we are feeling condemned, when the spirit of heaviness weighs us down, He will clothe us with a garment of praise. Such was the situation out of which David wrote Psalm 34.

It is finally clear that Saul has his heart set on killing David. David and Jonathan have had their tearful parting. David is on the run. He comes to the priest, Abimelech, at Nob. He's hungry. He takes the sacred bread. He lies about his mission. He lies again and gets the priest to give him Goliath's sword. Doeg, one of Saul's men sees him there. Wouldn't that be enough to "make his day?"

No! David, in fear of Doeg telling Saul, gets up and flees to Achish, the king of Gath. The servants of Achish say, "Isn't this the mighty king of Israel of whom it is sung, 'Saul slew his thousands, and David his tens of thousands?'"

And now David is afraid of Achish. So he feigns madness, scratching at the walls and letting his spittle run down into his beard. Achish says, "Get this crazy man out of here!" David, therefore, departs from there and escapes to the cave of Adullam. (All of this is found, by the way, in I Samuel 21. I didn't make it up!)

I can imagine David trying to make himself comfortable, leaning back against the rock-hardness of that musty-smelling cave, trying to put the pieces together. In these circumstances and out of this hassle, David begins to sing:

I will *bless* the Lord at all times;
His *praise* shall continually be in my mouth;
My soul does make her *boast* in You, Lord;
The humble shall hear of it and be glad.
O, *magnify* the Lord with me
And let us *exalt* His name together;
I searched for the Lord and He heard me
and *delivered me from all of my fears!* Psalm 34:1-4

Bless means to hallow, which means to respect greatly or venerate. It also means to consecrate which means to declare sacred. *Praise* means to worship, value with merit, commend; and glorify. Glorify means to shed radiance and splendor and resplendent magnificence by ascribing perfection. *Boast* means to display proudly, glory in, to leap for joy. *Magnify* means to extol, to praise highly, to laud, to acclaim, to hold in great esteem and respect. *Exalt* means to lift up on high.

And all that came from a dictionary! It sounds more like what we would do at a football game (when our team is winning) than in a cave of despair! How long will we let our dank hiding place of despondency echo with the groans of lament? Let us rather follow David's example and cause that cave to reverberate with praises to our King of Kings and Lord of Lords!

The result: He was delivered from all of his fears! We, too, can find His victory over all our fears as we allow Him to clothe us in His garment of praise.

Overcome

As Jesus walked among the Churches, He gave beautiful promises to those who were *overcomers.* To the Church of Ephesus: "To him who *overcomes*—conquers, is victorious—will I give the privilege to eat the fruit of the tree of life which stands in the paradise of God." Revelation 2:7 To the Church of Smyrna: "The *overcomers* cannot suffer the slightest hurt by the second death." Revelation 2:11 To the Church of Pergamos: "I will allow the *victors* to eat the hidden manna, and I will give them a white stone on which is written a new name...." Revelation 2:17 To the Church of Thyatira: "To those who *conquer* (and keep my works until the end) I will give authority over the nations." Revelation 2:26 To the Church of Sardis: "The *victorious* will wear white clothes, and I will never erase his name from the book of life, but I will confess his name before My Father, and before the angels." Revelation 3:5 To the Church of Philadelphia: "To him who *overcomes* will I make a pillar in the temple of God...." Revelation 3:12 And lastly, even in the Church of Laodicea, Jesus Christ had a message for the overcomers: "To you I will grant to sit with Me on My throne...." Revelation 3:21

In I John 2:13, John acknowledges that the young men have overcome the wicked one. In verse 14, John repeats their ability to conquer the evil one, but adds a phrase which no doubt is the reason for their victory: "You treasure the Word of God in your heart." If there is one thing I am trying to do in this study, it is this: To do what is necessary to get us to plant that treasure of God's Word deep in our hearts!

In his writing the Revelation of Jesus Christ, John describes three more means by which we are able to overcome. "And they overcame him (the accuser of the brethren) by the blood of the Lamb, by the Word of their testimony and they did not cherish life even in the face of death." Revelation 12:11

1) *"...by the blood of the Lamb."* The blood, the perfect, sinless blood of Jesus Christ, the spotless Lamb, was slain from before the foundations of the earth.

I don't particularly like the sight of blood. Now, I don't faint or anything like that. I just have a greater appreciation for it when it is in the veins and arteries where it flows and does its thing. So as my understanding of the "blood of Christ being shed for the remission of my sins" grew into adult comprehension, I still (secretly) wondered, "God, why did it have to be His blood?" Yes, I knew the life is in the blood, but...

Medical science has determined that there is no blood in the unfertilized egg. Further, the placenta forms a unique barrier that keeps the mother's blood separate from the infant's. This gave me new reason to appreciate what God knew all along, expressed in this song:

It's His blood that cleanses me;
It's His blood that gives new life.
It's His blood that took my place
In redeeming sacrifice
And washes me
Whiter than the snow, than the snow.
My Jesus, God's precious sacrifice.

And that's just the opening of the door to the depth of understanding of the blood of Christ. It is as we come into a fuller appreciation of the work of Calvary that we are able to more easily overcome—have victory over— the one who accuses us before the Father. For though the enemy may be there, we are able to come boldly into our Father's presence by the blood of Jesus Christ. See Hebrews 10:19.

2) *"...by the word of their testimony."* That testimony must be a vibrant, alive, current, attractive word; a "today" reason for our faith in Christ.

As Jesus said to the demoniac who had been delivered, "Go home to your people and report to them what great things the Lord has done for you and how He had mercy on you." Mark 5:19

It may be my background that is giving me reason to put such emphasis on this point. As I alluded to earlier, I was raised in a church that had some very "unique" practices. One was the testimony service. That they had a testimony service was not unique. It's just that this part of the service "had to" begin with Sister Smith. She was ninety-three years old at the time, but her word of testimony was always about the "glorious day when I was 12 years old and accepted Jesus into my heart." And again, nothing wrong with that "glorious day." But had He done nothing in her life in the intervening 81 years?

And then we knew the testimony service was over when Brother Brown looked around and stood and told us how badly things were going at his manufacturing plant. His "testimony" could possibly illicit pity, but I doubt it ever overpowered the evil one!

Peter tells us that we should always be ready with a quiet and reverent answer for the *reason* of the hope that lies within us. See I Peter 3:15. The hope of the believer is the return of the Lord. But what is our *today* reason for that hope? When you least expect it, ask yourself, "What is going on in my life today—right now—that makes me glad the Lord is coming back?"

David time and again gave a powerful word of testimony. He is standing on his roof on a cloudless night. The sky is spangled with zillions of stars. The Milky Way splatters its creamy effect from east to west. The constellation of Arcturus, Orion and Pleiades are identified. In one grand, effusive testimony of praise, he says, "The heavens declare the glory of God...." Psalm 19:1

Paul also gave a word of testimony of quite another sort: "Then I will glory rather in my infirmities...for Christ's sake: for when I am weak, then I am strong." See II Corinthians 12:9,10.

Can we identify with John's testimony? "And many other signs truly did Jesus in (my) presence... but these things are written that you might believe that Jesus is the Christ, the Son of God; and that believing you might have life through His Name." John 20:30-31

Our testimonies (like David's and Paul's and John's) may run the gamut from our rejoicing in the creative beauty of a crocus poking its spring-announcing colors through the snow to our finding a reason to praise Him for a disability to our witnessing the dramatic power of Christ's love. Whatever the content of my report, may the word of my testimony concerning Christ's work in my life—today—be an effective weapon from my arsenal of spiritual authority, thereby overcoming the evil one with praise and honor to Him who reigns eternal.

3) "...and they loved not life even unto death." I do not believe this is saying they wanted to die. They just had a right attitude toward life and death. Paul dealt with this issue in Philippians 1. As we come to understand that our life—our very breath—is in His control, we will be able to overcome the fear of the unknown, a powerful tool of the enemy. We share in the responsibil-

ity. As Jude said, "...by praying through the Holy Spirit keep yourself in the love of God...." Jude 20-21

Resist and Come Close
We have now looked at this aspect of spiritual authority from several perspectives:
1) Authority over the enemy is an aggressive, offensive action; there is nothing passive about it.
2) Praise is a powerful means by which to launch this offensive. We resist the spirit of heaviness (depression, despair) by clothing ourselves in His garment of praise.
3) To the Church (in whatever state it may be), Jesus gave beautiful promises to those who overcome.
4) Living victoriously (overcoming) is definitely aided by treasuring God's Word in our heart.
5) Overcoming by the blood of the Lamb, by declaring a positive testimony of what God has done in our lives and by having a right attitude toward life and death raises us to the place of victory in Christ. And places the enemy in defeat.

But the classic passage on this dimension of spiritual authority is found in the words of James. We are, no doubt, familiar with the abbreviated form: "Resist the devil and he will flee from you." But, dear friend, the abridged Word of God will deceive us every time! We need to back up at least one sentence. Well, we better make it two! Better still, would be to begin at verse one of Chapter 4. But we'll start at verse six. (One time when I began that process—of seeing where it would be best to start—I ended up back at the beginning of the Book!) We read, "God resists the proud but gives grace to the humble. For this very reason, submit yourself to God." James 4:6-7a

Never in a thousand lifetimes could we become good enough or powerful enough or "satan-resistant" enough to face the enemy without first submitting to God. We must acknowledge our total dependence on Him. In our own strength, we are no match for the enemy. There is no place for arrogance or flippancy. This is too serious a matter to joke about. It is only from a position of humble submission, protected by the armor of Christ, "strengthened with all might, according to His glorious power" (Colossians 1:11) and wielding the Spirit's Sword that we can stand against, oppose, and resist satan by saying, "Be gone, in Jesus' Name!" Or, to use Scripture, "The Lord rebuke you!" Jude 9 With a sharp slash of the Spirit's Sword, using the specific "It is written..." He has given us for that situation, we can cut through the umbilical cord of sin and stop feeding on death. See again James 1:14-15.

It is not healthy to prolong our encounters with the enemy. Therefore, the sooner and more swiftly we exercise this action—resist—the less time we are giving to satan. And he has to leave! Yes! Gone! Out of here! In Jesus' Name!

But before we do any reckless celebrating, we need to consider a basic law of physics. When something leaves a space, a vacuum is created. Unless we occupy that space with Someone else, knowing the tactics of the enemy, he'll be right back.

Thus, Scripture continues, "Come close to God and He will come close to you." The *resist* of verse 7 and the *come close* of verse 8 is a two-part action. The former is swift and brief. Coming close to God, however, is a process of life. "Thy Word have I hid in my heart...." Psalm 119:11 It has become a part of me; it has become the motivation of my lifestyle. I surround myself with a godly atmosphere. I create an environment in my home and in my heart that will actively encourage me to mind the things of the Spirit, giving no place for the things of the flesh. That emptiness in my heart is filled. My long-ings are for a deeper and fuller relationship with the Lord. "As the deer panteth for the water brook, so longeth my soul after Thee," the Psalmist penned. Psalm 42:1 Paul expressed this two-part process to the Christians at Ephesus. He said that they must not only "put off the former lifestyle of the *old man,* which is corrupt through lusts and desires that spring from delusion," but to "*put on the new man,* which was created by God for righteousness and true holiness." Ephesians 4:22,24

James continues his focus on the process of coming close to God by delineating six steps:

1) "*Realize that you have sinned and get your hands clean again.*" Is it possible James was remembering the Word of God through Isaiah? "And when you spread forth your hands, I will hide My eyes from you.... Your hands are full of blood. Wash yourself, make yourself clean.... Cease from doing evil." Isaiah 1:15,16

Our hands represent the instruments by which our deeds are done—evil or good. In the process of coming close to God, it is necessary to repent and "cease from doing evil." When Jesus said, "Neither do I condemn you," He added, "Go and sin no more." John 8:11

Was James also reminding his readers (us!) of the words of David? "Who shall ascend into the hill of the Lord? or who shall stand in His holy place? He that hath *clean hands,* and a pure heart." Psalm 24:3,4

Perhaps this was what Paul was referring to when he said to the elders of Ephesus, "I have no man's blood on my hands." Acts 20:26 (See also Ezekiel 3 & 33.)

James continues with the next step in the process:

2) "*Purify your hearts, you double-minded.*" James' readers included many who were double-minded, doubting, wavering persons. Their hearts were not steadfast. They were vacillating. They were asking for wisdom and then wondering if God could really give it. See James 1:5-6. They were asking and not receiving be-

cause they only wanted to consume it on their lusts. See James 4:3. James expresses the sad plight of the double-minded man: "Tossed about like a wave of the sea; unstable in all his ways; not able to receive anything from the Lord." See James 1:6-8.

To counter this dilemma, James says to purify our hearts. To be pure is to be of a single substance. (There is nothing wrong with mixing oil and vinegar, and a few spices for a great salad dressing! It's just not a pure substance any longer.) To eliminate all other substances—to purify—is often accomplished by the application of heat. Silver, being prepared for the jeweler, is put into the crucible. Heat is applied, but for only a short period of time. The impurities rise to the surface and are skimmed off. The precious metal is allowed to cool, and then heated again. Each time more of the impurities are separated. As it is said of the Words of the Lord: They are pure, as silver tried in a furnace seven times. See Psalm 12:6.

For months David had been trying to cover his sins—even going to the temple with burnt offerings and sacrifices. But when he was "nailed to the wall" with Nathan's story of the little ewe lamb (II Samuel 12:1-13), he cried out, "Create in me a *clean* heart... A broken and a contrite heart, O God...." Psalm 51:10,17

With the Psalmist may we pray, "Search me, O God and know my heart; try me (this is that refining process) and know my thoughts; and see if there is any wicked way in me, and lead me in the way everlasting." Psalm 139:23-24

James continues:

3) *"Be afflicted and moan and weep."* This is getting serious. It is an act of penitence he is talking about. A change of heart. Not treating sin—any sin—lightly. Paul tells us there is a worldly sorrow that leads to death but "the sorrow which is of God means a change of heart

and leads to salvation." II Corinthians 7:10

He goes on:

4) *"Let your laughter be turned to grief and your joy to heaviness."* As we are brought deeper into the realization of the awfulness of sin, our high-spirited laughter will become heartfelt shame for our sin.

At times I ask myself, "Why don't I hate sin like God does?" And I have to answer myself, "Because I too easily take for granted His forgiveness." Not that we should not rejoice in our sins being forgiven. But I believe that, if we (as we are contemplating those seed thoughts to sin) thought of the pain and suffering that it caused Christ as He took upon Himself the sins of the world, it would serve as a greater deterrent to our sinning. At least it does for me.

The sin being talked about in the context of James 4 is that of Christians trying to be friends with the world, and at the same time feeling like they are serving God. James asks them, "Don't you know that being the world's friend is being God's enemy?" The answer should be clearly *yes*, but he goes on and states, "So whoever chooses to be a friend of the world takes his stand as an enemy of God." James 4:4 James is encouraging them (and us) to give sober thought to our true position, to abandon the carefree, light-hearted attitude into which we have been lulled, and to become remorseful and aware of our spiritual need, even moaning over the bad situation into which we have gotten ourselves.

The capstone of this process follows:

5) *"Humble yourself in the sight of the Lord."* Humility is an attribute of wisdom; it is born of true wisdom. Jesus teaches this attitude with two illustrations: Better to stand in the corner beating your chest, saying, "God be merciful to me—a sinner" than to publicly pray with *yourself,* boasting, "Lord, how glad I am that I am not like him." Jesus ends this discourse with, "For eve-

ryone who exalts himself will be humbled, but he who humbles himself will be exalted." See Luke 18:10-14.

Again, "when you are invited to a marriage feast, do not take the chief seat, lest a more distinguished guest arrives and you have to be escorted to the lowest place. Better to sit in the back, so that when your host comes in he may say to you, 'Friend, here is a place of honor for you.'" Jesus concludes that story with the same principle: "Every one who exalts himself will be humbled, and he who humbles himself will be exalted." Luke 14:7-11

And this brings us full circle back to the opening statement of the lesson: "God resists the proud, but gives grace to the humble."

What then is the result of this process?

6) *"And He (the Lord) shall lift you up!"* The freedom—the exhilaration to know that my burden has been lifted at Calvary. The joy—the delight to know that "He brought me up out of a horrible pit, out of the miry clay, and set my feet upon a Rock, and established my goings." Psalm 40:2 What peace—what comfort to know that He has restored the joy of His salvation and that He upholds me with His free spirit. See Psalm 51:12. What perspective—what grandeur to be seated with Christ in heavenly places. See Ephesians 2:6.

In total dependence upon Christ we stand tall, victorious over the devil and his hoards of demonic beings. We turn every attack of the enemy into a compelling force, driving us deeper into the richness of God's provision of salvation. This is our desire; this is our prayer; this is our victory.

For there is victory in Jesus' Name! Out of His abundant resources of Heaven, He has provided all things necessary for godly living. *Cast out* and *resist!* Soldiers of the Cross, let us exercise our spiritual authority as we fight the good fight of faith.

PRACTICAL INSIGHTS

WHEN SATAN HASSLES CHRISTIANS

I believe that an overconfidence in "having it all together" or being fearful that "I will never have victory" are equally dangerous. Let's be sure to have a "sane estimate of our capabilities" as we look at these problems, and at some solutions I have found helpful.

Problem   The enemy tries to hassle me by getting my eyes off of God and onto problems or myself. This is usually a very subtle, gradual change of focus, which happens too often and too easily. We start looking only at our problems, at what is wrong, instead of to the Problem Solver. Even when we are concentrating on a way to solve our problems, the enemy tries to get our attention dwelling on that problem rather than the solution. The problem is known; the solution is still unknown, so it is easier to continue to think about the problem. It can become a very negative perspective. We tell everybody—even God—how wrong something is. The problem grows and grows and looks bigger and bigger until we can't see anything else. The problem can become *the* consuming issue.

Solution   James says, "If you don't know how to handle any particular problem, God will give you wisdom...." James 1:5 "Wisdom" is the solution to the problem of not knowing how to handle any particular problem! Tell God your *needs*, not your problems. Philippians 4:6 says, "Tell God the details of your needs (requests) in earnest and thankful prayer." The "need" or "request" is what we should ask God for, and with a thankful attitude. And Jeremiah 32:17 gives us the perspective of God's greatness and the realization that nothing is too hard for

Him. This is a totally different focus.

Another related thought: We need to be careful about negative self-talk. We all talk to ourselves all the time. Even if we don't do it out loud, in our thoughts are a constant monologue of self-talk. We are either talking constructively or destructively to ourselves. God tells us what thoughts to think about, and they are all positive. "If you believe in goodness and value the approval of God, fix your minds (focus your thoughts) on whatever is *true* and *honorable* and *just* and *pure* and *lovely* and *praise-worthy.*" Philippians 4:8 You can't get more positive than that!

So, we need to watch how we program our minds and what we reinforce in our own thinking.

Problem The enemy can hassle me if I allow an unhealthy dependency relationship to develop. This dependency can go either way—a person can become overly dependent upon me or I can become overly dependent upon another person. This is an area in which Christians can easily be deceived.

There are several reasons why we fall prey to the enemy here: 1) We may have been taught that it is selfish and "unchristian" to say, "No," to any person in need; 2) We may have a strong need to be needed and useful to feel worthwhile; 3) We may have developed a messiah complex—the thought that I am the only one who can help that person; 4) We may "need" to be in control of other people's lives— motivated out of *fear* of what would happen if we were to let go of that control.

There may be other subtle ways the enemy can lead us into an unhealthy dependency relationship. But these give some idea of the direction we are going. If we are looking to a person (or they are looking to us) rather than to God as the Source of our solution, there is a problem. If we are more concerned about what another person thinks of our actions than what God thinks, we might be overly dependent on that person. If we feel backed in a corner, manipulated, or controlled by another's need for us—they may be too dependent on us.

Solution In our involvement of helping others, there must be a balance with our other time commitments. And in our help, we must lead them to find their solutions in God and through His Word—not in us. It is healthy for all of us to be available for God to minister His love through us to others, recognizing that we are not the Messiah, but servants of the Messiah.

Problem The enemy tries to hassle me through condemnation. I am sure we have all experienced condemnation. We feel like a failures. We just can't do anything right. We might as well give up and quit! I missed reading my Bible for three days now. I might just as well not try. Or, how can I pray now? I just blew up and said some bad words. God doesn't want to hear me now. (Do you hear all the negative self-talk?) And, if we do quit, the devil has accomplished his purpose: To break our fellowship with God, and to stop our Christian witness—to immobilize us.

Solution Fight with the truth of Scripture. If you have not yet memorized Romans 8:1, now is a good time to do it: "There is therefore now no condemnation to those who are in Christ Jesus."

The devil condemns by starting with a true statement (or a half-truth). Then he goes right into a lie. He'll whisper the truth: "You did this." Or, "You didn't do that." But then he draws a conclusion that is a lie. "You failed." (A truth.) "You might as well give up." (A lie!) Or, "You didn't get what you wanted from God the last time you talked to Him. Why bother asking Him for anything else. Anyway, He doesn't have time for you." (Possible truth followed by two lies!)

You can agree with his truth—"Yes, I was tempted to do wrong. And I did it." But here is where you change it around. You continue to God, "Thank you Lord for forgiving me. And furthermore, thank You for Your Word assuring me that You don't even remember that against me any more." You get your focus right back on God and the truth of what the Word says. Fight his condemnation with the truth of Scripture.

Problem   The enemy tries to hassle me through discouragement. The discouragement may come because of our failure to do something, or when we don't see fruit in our personal lives, or by not seeing results from our work. Most of us tend to get impatient if we don't see results in hours or days or weeks. When things don't happen as we expect, we are disappointed. And that leaves us open and vulnerable to be hassled by the enemy through discouragement!

Solution   Encourage yourself in the Lord. You need to read most of I Samuel to get the full picture of the discouragement David was facing by the time of the story in Chapter 30. I will just say that he had been through a lot! And now his "faithful" men were about to stone him to death! Verse 6 says, "But David encouraged himself in the Lord."

There are many ways to encourage yourself in the Lord. Here are three ideas:

1) Become actively involved in a small group Bible study. It could be just two of you, or several, who have agreed together to keep each other accountable in the Word. It can be encouraging to sing

together, to study together, to pray together.

2) If you live in an isolated location, you can use Bible study and music tapes or CD's to build yourself up in the Lord. Read, sing and pray along with the tapes. Another option is to develop a correspondence commitment with a friend to do a Bible study together long distance.

3) Let the Word search you. If you are discouraged in your personal devotional life because things are seemingly dry and you're not getting anything out of the Word, keep a notebook. With every passage you read, ask yourself these questions: What is the overall message? What is the key point in this passage? In this passage is there an example to follow? Is there a sin to avoid? Is there a commandment to obey? Is there a promise to claim? Is there something in this passage that teaches me more about God—Who He is? What He is like? Is there a personal application that the Spirit could reveal to me? Is there something in the passage that I need to pray about?

If you have these questions (and others you may think of) written down before you read, then while you are reading, you will concentrate on finding the answers. That will help you to get something out of your reading, and getting something out of the Word will definitely encourage you!

I think the following testimony of patience that overcame years of discouragement is one of the best I know. Some friends of ours spent 17 years with a people group living in villages along a tributary of the Amazon River. They first had to make a peaceful contact with them, then learn their language, create an alphabet, write their language, learn and write their folklore stories and teach them how to read. Then, when they felt like they knew the language well enough, they began translating the New Testament for them.

Even though our friends were conversant in the language after a few years and they could communicate the love of Christ, during the whole seventeen years, there was only a single convert—one!

Then, the New Testament having been completed, they decided to make a last journey to all of the villages scattered along the river before moving on to other work. They stopped at the first village, greeted the people and preached the Word. Dan asked if there were any who wanted to commit their lives to Christ. Everybody stood up! He thought they had misunderstood him, so he had them all sit down. He then proceeded to explain the commitment more carefully. They all stood up again! In village after village there was a great harvest of souls. Almost 100% of that language group made a commitment to Christ.

What if they had been defeated by discouragement from the enemy and given up—even in the sixteenth year? I hope you will remember this story as an encouragement to you to stand strong when the enemy attacks through discouragement.

6

PRINCIPLES OF WAR

""...neither shall they learn war any more." Micah 4:3
"Prepare for battle...." Joel 3:9

I hate war! It is vicious. It is unfair. It is dirty. It leaves a path of devastation, sorrow and pain. There are casualties. Even in victory, there is loss. It seems so out of context with the peace-loving God of our culture.

Yet those who commit themselves to this business of war—those Christians who have left the country club comfort of the "pew"—must also study, understand and apply the principles of war. Our abhorrence for secular war cannot keep us from facing the realities of spiritual warfare.

But as I flip the pages of my Bible back and forth between Micah and Joel, the encouraging words of Micah are much more enjoyable to read than those of Joel: "In the last days...the house of the Lord shall be established...all people shall flow into it.... They shall beat their swords into plowshares, and their spears into pruning hooks. Nations shall not lift up a sword against nation, *neither shall they learn war any more."* Micah 4:1-3 That is music to my ears. I await that day.

Then I turn back to Joel. I don't even want to read the words, much less write them. But they are also a part of the Whole Counsel of God. Therefore, in this time of war, it is necessary to "*PREPARE FOR BATTLE*, wake up the mighty men, let all the men of war draw near.... Beat your plowshares into swords, and your pruning hooks into spears. Let the weak say, 'I am strong—a warrior!'" Joel 3:9-10

You have not studied the lessons of this book to this point without believing that Christians are indeed engaged in warfare. You must also be aware that it is imperative that those of us involved in battle apply certain principles to govern our actions.

(This chapter somewhat follows the outline of a book, Principles Of War. Authored by Jim Wilson, a military strategist, it puts forth eleven principles of war. These eleven principles, taken from secular strategy, have a striking parallel in spiritual warfare. Mr. Wilson has graciously allowed me to integrate many of his thoughts into this context. His complete book [a 96-page paperback] is available through Ransom Press, PO Box 9754, Moscow, ID 83843.)

Principle One: Objective

On the time line of history, periods of peace in this world barely appear as blips. If the full truth were known, there probably has been no period of time in which some region of the world has not been engaged in war. And in the council chambers where decisions are made, as men weigh the cost of battle, victory is their ultimate objective. For who would engage an enemy in battle if he were assured of defeat? Instead, he would send ahead envoys of peace. And appeasement. See Luke 14:31-32.

In spiritual warfare, however, ultimate victory is assured. The outcome is known. We have been told by our Commander-in-Chief. And we believe Him!

Victory in the inward battle is validated in Scripture: "You are of God, my children, and have already defeated and overcome (the evil spirits of anti-Christ), because He Who lives in you is greater than he who lives in the world." I John 4:4 "Thank God! It is our Lord Jesus Christ, who has given us the *victory* (over sin and death and the grave)." I Corinthians 15:57

The victory in the battle for lost souls is expressed in the triumphant words of the twenty-four elders. "You are worthy to take the book and break its seals, for You were slain, and by Your blood You have purchased for God men from every tribe and tongue, every people and nation." Revelation 5:9

Whether the battle rages in the inner recesses of our being or for souls throughout the nations of the world, when war on the enemy is declared, the objective is living in the *victory* won at Calvary.

The assignment of war is in the hands of Jehovah Sabaoth, the Lord of Hosts. He is the Commander of the armies of heaven. He, in turn, has passed on His commands to all subordinates. Our objective is victory in fulfilling the commands of God. Although none of us—in our particular arena of battle—can possibly comprehend the full compass and strategy of this war, we can read, study, understand and obey the commands God has given to us. How much more simply could He have stated them? Jesus declared the commands of God in four brief words: "Love God; love man." See Matthew 22:37-40.

From that basis of relationship, however, He does enlarge the objectives in our lives with further details:

Because we love God, we will "be perfect, even as He is perfect" (Matthew 5:48); we will "give our entire beings to Him as an act of intelligent worship." Romans 12:1

Because we love men, we will "go into all the world and preach the Gospel" (Mark 16:15); we will "go into all the world and make disciples of all ethnic communities." Matthew 28:18-19

If we are going to participate in the victory of the ages, we must clearly understand and fulfill His commands in our lives.

Unfortunately, history records that some wars have been deliberately protracted for the selfish financial or political gain that such a delay in victory might bring to the perpetrators. However, in spiritual warfare, we must be sure that we want victory—now! One who finds himself ensnared in battle over some "secret" sin, yet does not do what is commanded to gain victory over that sin is not likely to live in freedom from it.

He may time and again enter his closet of prayer and weep tears of sorrow and remorse. He may begin that trek to Calvary, wanting to reckon himself dead to that sin, convincing himself that this time he really means it. Yet, not having fully wrestled his will into submission to his God, when the jagged splinters of that cross dig deeply into his shoulders and the weight is more than he can bear, his resolve dissolves, and he finds himself in another defeat.

Victory for the believer is to live within the provision of the "abundant life" that Christ has won for us. See John 10:10. Victory in the battle for lost souls is to give them a clear, culturally relevant presentation of the Gospel. See I Corinthians 2:2. Unless we know what we are fighting for, all else is of little consequence. The objective is primary: *Victory!*

Principle Two: Offensive

The offensive is the attitude as well as the action by which the objective (victory) is achieved. There are three attitudes that have been employed in both secular and spiritual warfare that have not accomplished the goal of victory:

1) *Defense.* No territory is claimed or gained. One is

only trying to hold onto what he already has. Without
reinforcements from outside, defeat is imminent.

2) *Détente.* This word and attitude was made popular by Henry Kissinger during the Cold War when he
was Secretary of State. And it remains a compelling
worldly posture today. Détente is an attempt at coexis-
tence which leads to compromise which leads to appeasement which leads to infiltration which surely
leads to defeat. It is significant that the word, of French
derivation, means "slackened bow string." We don't
need to be an archer to know that an unstrung bow is
worthless in battle. In New Age lingo it comes out as
"Live and let live." Or, "Do your own thing." Or, "That's
beautiful. That's your reality!"

3) *Desertion.* One who is weak and cowardly and
without resolve or knowledge of the Commander's will,
by his desertion, proves that he lacks the "stuff" to
"stick it out." It is an attitude toward war that is easily
adopted by those who are raised on, "If it feels good, do
it!" Or, "Are we having fun yet?" Or, "Try it, you might
like it!" Yet, it is a trick of the enemy as old as history.
Solomon observed, "If you faint in the day of adversity,
your strength is small." Proverbs 24:10

Each of these *"d"* words initialized by their author,
the devil, has weakened, crippled, and then defeated
those trying to employ them.

There yet remains a fourth attitude. It is the position—the frame of reference—from which victory arises.
It is the only one that makes satan tremble.

4) *Offense.* Paul said (regarding the inward battle),
"Don't allow yourself to be overcome by evil, take the offensive; overpower evil with good." Romans 12:21 Jude
said (regarding the lost), "There are some who doubt.
Be merciful and have compassion for them. Some you
will save with fear, snatching them out of the fire. But
there are others whom you must pity with the utmost

caution, hating even their clothes stained by their evil deeds." Jude 22-23

An army (secular or spiritual) on the offensive has two distinct advantages over the enemy:

1) The aggressor has the advantage of making his decisions and carrying them out. The defender must first wait to see what his opponent does before he can make his plan of action.

2) The aggressor has the advantage of the initiative. He has overcome inertia so his forces are actively on the move. He has chosen whether to attack, and when and where to attack. The defender must wait for him.

In warfare the offensive is also the action by which the forces achieve their objective. That action may be directed against any point along the battle line. In military strategy two questions must be answered in the affirmative to determine a decisive point of battle; that is, the one which will most likely lead to victory:

1) *Is it worth taking?* Is the action strategic to the battle? Is it vital to put clothes on the aborigines and see them go to hell nicely dressed rather than naked? Is it not but humanitarianism to feed the starving children of the world and to not nourish them in the Word of God? Is it leading to the objective that "all men come to repentance" (II Peter 3:9) to make the hippies cut their hair or the skinheads grow their hair? The Slaughter of the Innocents taking place today makes Herod's actions in the region of Bethlehem look like child's play. It is grievous. It is barbaric. Yet, is there a deeper issue which, if addressed, would be a more decisive point of battle than killing abortionists?

2) *Can we take it?* Once the action is determined to be valid, those laying the strategy for battle must determine if the personnel and material resources are available to claim victory in that struggle. Do we have the resources to launch a campaign for moral purity? Do we

have the grace to allow the hippie and skinhead into our fellowship, following God's instruction to Samuel, "The Lord looks on the heart"? See I Samuel 16:7. Do we have the compassionate heart of Christ not only to fill the bellies of starving children but also to give them the Milk of the Word? Do we have the patience to let the Word convict the hearts of people regarding mini-skirts or tight jeans or aboriginal attire?

In short, the offensive is characterized by:

1) *An attitude that is bold, daring, creative.* "I am not ashamed of the Gospel of Christ, for it is the power of God unto salvation to everyone who believes," Paul strongly declared. Romans 1:16 Can we also say with this daring first-century Christian, "My life is of no importance to me when compared with the joy of completing the course laid out for me...to bear full witness of the Good News of the love of God"? Acts 20:24 What an attitude. Bold! Daring! Creative!

2) *Action against the enemy, not against the objective!* "Get thee behind me, *satan*" were the words Jesus used when He knew Peter was seeing things from a human perspective and not from God's. See Matthew 16:23. The vilest of sinners is not the enemy! He is a soul for whom Christ died.

3) *Using the most effective means at decisive points of battle.* "I have been made all things to all men so that by all means I might win some to Christ." I Corinthians 9:22

In spiritual warfare the most critical battle has been fought and won. It is history (HIS STORY)! The decisive blow was Christ's death for sin. The decisive point was on a cross on Mount Moriah outside Jerusalem. The decisive time was during the Feast of Passover, about 30 A.D. The decisive action was His obedience; His obedient giving of His life.

Those of the world who believe in a historical Jesus

look at His death as a failure—the ultimate failure. "But we see Jesus...crowned with glory and honor because of His having suffered death...." See Hebrews 2:9. When Jesus died on the cross, He cried with a loud voice, "It is finished!" See John 19:30. The battle was over. Victory had been won!

What then is there for us to do? Personally, as Christians, it is our privilege to live within the freedom that Christ has won for us. "Whom the Son sets free is free indeed!" John 8:36

In our relationship to the lost, it is our privilege to declare the emancipation to satan's captives—to proclaim the means of freedom so that in reality all men may live in the power of the resurrection. Paul told King Agrippa what he knew to be his part in the battle for souls: "To open their eyes, to turn them from darkness to Light, from the power of satan to God..." (and then he describes God's part), "...so that they may receive forgiveness of sins, and gain an inheritance among all who are sanctified by faith that is in Me." Acts 26:18

Principle Three: Concentration
As kids, wanting to have a good game of competition, we would carefully weigh the value of each player as we chose teams, trying to make the teams as even as possible. However, in the cold, cruel business of war, one does not count the warriors of the opposing side and make sure he has only an equal number. No! It is a military leader's calculated purpose to mass an overwhelming force of power to hasten the outcome of victory.

The principalities and powers of darkness outnumber us in every arena of battle. By employing the principle of concentration at decisive points of battle, though, Christians can win the victory. Biblical precedent for this is abundant. Jesus sent His disciples and then the

70 out two-by-two. He also taught them to pray in concentration. See Matthew 18:19-20. Certainly on that Day of
Pentecost there was concentrated unity of prayer. "They
were all in one accord." Acts 2:1

On Paul's missionary journeys we see the effective
use of concentration. He always had one or more companions with him. When he found himself alone in Athens, he sent a message calling for Silas and Timothy to
rejoin him as soon as possible. They delayed. After
some days of waiting "his soul was exasperated beyond
endurance at the sight of a city so idolatrous." He went
out on his own. To the synagogue. To the God-fearing
Gentiles. To the street corners of the market place. To
the Aeropagus. "With mixed reception Paul retired from
their assembly, yet some did in fact join him and accept
the faith." But there was no great revival in that city—
nor a riot! See Acts 17:14-34.

Paul went on to Corinth, reasoning in the synagogue. Not much action. But it was after Silas and Timothy arrived that "Paul was pressed in the spirit, showing as clearly as possible that Jesus is Christ." And
then followed the opposition and blaspheming (war!)
and many conversions. See Acts 18:1-11.

It must be noted that the enemy also applies this
principle. For, following 18 months of Paul's successful
preaching and teaching, "the Jews banded together in
one accord to attack Paul...." Acts 18:12 Another time,
"...the unbelieving Jews were aroused to jealousy, and
getting hold of certain lewd fellows of the baser sort,
gathered together a mob and set the city in an uproar."
Acts 17:5

And today, satan has large segments of the Church
of Jesus Christ amassed at non-decisive points of battle. Thousands of Soldiers of the Cross, having been
trained in warfare, yet are lounging in a perpetual apa-
thy! Yes, they know about armor. They have a brilliant-

ly polished set in their closet. Yes, they know about weapons. They have five or ten Swords—in as many translations—on the coffee table or on a shelf. Yes, they know about the authority that is available to Christians in Jesus' Name. They hear their pastors tell of the mighty deeds of warriors of days gone by. Yet, the leadership has not sounded the battle cry. Thus, they unknowingly fall prey to one of satan's most successful tactics: There is no war!

Some of our churches fit the description of social clubs, amusement centers, hospitals and psychiatrists' offices; as a result they cannot be regarded as induction centers, barracks, strategy rooms and deployment centers. May God help us to weaken our forces at nondecisive points of battle so that we may amass the Army of God in the homes and workplaces and marketplaces of the world where the people are being held captive, yet where spiritual breakthroughs are assured.

The very thought of partnership—a relationship with someone who is *really* with you—will seem foreign to the person with a strongly individualistic mind. To apply this principle of war, you must find another person or team of people to work with. Ask God for a "good man, full of faith and the Holy Spirit." Acts 11:24 Then study the Word together, pray together, talk together, reprove one another, find an openness and honesty between you—a unity of purpose. Then you can meet the enemy with combined power. You will fight in concentration.

A final lesson from Paul: "When I came to Troas to preach the Gospel of Christ, although there was an obvious God-given opportunity, I had no rest in my spirit because there was no sign of Titus. So I said good-bye and went from there." II Corinthians 2:12-13 So strongly did he believe in this principle that even though a "God-given opportunity" was there (it was worth taking), because he had no partner, he left (he sensed that he could not take it). Because both questions couldn't be answered in the affirmative, it was not a decisive point of battle.

Principle Four: Mobility
After 430 years of "entrenchment" in the land of Egypt, on a night to be remembered, about 600,000 Israelite men plus women and children and a mixed multitude of others—up to possibly three million people, together with flocks of goats and sheep and herds of livestock (and don't forget the mummified body of Joseph), went out from Rameses to Succoth. See Exodus 12:37-41. That is mobility!

As a principle of war, mobility is not measured against how well we moved yesterday, or how well we could move "if only." Rather, it must be compared with the enemy's mobility. We must move more quickly and farther and for a greater period of time *than the enemy*. Even in a temporary retreat, this principle must be measured against the enemy's mobility.

When one cannot attack, evade or retreat, he has become immobile. So devastating was the Jewish self-annihilation on the mountain citadel of Masada that today the one word, *Masada*, is the battle cry of the Israeli military. Worked deep into their being is the determination that they will never again be caught immobile so that they must choose suicide over surrender.

One of the greatest causes of spiritual immobility is the fear of man. Solomon says it "brings a snare." Proverbs 29:25 Fear of what others will say or think or do entangles and entraps. We discard a new method of presenting the Gospel because we fear change. We scrimp on the big ideas because we fear the costs involved. We stifle the creativity of God in us because we fear failure.

Oh, there is a healthy fear: The fear of God is the

beginning of wisdom (Proverbs 9:10) and of knowledge. Proverbs 1:7 And when that fear remains directed toward God, men have strong confidence (Proverbs 14:26), men depart from evil (Proverbs 16:6), and men enjoy long life. Proverbs 10:27 So strong an immobilizing factor is fear of man that the Word contains 365 "fear nots!" Let us break the bars of fear that imprison us. Let us strive to live more and more in the "perfect love" of I John 4:18 that "casts out all fear."

And let us listen to our Commander-in-Chief who is mobilizing His Army. He stood on the Mount of Ascension and said, "Go! I will be with you!" See Matthew 28:19-20.

That clear and simple command to be mobile rings through the corridors of time and is today the clarion call to aggressively take the offensive, overpowering evil with good, striking a death blow against the enemy (victory in the inward battle). And, finding ourselves free in Christ, we mount an attack against the devil, wresting from his clutches those for whom Christ died (victory in the battle for lost souls).

All over the world the Spirit is moving. The ways and means of going to the battlefields of the world today are limited only by our lack of creativity. Nations and people groups formerly closed to the Gospel message now are waiting for Christians who know how to get up and go—to get up and go! As with Isaiah, the Lord is still saying, "Whom shall I send? Who will go for Us?" Isaiah 6:8 Whether to our own people (as was the case with Isaiah) or around the world, may we arise and go forth!

(I was tempted in this context to launch into a discourse on cross-cultural outreach ministry. But I am restraining myself by writing just that one paragraph. The primary work of Emmaus Road International is mobilizing

and training churches and teams for cross-cultural minis-
try. If the above spoke to you about your possible involve-
ment cross-culturally [either as a "goer" or as a "sender"],
please contact us for more information.)

Yet, wherever we are going, our primary concern
should be sending the Word of God—by whatever
means—to all parts of the world. For the Word of God,
the Sword of the Spirit is the primary weapon in spiritual warfare. Paul, in prison, exhorts the Christians at
Colossae to pray for him that God would open for him a
door for the "entrance of the Gospel." Colossians 4:3 To
the Christians at Thessalonica he said, "Pray for us,
that the Word of the Lord may run free and bring Him
glory." II Thessalonians 3:1

Beyond our physical presence, the means by which
the Word can be mobilized today are mind-boggling: A
hand-written copy of the Word secretly shared with 300
believers in an underground church in China, correspondence, books, records, audio tapes, CD's, video
tapes, DVD's, MP3 and MP4, streaming, downloads, radio, TV, satellite dishes, telephone, fax, e-mail, blogs,
web sites, and the communication super highway...!
And who knows what further telecommunication wonders are about to broaden the means to mobilize the
"entrance of the Gospel"? We rejoice with Paul: "The
Word of God is not bound!" II Timothy 2:9

What about our other main weapon in spiritual warfare—prayer? Is it bound or is it mobile? It is not bound
and it is mobile. No satellite power failure can hinder
its effectiveness. No busy signal can delay its transmis-
sion. No human agent can deny our access to the Father.

We can enter our closet of prayer anywhere in the
world. With the simple acknowledgement of "God," we
are transported beyond the dimensions of time and

space and are ushered to the very gates of the eternal Kingdom. And with thanksgiving in our hearts, those portals of Heaven open to us. And with praise on our lips, we walk into the Courts of the Lord. See Psalm 100:4.

And then, by the miracle of miracles, because we "have a High Priest Who shared fully in our experiences of temptations (yet without sin), we walk boldly into the very presence of God, and bowing at His throne of grace we are able to obtain mercy, and find grace in our time of need." Hebrews 4:15-16

Is our heart broken with compassion for the lost in Tibet or the lost in our neighborhood? We can present this need to the Father. Is our heart grieved because of the "sin that so easily trips us up?" Hebrews 12:1 We can ask for forgiveness. And heed Christ's Words of comfort and exhortation: "I don't condemn you; go and sin no more." John 8:11 Do we see the holy wrath of God about to be poured out on a nation that has turned from Him? We can "stand in the gap and fill in the hedge of protection against His holy anger" (Ezekiel 22:30), begging for a little more time for their repentance. See Genesis 18:23-32. We can live by the Promise of God, "If my people who are called by My Name will humble themselves and pray, and seek My face and turn from their wicked ways; then I will hear from Heaven, forgive their sins and heal their land." II Chronicles 7:14 We can rejoice that both of the main weapons of our warfare (the Sword of the Spirit and Prayer) are fully mobile. Let us not put limitations on them by our immobility.

Principle Five: Security

Looking for a safe place from the world (and from other Christian groups), some segments of the Church have retreated into their own little world. In fact, at one point the Church almost "retreated" itself into oblivion through monasticism. Today's retreats generally focus on how to make *my* life better, easier, more fulfilling with the pleasures of this world.

In military terminology, a retreat (or, more accurately, retrenchment) is for the purpose of regrouping, getting our signals clear and laying strategy for the next advance. Thus, some groups now call their conferences, Advances; however, we have generally made the retreat centers so comfortable that no one wants to "get out of the 'pew' and into the battlefield!"

Security, as a principle of war, however, does not even relate to finding a secure hiding place from the enemy. Rather, it encompasses these three aspects:

1) *Security requires intelligence of the enemy.* Is there an enemy? The first issue here is acknowledging that there is an enemy. A nation or person without an enemy is very secure. A nation or person who has an enemy but does not know it is very insecure! A nation or person who knows there is an enemy but tries to ignore him is most frightfully insecure!

Who is the enemy? The enemy of our souls is satan. Lucifer, the fallen angel of Light, is a created being, and—for reasons known only by the counsel of God's wisdom—he has been given license to hassle mankind.

What are his intentions? Isaiah, by the Holy Spirit, penned the five prideful "I will's" of Lucifer which led to his downfall: "I will ascend into Heaven; I will exalt my throne above the stars of God; I will sit also upon the mountain of the congregation, in the sides of the north; I will ascend above the heights of the clouds; I will be like the Most High God!" Isaiah 14:12

What are his methods? Covered at length in Chapter 4, they are briefly summarized here:

a) Initially, to distract us from war.

b) If that doesn't work, to get us to fighting with each other.

c) Next, to get us so confused in our priorities, that we "burn out."

d) Or, without need for logic, to isolate us or herd us into majority thinking.

e) Or, behind a façade of wisdom, to get us to focus on non-essentials.

f) Or, lead us into sin.

g) Or, bind us in his stronghold.

h) Or, lead us into an addiction.

i) And ultimately, to try to destroy the validity of God's Word.

We know the enemy and his tactics. We are secure.

2) *Security involves continual protection against the enemy.* Our primary objective is to preach the Gospel to every person of our generation. But those who have not trusted in Christ as Savior are "enemies of God through the evil things they have done." Colossians 1:21 Living in this "evil and perverse world" (Philippians 2:15), there is a continual barrage against the children of God. Yet, we are not to isolate ourselves. See I Corinthians 5:10. And Jesus prayed that we should not be taken out of this world. See John 17:15. It is His will that we be exposed to attack, but not defeated. With Paul, we might say, "We are pressed upon on every side, but not crushed. We are perplexed, but not driven to despair. We are persecuted, but not deserted. We are knocked down, but never knocked out." II Corinthians 4:8-9 Therefore, since this is the nature of the war, we "put on the whole armor of God." Ephesians 6:13

We wrote extensively of this armor in Chapter 1. However, in brief summary here: To find that continual protection against the enemy, we must "put on" Jesus Christ. He is Truth; He is our Righteousness; He is our Peace; He is our Source of Faith; He is our Salvation. Again, "...let us put on the armor of Light; let us put on the Lord Jesus Christ." Romans 13:12,14 Where the Light of Life is radiating, no darkness can penetrate. See Psalm 139:11-12. We are secure.

3) *Security also concerns itself with the final stand against the enemy.* So astounding was the revelation of truth about the final stand to me, that I still get excited every time I think or speak about it. Yes, the contrast comes from my early erroneous theological understanding:

I had come to believe that the phrase in Ephesians 6:13—"...and having done all, to stand"—meant: The enemy has me in a corner. He's beating me to a pulp, but I have done everything that I can do. "Lord, help me to keep standing!" And most modern translations do no better than the KJV to explain otherwise.

However, studying the language and the culture of Paul's day let me understand and interpret an entirely different picture: This is a military term that describes the final stand against the enemy. It is the turning point of the war. It is called the defensive-offensive battle. It is that point in time when we engage the enemy in defense but emerge on the offensive. It is the point in life when we are no more "overcome by evil," but we take the offensive and "overpower evil with good." Romans 12:21 It refers to that point in warfare when we are no longer trying to "protect (defend) what we believe" and instead we boldly "declare God's Word—that sacred mystery which up until now has been hidden in every age and every generation, but which is now as clear as daylight to those who love God." Colossians 1:25-26 It is the time in our life when we say, "Enough is enough! We will stand for righteousness in our neighborhood, our schools, our community, our nation and our world!"

If in this discussion of "taking the offensive" you have felt a bit uncomfortable, you have a lot of Christian company. Somehow it seems "right" to defend and "wrong" to take the offensive. When we were kids, nobody had to teach us to say, "He started it!" And we quickly discovered that that declaration (if proven true) brought little or no punishment. We are for the underdog. Defense is associated with the innocent party, as though we expect only the wicked to take up the offensive. We are passive. We are *A Nation of Sheep* as William J. Lederer declared in his book by that title. Thus, (along with many other factors), our culture has taught us to be reactive rather than proactive. Something really bad has to happen before we take action—be it Pearl Harbor or Roe vs. Wade or the Twin Towers.

In our Christian culture, then, this can develop to the point of enjoying defeat. Some may even (mis)use the half-scripture, "Blessed are you when men persecute you...." Matthew 5:10-11 But the full context gives a different picture. Why are men persecuting you? Because you are taking a stand for righteousness! We must remember that in the business of war a defensive attitude will ultimately lead to defeat. There has to come the point in time when we take a proactive, offensive (not *being* offensive) stand for righteous living and His Kingdom's sake.

Principle Six: Surprise
As with each of these principles of war, numerous examples can be drawn from secular war and spiritual warfare—from the pages of world history and from God's Word. But a classic illustration of surprise has to be the story of Gideon. Nobody fought at night in those days. Nobody pitted his three hundred men against 140,000. Nobody used lanterns, pitchers and trumpets as weapons. And, for sure, nobody used the battle cry, "The sword of the Lord." Yet, in the confusion of that surprise midnight battle, fewer than 15,000 Midianites escaped. And they were pursued and destroyed before

the war was over. See Judges 6-8.

Salvation, itself, is a surprise. It is a free gift of God, lest any man should boast. See Ephesians 2:8-9. You can't earn it, barter for it or buy it. You can't beg, borrow or steal it! All who will drink freely of the River of Life will be saved. See John 4:14.

There are five elements in surprise as a principle of war:

1) *The Time.* Remember Pearl Harbor? It happened on a Sunday morning in a culture when Sunday was still a day of rest for Americans. And, just like Gideon's attack, it began at the change of a watch.

2) *The Place.* Pearl Harbor was a strategic location of naval and air power.

3) *The Method.* The method in that the battle was not so surprising, but certainly the ending of that World War was brought about by a surprise method— the dropping of an atomic bomb!

4) *Ignorance of one commander...* By incompetence (there had been warnings that went unheeded) or by deception (a Japanese delegation had just left Washington, D.C.), coupled with

5) *Intelligence possessed by the other commander.* It was later learned that the mastermind of this battle had been an international student in the Pacific Northwest who had been culturally abused. In his anger against America, he conceived this gruesome battle as retaliation!

Any one of the first three (or any combination of them) can yield surprise. But elements four and five must be employed together to be an effective strategy. II Samuel 11 begins, "At the time of year when kings went out to battle, David sent Joab." The element of surprise was certainly not applied to those battles. Yet, as the story unfolds, satan applied this principle of surprise in David's inward battle, using all five elements. For David found himself in the wrong *place*, at the wrong *time*, using the wrong *method* of relationships. Though David was *deceived* into believing he could cover his deed, satan *knew* that the repercussions of this sin would affect David's relationships for the rest of his life. See Proverbs 6:32-33.

Does the Church of Jesus Christ employ the principle of surprise in evangelism? When, where and how does most evangelism take place? On Sunday or Saturday evening, in church by one person in the pulpit. Or late at night on TV by one person on stage. We have developed a *salt block* mentality. "You bring 'em to church and I'll get 'em saved," the evangelist assures. Or, "Bring 'em to the crusade. We'll all walk out on the field together." Rather, as Rebecca Pippert so well teaches in her book, we must get *Out of the Saltshaker and into the World!* Meet them where they are.

No one—saint or sinner, nor the devil himself—is surprised by the evangelistic message given on so many Sundays at as many churches. Even if everyone in attendance is known to be a Christian, the salvation message must go forth. And the altar call must be given. But no one goes forward. So the next appeal: "Is there anyone who is not sure of his salvation?" All are sure. No one goes forward. The pastor, being watched by his Board of Deacons, is getting nervous. "Well, is there anyone who wants to rededicate his life to the Lord?" And we play church, ad nauseam!

Rather, I have heard of creative churches that, when they have gotten too large for their auditoriums, instead of building bigger barns (oops! I mean *sanctuaries!*), have rotated their congregation. One-fourth of the congregation each Sunday of the month is not allowed at church. They are to be out in their neighborhoods talking with the unchurched! Talking about Jesus Christ and Him crucified! That's surprise!

It was in the middle of a secular movie on television when, at the commercial break, a man in white buck shoes came out offering to send me a free Bible. That's surprise!

A friend of mine pastors a church in Olongapo, Philippines, a city made "famous" for its prostitutes when the U.S. Subic Bay Naval Station was in operation. He told me that they never bothered the girls when they were "working." But the people of his church knew where those girls lived with their mothers and children. And the church members would go to their homes to share the love of Christ with them. That's surprise!

On the other hand, two ladies who were ministering among the skinheads, punkers and prostitutes of London, one Christmas, were allowed into the basement rooms of a brothel. They knocked on each door, handing each girl a long-stemmed rose, saying, "Merry Christmas. Jesus loves you." That, too, is surprise!

On the last day, the Great Day of the Feast, the Man stood on the paved courtyard and shouted, "Hey! Are you still thirsty? Come to Me, and drink!" To us it may be just a story. But to the people listening, it was surprise!

The timing was strategic. This Jewish festival celebrated the time of the Children of Israel arriving in the Land flowing with milk and honey. For six days, the priests went down to the Brook Kidron and brought jugs of water up to the Temple Mount. The water was poured out. It ran over the people's feet, and they thanked Jehovah for His provision in the Wilderness. On the last day, the Great Day of the Feast, again the people gathered. But this time, no water was poured out. They were to celebrate His provision in the Land flowing with milk and honey. See Exodus 23:16 and Zechariah 14:16-19.

And it was on *this* day that Jesus questions, "Hey!

Are you still thirsty? Come to Me, and drink." That's surprise! See John 7:37-39.

On the other hand, Jesus Christ can never be surprised. He has no limitations on His intelligence, nor can He be deceived. "No creature has anything to cover himself from the sight of God; everything lies naked and exposed before the eyes of Him with Whom we have to relate." He had just said that His "Word is alive and active: It cuts more keenly than any two-edged sword; it strikes through to where soul and spirit meet, to the innermost intimacies of a man's being; it exposes the very thoughts and motives of a man's heart." Hebrews 4:12-13

This is not true of the devil. From his very first act of rebellion, his lack of intelligence led to his defeat. In the most critical battle of the ages, his incompetence led to the surprise of Calvary. "But we speak the wisdom of God (a mystery, even hidden wisdom) which He planned before the creation for our glory today; wisdom which none of the princes of this world knew; for had they known, they would not have crucified the Lord of glory!" I Corinthians 2:7-8

We must take the offensive and employ the element of surprise in our battles. On the defensive we have no choice but to fight. But when we take the opportunity to surprise the enemy, the decision to fight is ours.

For us to devise and employ the element of surprise in our warfare, three ingredients are necessary:

1) *We need creativity.* We cannot vegetate in front of the TV or video games for hours on end and then expect the creative juices to flow. We need to think and reason and question and meditate and imagine and wonder! We need to exercise the mind of Christ that is ours as His spiritual body. See I Corinthians 2:16.

2) *We need to take the initiative.* The "get-up-and-go" has to really get up and go! A thousand mile journey still has to begin with the first step. Moses was saying,

"Stand still and see the salvation of the Lord!" But the Lord said, "What are you doing talking to Me? The enemy is coming! Tell the people to get going!" (Another one of my rather loose paraphrases of Exodus 14:13,15. But it is there. Read it for yourself.)

3) *We need determination.* The bulldog "stick-to-itiveness" that moves the plan forward; the "nubbies" on the off-road bike tires that dig into the dirt and give it the traction to move forward.

In the final analysis, Jesus is our example: *When* was He about His Father's business? "From 9 to 5. Them's my working hours!" No! That doesn't sound like God Incarnate. Jesus ministered to Mary Magdalene at the break of dawn on that Resurrection morning. He met with Nicodemus at midnight, for this teacher of the Law feared the Jews. And Jesus was focused on His Father's business every hour in between. "I do nothing but what the Father has shown me." John 5:19 Often, Jesus was so involved that He and His disciples had no time to eat. See Mark 3:20.

Where did He spend His time? In the synagogues, yes. But also in the homes of sinners. In fact, his reputation was that He was a friend of publicans and sinners, mainly tax collectors and prostitutes! In a town where He was experiencing some popularity, His disciples came looking for Him: "The people are calling for You." He said, "Then we had better go on to the next town, so I can preach there, too—for that is why I have come." See Mark 1:37-38.

How—by what methods—did He do the Father's work? The variety is beyond cataloging: Go dip in the pool. Neither do I condemn you. You must be born again. He spit in one guy's eyes: He stuck His fingers in another man's ears. He turned water into wine. He waited until Lazarus' body was decaying before He brought him back to life. I say, do you catch any element of surprise in His methods?

"But you shall receive power, after the Holy Spirit has come upon you, and you shall be witnesses unto Me both in Jerusalem, and in all Judea, and in Samaria, and unto the uttermost parts of the earth." Acts 1:8 Again, to us that may be just another sentence in the Bible. But to those to whom He was speaking, it was *surprise!* For they were hoping that He would at that time set up His Kingdom on earth.

Principle Seven: Cooperation
"Among the large number (estimates of up to 20,000) who had become believers, there was complete agreement of heart and soul. Not one of them claimed any of his possessions as his own, but everything was common property—a wonderful spirit of generosity pervaded the whole fellowship. Indeed, there was not a single person in need among them." Acts 4:32-34 There was fellowship; there was harmony; there was cooperation in this early church in Jerusalem.

An isolated Christian is an anomaly just as *"But, Lord...!"* is an anomaly. Those two concepts just don't fit together. To the degree that we *But (butt)* Him, He is not truly our Lord, or Master. Another example: "He is *deceptively honest."* Wait! Those two words cannot come together to describe one action. Likewise, the thought that a Christian can isolate himself should be as unbelievable.

Yet, a culture that glorifies individualism says, "I can fight my own battles. I can make it on my own." The self-made man, pulling himself up by his bootstraps, climbs the corporate ladder from janitor to president! He is applauded, and he is proud!

Having grown up in such a culture, the Christian applies this technique to his personal spiritual warfare: "I can do it by myself." Some misleading Christian songs even supported this mistaken concept. "On the Jericho Road, it's just Jesus and me; no more and no less, for two is the best...."

How conveniently this fits into one of satan's tactics, "Shush! You're the only one doing this. Don't tell anyone. You will be kicked out of the church if they know," he whispers in your ear. And the struggling Christian goes deeper into isolation.

Thus, when it comes to the greater battles for the souls of men, we don't know how to cooperate. Yet, cooperation is essential to concentration at a decisive point, and concentration is necessary for victory!

Cooperation demands two prerequisites:

1) *Cooperating forces are allies, not belligerents;* and

2) *Cooperating forces are under one Commander.*

Allies form when people share common goals. Even in such a multi-faceted objective as the evangelization of the world, it is good to be able to state and agree upon a very simple, easy to understand phrase such as Habakkuk's, "The just shall live by faith" (Habakkuk 2:4) or Joel's, "Whosoever shall call upon the Name of the Lord shall be saved." Joel 2:32

But what do we find in the Christian community?

Paul looked for cooperation with Apollos: "As for our brother Apollos, I pressed him strongly to go to you with the others, but his will was not at all to come at this time...." I Corinthians 16:12

A young man came running up to Moses and reported, "Moses, Eldad and Medad are prophesying in the camp!"

"Moses, forbid them!" Joshua urged.

But Moses said, "Are you jealous for me? Wouldn't it be great if all of the Lord's people were prophets, and that the Lord would put His Spirit on all of them?" Numbers 11:27-29

John, later to be called the Apostle of Love, at one

time bragged to Jesus, "Master, we saw someone casting out evil spirits in Your Name, but we stopped him,
for he is not a part of our group."

Jesus replied, "You must not stop him. No one who
exerts such power in My Name would readily say anything against Me. For the man who is not against us is
on our side." Mark 9:38-40

One says, "I am a follower of Paul!" Another boasts,
"Apollos is my favorite TV evangelist. Such eloquent
speech!" "Peter is an *Apostle*; I listen to him," yet another chides. In assurance of his position, a quiet voice
declares, "I am of Jesus only." "What?! Is Christ divid-
ed?" Paul demanded. See I Corinthians 1:12-13.

Has anything changed?

In a Christian context, today, the question "What
are you?" is meant to elicit the response of Presbyterian
or Nazarene or Lutheran or Baptist or Pentecostal or
any one of the thousands of Christian denominations.
Anymore, I don't even want to say, "I'm a Christian!"
For, even Christian has come to lose its true meaning,
Little Christ.

Whether it be denomination or non-denomination or
mission society or some theological position of my
group, these distinctives tend to keep us from cooperation. Jesus prayed, "Father, that they may be one as
We are one." John 17:22 He had previously instructed,
"They will know you are My disciples by you love for
one another. John 13:35

The greatest single deterrent to cooperation is pride.
On a personal level, pride may keep us from admitting
our needs to even ourselves, let alone to anyone else. A
proud person will struggle alone so that if he wins, he
may take all of the glory; or so that if he loses, nobody
will know about it.

And Scripture describes him, "He who covers his
sins shall not prosper." Solomon goes on to say, "But

whoever confesses and forsakes them shall have mercy." Proverbs 28:13 James instructed, "Get in the habit of confessing your faults one to another and praying for each other so that you may be healed." James 5:16 The Word further says that a prideful look (which arises from a proud heart) is one of the seven abominations of God. See Proverbs 16:5; 6:16-17. "Pride goes before destruction; a haughty spirit before a fall." Proverbs 16:18 The Lord, having just said that He ponders the hearts of all men, declares that a proud heart is sin. See Proverbs 21:2,4.

But the ultimate passage in painting the dismal state of a proud person has to be Proverbs 26:1-12. Solomon has just described eleven characteristics of a fool, ending with "...as a dog returns to its vomit, so a fool returns to his folly." And then (and to get the full impact of what follows, it would be good to read all eleven verses first), Solomon notes that "...there is more hope for a fool than for a proud person!" (v.12) And if you are quick with your words to defend your pride, Solomon also said, "There is more hope for a fool than one who is hasty in his words." Proverbs 29:20 May we heed the further instruction of James who wrote, "Humble yourself (and humility is the opposite of pride) in the sight of the Lord, and He will lift you up." James 4:10

There are four attitudes we can assume as we encounter other Christian warriors on the same battlefield:

1) *We can oppose them.* "We were here first! We have a better strategy than you! You don't share (insert your particular theological distinctive) with us. Go home!"

2) *We can tolerate them.* "Okay, if you have to be here, work in those areas where we choose not to work."

3) *We can ignore them.* "Oh! I wasn't aware of any other warriors on this battlefield." Or,

4) *We can unite with them.* "How good and pleasant it is for brethren to dwell together in unity." Psalm 133:1 Or, as Paul exhorts, "Endeavor to keep the unity of the Spirit in the bond of peace." Ephesians 4:3

In the final analysis, the attitude of Paul is classic and one to be emulated: He is in prison for preaching the Gospel. This emboldens others to preach. Some are preaching out of their strong love for Paul. Others, though, are preaching just to make the fact that he is in prison hurt more. What a motivation! Yet, Paul, knowing this, still says, "What should I say? I will say this: Praise God! The Gospel is being preached." See Philippians 1:14-18.

Principle Eight: Communication

In military language, the "lines of communication are all the land, water and air routes which connect the army with its base of operation, along which supplies and reinforcements move." History is replete with failed military engagements because the army moved too fast for the more cumbersome supply train to keep up. Or, in their advancing, the thinned-out supply line was cut off by the enemy.

In spiritual warfare, we are grateful for a fail-safe communication network—at least from the Commander's perspective. He said, "I will never leave you nor forsake you." Hebrews 13:5 And, "Behold, I am with you always, even unto the end of the world." Matthew 28:20 He is omnipresent; so, although we picture Him seated at the right hand of the Father, highly exalted, He is also as close to us as our spiritual beings will acknowledge Him to be.

It has been humorously said that in the Oval Office of an earlier President a new, pure white phone had been installed. One day the Secretary of State entered the room and noticing the phone, inquired of it. "Oh," said the President, "with the difficulties of this office, I have installed this direct line to God!" Upon using it, the Secretary was about to leave. But the President, calculating the price of that call, gave him a bill. Surprised by the high rate, the Secretary still paid it, for the advice was good.

A number of months later the Secretary was in Israel. Walking into the Prime Minister's office, he saw a similar white phone. After using it, he pulled out his wallet, again expecting the same high rate. The Prime Minister said, "No. No. It only cost you a dime. It's a local call!"

Whether we are in Israel, the United States, on the highest mountain or in the deepest sea, we have the assurance of His presence with us. See Psalm 139:1-12 and Romans 8:38-39.

But if we overextend ourselves (burn out) or allow the lines of communication to be severed, we can expect spiritual defeat. How many campaigns against the enemy have been lost because those involved got so busy working *for* the Lord, that they neglected personal or corporate time *with* the Lord? The battle was going great. Victories were being won. Advance. Advance! Claim more territory in Jesus' Name. Then one day the warriors wake up to realize that yesterday's prayers, last week's Bible reading and last month's Bible studying is not sustaining them in the thick of the battle today. Open and vulnerable to the enemy, unless a rapid retreat can be executed, they will fall prey to the devil. And the new believers left behind are vulnerable to the enemy.

Physical proximity was not what distanced Martha from her Lord. But His rebuke to her certainly lets us know that she had overextended herself. Her good works, her good deeds—I'm sure the aroma of her cooking filled the house—had caused her heart to miss the "better part." See Luke 10:38-42.

Equally, we are warned in Scripture of other practices in our lives which can sever those lines of communication. To mention a few:

1) "Whoever stops up his ears from hearing the cry of the poor, he also will cry, but shall not be heard." Proverbs 21:13

2) "But your iniquities have separated between you and your God, and your sins have made Him hide His face from you so that He will not hear you." Isaiah 59:2

3) "Husbands, live with your wives in knowledge and with understanding, giving honor to them as to a weaker vessel, yet equally heirs with you of the grace of God. If you don't do this, you will find it impossible to pray effectively." I Peter 3:7

Whether it is a hearing problem, our iniquities and sins, or how we treat our spouse, the Word declares it will sever—or at least cause disruptive static on—that line of communication.

Jesus said, "I am the Vine, you are the branches...Abide (stay connected) in Me." John 15:5 Have you ever used a phone where the little safety clip on the connector was broken? Nobody else knows of the danger—maybe not even you. As long as you don't move the phone or pull on the cord everything is okay.... But you reach for something across the desk and the cord falls out. You are still there with the phone to your ear. The party on the other end is still there saying, "Hello? Hello?" Such a little piece of plastic, but how devastating the results—especially if it is a call to your Commander-in-Chief, Jesus Christ, the righteous.

Paul encouraged the Christians at Thessalonica to "pray without ceasing." I Thessalonians 5:17 It is an exercise of faith, but it can be done. We are spiritual beings. By the Holy Spirit we are drawn to the Father through Jesus Christ. Our spirits are alive even while the earthly part of us can be stuck in a freeway traffic jam or be in a nose-to-nose confrontation with the neighbor's bulldog. Thus, by the simple acknowledgement of God, we are able to transcend the dimensions of time and space and dwell in the shadow of the Almighty. And under His wing find the security of His peace. See Psalm 91:1,4. And by just breathing His Name we find safety in a strong tower. See Proverbs 18:10. By faith, our spiritual communication need not be broken. While I sit at this desk with all the sights and smells and sounds of my physical environment to distract me, and with my mind struggling to put pen to paper in order to clearly communicate that which is in my heart, I am also conscious that my spirit is alive in God through Christ and that I am connected to the Source of my life. This is unbroken spiritual communication. This is "praying without ceasing."

The strength, the vitality of our spirits comes from the Source of all Life. We, as Soldiers of the Cross, must maintain communication with our Commander-in-Chief at all times. He is our "base camp"—our Source of supply for spiritual food, ammunition, strategy and specific orders.

Further, God's Word is the ultimate authority. Spiritual communication—from any other source—that does not align itself with Holy Scripture is not of God. Even when a spiritual leader is teaching from this Source— even when that leader is as brilliant as Paul, the Apostle—we are encouraged to "search the Scriptures to see if what he is saying is true." Acts 17:11

Why have I filled these pages with Scripture references? To make it easier for you to align what I am saying with the Ultimate Truth, the Word of God. For, unless what we are writing finds its substance in His Precepts, we are merely putting printer's ink on some finely processed trees!

E.V. Hill, concluding a dynamic presentation on the power of the Word to transform society, crescendoed to this climax: "The Word; The Word; The Word! The Word! The WORD! THE **WORD**! **THE WORD**! It is the power of God unto Salvation!" See Romans 1:16.

In concluding this section, while my mind is searching for a word to more appropriately express... (Here I just crossed out the word "say" and wrote in "express.") ...what I am thinking... (What *am* I thinking? I'm thinking how sloppy this page looks with all its scratch overs and arrows trying to give direction to my secretary to help her follow my thoughts.)...   ...(and before I could write another word, I took a break. It's a cold day so my wife just brought in a hot cup of herb tea!)

In spite of all of that, my spirit is *still* alive in God through Christ, drawn by the Holy Spirit into His presence with joy and adoration. I'm not a pious, hyperspiritual sort of guy. But I assure you, just the same, that while my conscious life is full of a thousand thoughts, my spirit is in communication with God. To the praise of His glory! I am abiding in the Vine. I will not distance myself from my line of communication.

Communication with my Creator is like the umbilical cord of an unborn baby; it is like the tether of an astronaut's space suit; it is my Lifeline!

Principle Nine: Pursuit
The battle has been engaged. Principles of war have been observed. The enemy has been defeated. He is on the run. Is the war over? No...not yet. Victory—ultimate victory—is declared when the last enemy is pursued and found; when he is taken captive and rendered useless to the cause of hostile forces.

Though some may think pursuit is the "easy" part of war, there are two factors which identify it to be as critical as any other principle:

1) The conquering army is mobile and in pursuit. Not having to engage in battle, they are covering territory rapidly. One danger they face is outrunning their supplies. However, the retreating forces are falling back on their reinforcements, growing stronger all the time. Even to the point of again launching a new defensive/ offensive attack against their overextended conquerors.

2) The greater factor, however, is psychological, not material. The tension of the battle is over for the pursuer. The adrenalin rush is not there to keep him alert. "The end is in sight. I'm as good as home," he thinks. As these thoughts fill his mind, the pursued is thinking, "I've got to get out of here!" His senses are keener as he retreats over ground more familiar to him than his pursuer. And he gets away.

With tragic consequence, successful pursuits in the history of war have been few; the escape from a lost battle have been many.

And with eternal consequence, the spiritual war for men is not much different. The battle for souls has been engaged. A Spirit-anointed message goes forth in power. Conviction of sin is in the hearts of many. An opportunity to surrender their lives to Christ is given. Some respond. Many hold back.

Spiritual pursuit, at this point, must be directed toward two groups: Those who responded and those who are holding back.

Those who have surrendered have just capitulated to the Lord. "Having been taken captive by the devil at his will, by the instruction of the Word, they have recovered themselves out of the snare of the devil." See II Timothy 2:24-26.

Follow-up by traditional usage is too weak a word to describe what must take place. *Follow-through* may be better. But let's go for the best: *Disciple* those who have trusted in Christ. Jesus said it: "Go into all the

world...teaching them how to live by My Commandments." Matthew 28:18-20 Make them followers—disciples—of Christ. Encourage them (by your words and
your lifestyle) to enter an accountability group. Have
them join themselves in the study of the "Apostles' doctrine, in fellowship, in breaking of bread and in
prayers." Acts 2:42 By these four means the first 3000
converts on the Day of Pentecost were discipled.

To change the analogy, these new converts are babies. They need someone to choose the right formula—
the Milk of the Word—and hold the bottles in their
mouths; to spoon-feed them on the pabulum of the
Word. And, yes, to change their dirty diapers, also!
They will fall; they will sin. And satan will be right there
to condemn them. But you will be there, too, to sustain
them—to lift them up again. Yes, you will, if you are
discipling them and not just offering them a New Testament and the first in a series of *follow-up* sheets.

But there are also those in whose hearts the battle
is still raging. They stand there. Tears of regret may be
streaming down their faces. Their eyes have been
opened to the spiritual realm. Flashing before them is
the contrast of darkness in which they have been living
and the Light of Life, Jesus Christ. But the power of satan still keeps them from turning to God. See Acts 26:18.
This is a vulnerable moment.

While you are rejoicing in the success of the campaign, those scared of the uncertainty of exchanging
death for life eternal have time to retreat into their
thoughts of the pleasures of sin. While you are counting those who went to the altar, those who have been
given just a glimpse of eternity escape to the familiar
territory of earthly pursuits. As their reinforcements accumulate, they come back at you with a greater ven-
geance.

Rather, at that vulnerable moment, press in with

even greater force. A number of years ago I was an elder at a very evangelistic church. Often on Sunday evening, rather than going to the front to deal with those who had surrendered, from the back of the auditorium I would look around for those in whose chests such a battle was still raging. I would go to them. Stand next to them. Sense by the Spirit the words to speak. As a result many who would otherwise have left the church in their unrepentant condition bowed in submission to their Savior and Lord.

On that great Day of Pentecost, when the Church was birthed, "3000 trusted in Christ as Savior." Acts 2:41 "And they continued daily in the temple and from house to house...and the Lord added to the Church daily such as should be saved." Acts 2:46-47 Days or weeks later "many of them which heard the Word believed, and the number of men rose to about 5000." Acts 4:4 Some time later "...more and more believers were added to the Lord, multitudes both of men and women." Acts 5:14 "The High Priest said, "Didn't we tell you to stop teaching in this Man's Name? Look, you have filled Jerusalem with your doctrine." Acts 5:28

Did they stop? No! The pursuit continued. "And daily in the temple and in every house, they continued teaching and proclaiming the Good News that Jesus is the Christ." Acts 5:42 This is pursuit to ultimate victory!

Principle Ten: Obedience
"Behold, to obey is better than sacrifice." I Samuel 15:22 This was a tough rebuke to one who had just annihilated the enemy. However, it was a hollow victory of triumph for Saul, since he had not obeyed the commandment of God.

In one of satan's most subtle ploys, he has lifted up one word as our standard for involvement in Christian service. And he has caused us to overlook the scheme of God's design. (Bear with me as we look again at this critical issue in war. We considered it in Chapter 3.)

The word is *volunteer*. It is a high-sounding word. It speaks of bravery. Of sacrifice, Of doing something dangerous—above the call of duty. We would rather volunteer than obey because the choice of involvement rests in our decision. We have time to think about it. "Yes, that's something I would like to do," we muse. "I will stand up. They will see me step forward. I like that."

To volunteer is to respond to a challenge. The gauntlet is most often thrown down, surprisingly, by our own leaders. Those enticing us into Christian service paint the dangers and difficulties of a particular task in such a way as to provoke in our minds a human pride that draws us in.

In secular war, the military also appeals to pride to get a young person to volunteer. But once the ink is dry, it is a matter of obedience. There are no more appeals. The system has changed. There are only commands to obey. But the church wields no such authority over its adherents. Therefore, week after week the appeals must be repeated: "We are looking for more volunteers."

We should recognize that it is a flawed system. Let's learn from the Master. God is not looking for volunteers, nor does He challenge His own children. When Jesus called His disciples, it was in the simple imperative: "Follow Me." There were also a great many volunteers who followed Jesus. But they wanted to bury their dead first or care for their possessions. Or say good-bye to their family. Or.... See Luke 9:57-62.

And when His sayings got tough, thousands left Him. So great was the exodus that He turned to His disciples and said, "Will you leave Me, also?"

"Where would we go? You have the words of eternal life," Peter declared.

Jesus answered, "I have *chosen* you." See John 6.
To volunteer is to respond to a challenge. To obey is
to respond to a command. In John 14:15, Jesus did not
say, "If you love Me you will *volunteer.*" Rather, He said,
"If you love Me you will *obey* My commandments."

There are two obvious problems with this business
of obedience. First, we are not used to Kingdom living.
Even in earthly kingdoms today, there is a great emphasis on individual rights. Thus, the concept of a su-
preme monarch is lost. However, God is not running an
earthly monarchy, nor is He running a democracy. It is
a theocracy, a benevolent dictatorship! When God
speaks, He speaks in directives. And He expects obedience—a willing, or if necessary, an unwilling carrying
out of His commands.

This leads to the second problem. As a child, we
learned an obedience that was reluctant—an unwilling
obedience. What we might have even volunteered to
do—such as rake the leaves—when it became an order
to obey, all the *fun* was taken out of it. And now, because we *had* to do it, we avoided it until threatened.

Thus, whether we find our obedience of the reluctant kind (Refer again to the story of Moses in Exodus
3-4.) or of the willing kind (Refer to the story of Mary,
the mother of our Lord in Luke 1:26-38.), it is obedience that will keep us by the side of our Commander-
in-Chief. Men may become active in His Army because
of a challenge or desire to volunteer (though that motive
is inferior to simple submission to His will), but obedience—a gut-level discipline of commitment—will keep
them there!

"If you are willing and obedient, you will eat the
good of the land," God spoke through Isaiah. Isaiah 1:19
I believe it is consistent with His character to affirm
that principle for us today, as well.

The Holy Spirit through Paul told Timothy (and us),

"The goal of the *commandment* is charity out of a pure heart, and of a clear conscience, and of a genuine faith." I Timothy 1:5

May we with Paul discover the greatest motivation of service to our Master: "For the love of Christ constrains me...the love of Christ compels me...God's love for me leaves me no choice...It is His love for me that is the very well-spring of all of my action...." II Corinthians 5:14

Say it as you like it. Choose your translation. It all comes down to mean that when I come to comprehend and apply to my life the depth and height and breadth of His love for me, in humble willingness, I bow my knee to the King of Kings and say, "Yes, Lord!"

Principle Eleven: Economy of Force
The combined application of all principles of war yields an economy of force. Thus, to the degree that the foregoing principles can be brought to bear on any given engagement, there will be victory with the least amount of force.

There was only one "perfect" battle. It took place on Mount Moriah overlooking Jerusalem about 2000 years ago. Let's look at it:

Objective: Victory over death, hell and the grave. See I Corinthians 15:54-57.

Offense: He set His face toward Jerusalem. "For this reason I was born," He said. See Luke 9:51 and John 12:27.

Concentration: This one principle alone was not employed, for "all the disciples deserted Him and fled." Matthew 26:56 And while on the cross, Jesus Himself cried, "My God! My God! Why have You forsaken Me?" Matthew 27:46

Mobility: His body was nailed to a cross, yet He freely gave His life a ransom for many. See John 10:18 and Mark 10:45.

Security: The enemy was so deceived regarding the

purpose of this battle that he (through the "princes of this world") was cooperating with it! See I Corinthians 2:7-8.

Surprise: Why seek the living among the dead? He is risen!" Luke 24:5-6

Cooperation: "Father, into Your hands I commend My spirit." Luke 23:46

Communication: "After this, Jesus, knowing that all things had been accomplished, that the Scriptures might be fulfilled, said, "I thirst." John 19:28

Pursuit: "Go tell the disciples—and Peter—that I will meet them in Galilee." Mark 16:7

Obedience: "Nevertheless, not My will but Thine be done." Luke 22:42

"It is finished!" were His last words from the cross. Indeed! "For the joy that was set before Him He endured the cross, despising the shame and has now taken His seat at the right hand of the Father." Hebrews 12:2 Victory was His so that victory can be ours.

"Now unto Him Who is able to keep you from falling, and to present you faultless before the presence of His glory with exceeding joy; to the only wise God our Savior, be glory and majesty, dominion and power, both now and forever. Amen!" Jude 24-25

PRACTICAL INSIGHTS

WHEN SATAN HASSLES CHRISTIANS

There is joy in knowing that "in Christ" there is a solution for every need. We can cast *all* of our cares on Him because He cares for us. Let's live victoriously in the solutions His Spirit reveals to us.

Problem   The enemy tries to hassle me through temptations which can be very subtle. Too often we don't even see the problem coming, and so we fall. Or, just the shock of being tempted by something that we didn't think could be a temptation, can be unnerving to us.

Solution   Temptation is not sin! If a thought to do wrong comes into your mind, that is not sin. If you entertain that thought, however, it can follow the downward spiral that James talks about: "Every man is tempted when he is beguiled, allured and enticed by his own evil desires, passions and lusts. Then passion conceives and brings forth sin. And when sin is fully matured it brings forth death." James 1:14-15

Paul warned Timothy (and us) to "flee youthful lusts." II Timothy 2:22 Avoid setups—situations which make it easy to follow that downward pattern. If you know that you are easily tempted to over indulge in sweets, don't go into the bakery when you are hungry. Don't even walk past it!

If something is continually, consistently a temptation—a real problem in your life over a period of time—follow concrete plans to gain a permanent victory: 1) Meditate on Scripture passages that are relevant to the solution. (Notice I didn't say, "relevant to the problem," for our focus always needs to be on God's solution.) For example, take the problem of being tempted to talk in a negative, destructive way.

In just the Book of Proverbs, there are scores of Scriptures that teach us how to communicate in a healthy, constructive way. Allow the Spirit to direct you to the passage that will help you overcome this temptation. Then go over and over that Scripture until it becomes a part of you. Make it personal. Rewrite it with your name in it. 2) Get into an accountability relationship with a person with whom you can and will be totally honest. 3) Have the elders of your church, your home fellowship group or a few close friends pray for you.

Problem The enemy tries to hassle me through confusion. There are so many ways that confusion can cause trouble—it's confusing! Confusion can come through distractions. You have heard from God; your direction is clear. Then other good ideas come along, or maybe your leader proposes a different direction, or you begin listening to the many voices (of real people or thoughts in your head) that are trying to get your attention.

Confusion can come through timing. For example, there is a delay in scheduling. Or a change in a law now blocks your plans. Or something broke. Or you got sick. Or there was a family problem. Or a financial problem. Stop! It's too confusing!

Confusion can come through trying to live in a role that is not yours to fulfill. You just don't know how to function in that position. You feel like a round peg in a square hole! It's not what God planned for you. You just sorta' got there...somehow!

Confusion can come through your claiming other people's problems. It can be very confusing to try to solve someone else's problems *for* them—especially when they don't want you to. This does not mean that we are not to help another person who is asking for help—if God is also saying we are the ones to help.

Solution   God is not the author of confusion. There had been some confusion going on in the Corinthian church. Paul wrote some instructions about what they were doing and what they should be doing. Then he gave the basis for getting this issue sorted out: "For God is not the author of confusion." I Corinthians 14:33 He does not contradict Himself or change His mind.

Once we understand the source of confusion, we can exercise authority over the enemy to leave. This may clear up the confusion immediately. At least you will be thinking more clearly. Good questions to ask are, "Is this my problem? Is this what God wants me to do? Am I submitting to the authority structure God has put me under?" Often the issues that confuse us are out of our realm of responsibility, or beyond the scope of our role. When we see that it is not our problem or business, we need to learn to let it go.

Confusion can also just be the natural fruit of disorganization, and not to be blamed so directly on the enemy! Some people may lack the discipline to order their time, their household, and their work. But that's an issue for the next problem.

Problem   The enemy tries to hassle me when I don't establish priorities. To be totally unorganized, lacking clear goals—just drifting—makes me very vulnerable to the enemy's attack. Just think about it—nothing drifts upward; everything drifts downward. When we don't have our time planned, it gets used up by whatever comes along. So it is with our priorities, as well, if we don't understand them; if we don't have them clearly in our minds. When all we set out to do does not get done, the frustration that

follows could make a place for the enemy to attack.
Solution Make a plan and follow your plan.
This applies to any area of your life. Your plan will
begin with goals, the objectives that you want to accomplish. Then each goal needs specific steps to follow in order to achieve that goal. You look over
those steps and set them in order of priority. You
might want to have yearly, monthly, weekly and
even daily priority sheets. Personally, I am a "list"
person. Every night I make a list of what I need to
do the next day. I can't think without my list! (Well,
that might be a little extreme.) But I do make a daily
list. Then I put numbers next to the items I have
listed. That becomes my order of priority for the
next day.

Your plan is to be a guide, not a law. Interruptions (which *may* not be interruptions but really
God's plan), changes in other people's schedules
which affect you, and any number of things as the
day progresses can lead you to alter your plan.

When my husband drove our family (and his sister who was living with us) to the harbor one Saturday morning, I already had plans for that weekend.
But he stopped, pulled a suitcase out of the trunk
and said good-bye to his sister and our children. We
were off to a surprise weekend on Catalina Island!
Do you think I insisted on following my previously
determined plans?

Having no plans or priorities can be a great thief
of your time. When Paul was telling the Ephesians
to be wise and have a clear understanding of the
will of God for their lives he said, "Make the best use
of your time, despite all the difficulties of these
days." Ephesians 5:16 Make a plan and work your
plan!

Problem The enemy tries to hassle me through

pressure from other people. Partners, roommates, spouses, our children, parents, friends, in-laws! The enemy can use anybody—especially those close to us—to bring pressure. People with poor self-images suffer the most by this trick of the evil one. We all want to be accepted and approved of, but if we do not have the security of the realization of who we are in Christ—on a heart level—then we will have an even stronger need to please people. Thus, pressure from people who are close to us has a lot more effect on us.

Solution We must be in a close fellowship with God. A healthy Scriptural view of God and our relationship with Him gives us a security that can resist the pressures of other people's demands. We should certainly ask for, listen to and consider godly counsel from people. But we should not waiver in what we know to be God's will for our life. We take all of their godly counsel before the Lord and ask, "Lord, out of all this advice, what is Your will for me." See Proverbs 19:20-21.

We build and continue in a strong relationship with God just as the first Christians did: "And they remained steadfast in the Word, in fellowship, in breaking of bread (that's having meals together) and prayers." Acts 2:42

Also, we need to choose to develop a realistically good self-image as sons and daughters of God, the Creator of the Universe! When we have this "in Christ" estimation of ourselves, we can more clearly see things from His perspective and respond to others in love. And, as we have already noted, a healthy self-image comes from dealing with each issue—one at a time—with the truth of God's Word.

Problem The enemy tries to hassle me by keeping me busy doing good things instead of the things

God wants me to do. "Don't be so extreme. You'll be too different to relate with other people. Be reasonable; you've done your share; relax. Let someone else do their part," the enemy whispers in our ear. Mediocrity becomes the normal way of life. Thus, we find our time and our energy used up in good and acceptable things. And we are robbed of being and doing the best that God has for us.

Yes—we can miss the best in the big things—like whether to be a missionary or which profession. But the more subtle, daily way the enemy tries to block the Christian from God's best is by putting many small, very good things to do in our paths. The story of Mary and Martha is all too familiar. Martha was doing good things—exercising the gift of hospitality, serving Jesus and His disciples. See Luke 10:38-42. We can become so busy doing many good things that we miss the best and most important that God has for each of us.

Solution Sometimes to do the best involves risk, sacrifice, or people's questioning disapproval. Each of us has twenty-four hours a day. First, we must realize that it is impossible to do everything that we would like to do. Some of our dreams will remain just that—dreams. This may involve having to say, "No," to many things we would really like to do.

Second, we must prioritize those great plans that God has given to us by determining His will for our lives. And begin fulfilling them—one at a time.

Third, we need to have time for reflecting to be sure we are continuing in His priorities.

"In all these things we are more than conquerors through Him who loves us." Romans 8:37

7
STRATEGIES FOR BATTLEFIELD LIVING

*"No soldier on active duty gets himself entangled
with the affairs of civilian life because he wants to
please the One who has chosen him to be a soldier."*
II Timothy 2:4

"We do not want to give the enemy any advantage
over us, for we are not ignorant of his schemes." II Corinthians 2:11 As we learn how to live on the battlefield, this
concept again stands as the backdrop. Even in the area
of conducting ourselves on the battlefield, we see the
enemy trying to take advantage of us. Let's look at a
number of strategies that we can develop for overcoming the evil one and for living successfully on the battlefield.

Move Out Of The Pew
At some point in our Christian walk, we become aware
that we are Soldiers of the Cross. And that means spiritual warfare. But actually getting out of the country
club comfort of our *pew* (any aspect of our Christian life
that denies, ignores or fights against the realities of
spiritual warfare) and into the *battlefield* (every place in
our inward battle or in the battle for lost souls where
we have laid down the gauntlet, declaring war on the

enemy) can be quite a struggle. The Holy Spirit's work in our lives to accomplish this move is not unlike that of Mama Eagle as she begins to teach her young to fly. You have seen pictures of it, I am sure. Up on that craggy cliff, a nest is hanging over the canyon. It has been well made. A strong scaffolding of branches has been wedged into the cracks of the cliff. Woven into these pieces are smaller branches and twigs; and finally, the soft down that Mama plucked from her own body lines the nest. Deep in that soft, warm, fuzzy refuge the baby eaglets are hatched. And they romp and play. Mama keeps bringing them food. "Hey, this is really livin'!" they tweet to each other.

And that's what a lot of Christians like to do. They just stay snuggled deep in the nest (pew) because it's so comfortable there. But one day Mama Eagle wakes up, spreads her mighty wings, and starts tearing the nest apart. And the little eaglets think Mama has gone crazy! "You're ripping my home away from me! This can't be. It's getting uncomfortable. (It's not like it was when I first got saved!) You are my Mama, aren't you? Aren't you going to keep bringing me my food and masticating it for me and placing it into my beak?"

Ignoring their peeps, Mama just keeps pulling the twigs and branches out and lets them fall to the canyon floor below. As if to instruct her, an eaglet protests, "Mama, you built this beautiful home for us. Maybe I haven't fully expressed my appreciation for it, but you don't have to be this radical. You can't just keep pulling it...apart!" His last words are interrupted as he hops off a twig Mama is pulling out. He catches his balance on a safer branch.

In his insidious, illogical effort to keep us off the battlefield, satan could even suggest to our minds that this restlessness created by the Holy Spirit to mature us is "just the devil" trying to disrupt our lives.

But pretty soon, just the framework alone is left. And the little eaglet is looking down, down through the sticks to a rushing river a thousand feet or more below, wondering what is going to happen next.

Then Mama Eagle starts hovering over the disassembled nest. That huge expanse of her wings blocks the sun. Little eaglet looks up and tries to say something nice: "That's beautiful, Mama! That's your reality!" He is oblivious to the fact that his little wings are about to learn how to soar.

Mama Eagle carefully snuggles down into the skeleton of the nest and begins nudging little eaglet right up to the edge. "Afraid" isn't the word for it. His knees are shaking; his eyes are bugged wide open; perched on that framework he totters, holding on for dear life! But Mama comes along and gives him a shove right off the edge!

Ooohh! aaahhh! the little eaglet's baby voice echoes down into the canyon. Frantically flapping his wings, yet not knowing what to do with them, he free falls for several hundred feet. He's sure that this is his end. But in the nick of time, Mama swoops down underneath him, catches her baby on the pinions of her wings and takes him up again.

His heart is pounding out of his chest. "Whoosh! Mama came to her senses and she rescued me. Now she's going to build the nest so I can be comfortable again," little eaglet thinks. But, no! She pushes him off again...and again...until eventually that eagle learns how to soar on the currents of the wind. And he finds that life has new meaning. He sees things from a totally new perspective.

Might your experience have been similar? Sunday after Sunday the pastor bottle-fed you with the milk of the Word. Your friend spoon-fed you the pabulum of the Word. Your home fellowship group provided you with the warm fuzzy comfort. All was well. And you sank deeper and deeper into the nest (pew).

Ah, yes! Being a baby is wonderful. Carried, fondled, fed, diapered, patted, petted and passed from one adoring relative to another. The center of attention! My comfort zone! So also Christians come into the family of God as newborn babes in Christ. And it's all very wonderful. They don't care who pays the taxes or the gas and light bill. They're getting along marvelously. The whole world loves a baby. But when a 25-year-old has pabulum dribbling off his chin, we say something is very wrong.

Likewise, there is a God-implanted genetic pattern in our spirit that says, "Let's grow up."

The day will come when you hear Him say, "At a time when you should be feeding others, I am still having to hold the bottle in your mouth. Let's go on to maturity." A rather loose paraphrase of parts of Hebrews 5:12 and 6:1. Read the whole passage in its context.

Getting out of that pew and into the battlefield is that time in our Christian experience when the focus changes from "Me 'n' my God" to "*God!* What an awesome privilege that *You* would allow me to participate in *Your* great Plan of the Ages!" See Ephesians 2:10.

Now "getting out of the pew" does not mean "not going to church!" But when you are at church, you view it as a war college or strategy room. Granted, the church is also a nursery, a hospital and a rehabilitation center. But for the purposes of this discussion, we see it as Annapolis or West Point! Developing the mental image...No, it is more than that! Developing the *life style* of getting out of the pew and into the battlefield is the first step to successful battlefield living.

Focus on Proper Motivation
We find Paul instructing Timothy in matters of battle-

field living in II Timothy 2:4. He is saying that anyone who goes to war is not going to get entangled with the affairs of this world. (We will deal with that part of the verse next.) He goes on to emphasize the compelling force for living on the battlefield: "...that he might please the One who has chosen him to be a soldier." That is our motivation. We want to please the One who has chosen us. It's not that we have volunteered, but that He has called, commanded and commissioned us. He has chosen us to be Soldiers of the Cross. "You have not chosen Me, but I have chosen you—I have appointed you...." John 15:16 We want to fulfill His calling on our lives.

When I follow the owner's manual for a new tool or appliance, using that piece of equipment for its intended purpose, it works so well. But when I try to use a table knife as a screw driver, for example: Watch out!

"We were created for His pleasure," John writes into the Owner's Manual in Revelation 4:11. Thus, when we set our hearts on pleasing the Lord—since that is what we were created to do—we live in harmony with the purpose for our existence. And it works so well!

Develop Disciplines Of Christ-Like Living
To live on the battlefield we must practice the discipline of Christ-like living. To be a disciple of Christ is to be disciplined. Now, I realize that His disciples seemed a rather motley crew during their 3 1/2 years of training. However, from Pentecost on, things changed! Within months they had "filled Jerusalem with their (His) doctrine." Acts 5:28 And within years they were preaching the Word and making disciples of Christ as far as Antioch. See Acts 11:19.

Though a whole volume could be written on just this subject, let us look briefly at five disciplines:

1) *Toughen up!* "Timothy, endure hardness—join

the ranks of those who suffer hardships—as a loyal soldier of Jesus Christ." II Timothy 2:3 The succinct wording speaks clearly of the discipline that is necessary for a soldier to become ready for active duty. Jesus bluntly said, "The world is going to hate you." John 15:19 James added, "If you are going to be friends with the world you are an enemy of God." James 7:4 Jesus another time said, "In this world you will have tribulation...." John 16:33 James again enlarges, "When all kinds of trials and temptations crowd into your life...." James 1:2 Peter said not to think it strange to be partakers in Christ's suffering. See I Peter 4:12-19. Warriors need to become tough for the tough times of war.

For perspective, it might be good to review the hardships—the tribulations—Paul experienced as a Soldier of the Cross. "I have worked harder than any of them. (Those with whom he is *foolishly* comparing himself.) I have served more prison sentences. I have been beaten time without number. I have faced death again and again. I have been beaten the regulation thirty-nine stripes by the Jews five times. I have been beaten with rods three times. I have been stoned once. I have been shipwrecked three times. (Another time would come on his way to Rome.) I have been twenty-four hours on the open sea.

"In my travels I have been in constant danger from rivers and floods, from bandits, from my countrymen, and from pagans. I have faced danger in the city streets, danger in the desert, danger on the high seas, danger among false Christians. I have known exhaustion, pain, long vigils, hunger and thirst, doing without meals. I have been cold and have lacked clothing.

"Apart from all external trials, I have the daily burden of responsibility for all the churches. Do you think anyone is weak without my feeling his weakness? Does anyone have his faith upset without my own longing to restore him?

"Oh, if I am going to boast, let me boast of the things which have shown up my weakness! ...In Damascus...I escaped by climbing through a window and being let down the wall in a basket. That's the sort of dignified exit I can boast about!" II Corinthians 11:21-33

And then meditate, if you will, on his words in reference to his hardships: He called them "light afflictions!" See II Corinthians 4:17. Paul goes on to say, "One who goes to war doesn't ever get himself entangled in the everyday business affairs of this world." II Timothy 2:4 We must keep focused. We must keep our "eyes fixed on Jesus, both the source and the goal of our faith." Hebrews 12:2

A hymn of the Church has this refrain:

Turn your eyes upon Jesus;
Look full in His wonderful face,
And the things of earth will grow strangely dim
In the light of His glory and grace.

It is not a matter of looking for the hardships of wartime austerity, but the Bible does warn us that they will come and that to please the One who has called us to be a soldier, we need to toughen up.

2) *Bring Your Thoughts Into Captivity.* Paul emphasized to the Christians in Corinth that though we live in this world, it is not a *flesh and blood* battle that we are waging. Therefore, "...the weapons of our warfare are not of human design and forge, but are divinely potent for the destruction of the enemy's strongholds in our minds, casting down imaginations and every imposing defense that exalts itself against the knowledge of God." II Corinthians 10:4-5

Have you ever asked your friends, "What are you thinking about?" And they answer, "Nothing." You know that is impossible. Our minds are always active—even in our sleep. The research that is currently being conducted on the brain and how it functions is yielding fantastic insights to the Scripture, "I am fearfully and wonderfully made...intricately and curiously fashioned...." Psalm 139:14-15 The capacity of our minds to think, to reason, to draw conclusions, to analyze and to dream is phenomenal.

And to make choices. There is the key. We have a choice not only in our actions but also in the very thoughts we think. In fact, it is the thoughts of our yesterdays that become the actions of our todays. Thus, Scripture admonishes us to think on these things: "Whatever is true and honorable and just, whatever is kind and gracious, whatever is pure and praiseworthy, fix your mind on these things." Philippians 4:8 This is the *ounce of prevention* that saves us from *pounds of cure*.

But when cure is necessary, when we have allowed the enemy to establish a stronghold in our minds, we must "declare war." When we have allowed another person's unkind word to turn into a dislike of him, which has mounted into animosity and mushroomed into hatred, and we have vowed, "I will *never* forgive him."— satan has built a stronghold (a fortress within) from which he can launch a continual barrage of missiles, making direct hits on our tender consciences. That stronghold must be destroyed—in this case by humbling ourselves and asking the person for forgiveness.

What if's and *If only's* also erect huge enemy strongholds in our minds. "If only I hadn't done that," we lament. And though we have asked forgiveness of God and the others involved—and they have assured us of their forgiveness, we cannot forgive ourselves. The stronghold the enemy has built around those thoughts keeps them going 'round and 'round in our minds to the extent of causing despair, and even causing thoughts of suicide.

Whereas *if only's* refer to laments of the past, *what*

if's speak of the anxieties of the future. These walls of anxiety—fear—that are built up around our minds disallow us the freedom to think God's thoughts of creativity and determinative action. They keep us locked in a prison of immobility. Jesus said in His discourse on healthy living, "Take *no* anxious thought for tomorrow." Of course, what He said next certainly brings us back to the reality of today: "Every day has trouble enough of its own!" Matthew 6:34

Thus, also to be dealt with are the *what, where, when, why and how's* of today. The frustrations of the present can be equally immobilizing. Having a firm grasp on His will for my life and walking with Him in those chosen steps does a lot to keep me focused. Trusting in His sovereign Plan frees me from assuming responsibility for more than He expects of me. I am challenged to the maximum with just what He shows me He wants me to do.

All of these negative thoughts concerning regrets of the past, frustrations of the present and anxieties of the future can be brought into captivity. His Word declares it!

The same discipline of Christ-like living is necessary to "cast down imaginations." Use your imagination in a good way. Picture yourself standing on a high mountain with Jesus. And then imagine the enemy, the devil, showing Jesus all the kingdoms of the habitable world in a moment of time. Jesus' thoughts (whatever they were) are interrupted by satan, "To you I will give all this power and authority and their glory...." We know what Jesus does: "It is written '...worship and serve only God.'" See Luke 4:5-8.

Any moment's hesitation of our combating that offer with a strong "It is written," would allow our imaginations to go wild. "Yes! Let me be in charge!" Any moment's hesitation of allowing Jesus to be our model in response to all the *imaginations* the enemy brings to our minds is dangerous. Whether the imagination is as (apparently) mundane as wanting that new *gismo* for our car or as radically serious as "coveting our neighbor's house, wife, manservant, maidservant, ox, donkey or anything that is our neighbor's" (Exodus 20:17), it is most easily *cast down* with a strong, "It is written...!"

Another area in which our thoughts must be brought into captivity is the area of knowledge. Knowledge is increasing at a rate that can barely be measured. Much of the *knowledge* of the world, however, stands in opposition to the knowledge of God. With minds programmed to accept detailed data and researched findings, the stacks of *evidence* can erect an "imposing defense that exalts itself against the knowledge of God." When the knowledge of this world and the knowledge of God don't seem to line up—though it may leave us momentarily in a tenuous position—it is best to wait for *all* the evidence to come in. Theory after theory that previously had been held inviolable has fallen to new information and ultimately has aligned itself with the knowledge of God. We fight to capture every thought until it acknowledges the authority of Christ.

Words, and more words, could be written. But, in the final analysis, the Words of Scripture—already written—will bring the thoughts of our mind into obedience to Him. This also is the discipline of Christ-like living.

3) *Renew Your Mind.* This principle of Christ-like living presented in Romans 12:2 was quite completely covered in Chapter 1, but we mention it here, also. For no one can survive on the battlefield without the continuing, regenerative intake of His thoughts—of His very life. On the battlefield, we are in daily contact with the world and the ways of the world. In such a setting it is so easy for the enemy to squeeze us into his mold of conformity. Jesus prayed, "It is not that I want You to

take them out of the world, but to keep them from the evil one." John 17:15

If we are going to please the One who has chosen us to be a soldier, we will learn His thoughts and His ways. In this way we are submitting to the discipline of Christ-like living.

4)   *A Light Touch On All That Is Earthly.* As an introduction to this section, I want to emphasize that though I do not believe in the concept: *Prosperity—Your Divine Right,* neither do I believe that a Christian—in order to be a "really good Christian"—has to be a pauper.

There is in the Word the story of a rich, young ruler. In the final analysis it was necessary, Jesus said, for him to sell everything, give the proceeds to the poor and then follow Him. This was not because he was rich. Jesus knew his heart. Though he had done a commendable job at keeping the Law—even from his youth—it was his wrong attitude toward his wealth that was holding him back from following Jesus. See Luke 18:18-23.

On the other hand, a family of Bethany—Mary, Martha and Lazarus were also very wealthy. They had in their own backyard a hewn-out tomb. They had a house large enough for Jesus and his entourage of followers to come whenever they wanted to stay in Bethany. And think of the food bill! Jesus never once told them to sell all, give to the poor and follow Him, because they were evidently using their wealth wisely.

I like the counsel of Agur's prayer in Proverbs 30:8-9: "Give me neither poverty nor riches, but just enough; lest I be wealthy and say, 'Who needs the Lord?' Or, lest I be poor, and steal, and blaspheme the Name of my God." Whether you are a millionaire or a *nickelaire,* it is a matter of your attitude, which must be: A light touch!

In the discourse which has come to be called the Sermon on the Mount, Jesus instructed us about our attitude toward wealth, or lack thereof. Listen to the wisdom of His reasoning:

a)   Regarding investments, they are most secure in Heaven's repositories. For where your treasure is your heart will be also.

b)   You cannot serve two masters. You will love one and hate the other. You cannot serve God and the power of money.

c)   Life is far more than food, drink and clothes. Consider the birds of the air. God feeds them. Aren't you more important than they? Consider the lilies. Solomon's splendor does not compare. Will He not more likely clothe you?

d)   Set your heart on His Kingdom and His righteousness and all these things (food, drink, clothing) will come to you as a matter of course. See Matthew 6:19-33.

"What will a man give in exchange for his own soul?" is a question that Jesus uses in order to teach another aspect of our attitude toward the wealth of this world. In Matthew 16:24-26, Jesus is not talking about self-denial: "I'll be happy to give up spinach for the rest of my life, Lord!" (For most that isn't even self-denial.) But He is talking about denying self. And we prove that we have denied self by taking up our cross and following Him. "For what is the profit to a man if he should gain the whole world and lose his own soul?"

In the early days of our marriage, when college and kids took all our cash, my wife and I practiced what we then thought to be a rather innocent (and inexpensive) pastime: window shopping—now called "malling." We walked along the streets looking in the store windows at all we knew we could not afford. Of course, neither of us admitted to the other that there might have been the least bit of lusting in our looking.

However, in many communities today, the edifices of hedonistic worship rise as monuments to a society gone wild on self-indulgence. Fed by the bumper sticker philosophies—"Shop 'til you drop" or "I'd rather be shopping at ..."(name your favorite store)—the malls are open for *worship* every day—not just Sunday morning.

There is nothing wrong with most of the world's goods. But when *bigger and better* has you indebted to the creditors, or if you are even just lusting for the *bigger and better*, Christ's words of warning, "What shall it profit a man..." need to be heeded.

"He who dies with the most toys, wins!" is a bumper sticker philosophy of the world, feeding a materialistically–minded society with diabolical lies of hell. And the *bigger barns* of Luke 12:18 are lost in the shadows of the thousands of self-storage sheds that are being used to hold those *toys.*

He who dies with the most toys...dies! just like everybody else. And then the judgment. See Hebrews 9:27.

A light touch on all that is of this world is a demanded discipline for battlefield living.

4) *Crucified With Christ.* In Galatians 2:20, Paul captured the very essence of Christ-like living: "I am crucified with Christ, but wait a minute—I'm still alive! Yet, it's not really me, but Christ who is alive in me. And the life that I am now living in this body, I live by faith in the Son of God who loved me and gave Himself for me." We need to readily pick up our cross—daily— and follow our Master to Calvary. By an act of faith we must reckon ourselves dead to our sinful nature—to the appeal and power of sin, and our spirits alive and sensitive to the call of God through Jesus Christ our Lord. See Romans 6:11.

The disciplines of Christ-like living are demanded of those who are determined to live on the battlefield.

5) *Active Duty.* Once we have been called, commanded and commissioned to be a Soldier of Jesus Christ, and we want to please the One who has called us to be a soldier, battlefield living demands that there

are works of righteousness in which we are to be actively involved.

Ephesians 2:10 reads, "We are His *most finely crafted work of art...*" (KJV says *workmanship;* the Greek word is *poema,* from which we get our word, poem). We are His most beautiful poem created in Christ Jesus to "...sit back and wait for the rapture." Is that what the rest of the verse says? Does that even sound like God talking?! No! A thousand times, No! "We are His most finely crafted work of art, created in Christ Jesus *to do those good deeds* (works) that He beforehand prepared that we should walk in."

God has planned for each one of us to be "a doer of the Word and not a hearer only." James 1:22 And those good deeds were probably planned even before the foundations of the earth. Works *for* salvation? Definitely not! We don't want to get caught up in that. Salvation is a gift of God, giving us no room to boast. In Ephesians 2, notice how Paul deals with the "work" of believing (verse 8-9) and follows it with the "works" of righteousness (verse 10). Note also in Titus 3:8, Paul instructed "that they which believe in God (they had been saved by grace) be careful to *maintain good works.*"

Once we recognize the privileged position that He has given us to be part of His eternal Plan of the Ages, we jump in with a firm grasp on His will for our lives (Ephesians 5:17) and do the works of the One who has sent us. For Jesus said, "As the Father sent Me, so also I send you." John 20:21 The Father certainly sent Jesus to accomplish specific tasks. In John 5:36, He said, "The works which the Father has given Me to finish, I am doing..." So in His prayer in John 17, Jesus was able to say, "I have finished the work which You gave Me to do." John 17:4

As Queen Esther learned so long ago (Esther 4:14), we too have been called to the Kingdom for an hour such as this. There is Kingdom work to be done. Let's not just talk about it or listen to others talk about it or applaud those who are doing the work of the Kingdom. Let's be doers of the Word. This *is* battlefield living. Let me say it again: Battlefield living *is* doing the works of the One who called us to be His soldiers and thus please Him Who has commissioned us into His service.

Develop A Working Relationship With All In The Army
The uninitiated in battlefield living may think that the most difficult aspect is the distress of the job or the long hours, the tough living conditions or the thankless labors. But reports from the front lines say that the most difficult aspect of battlefield living—of all Christian ministry—is the business of getting along with the other soldiers, that of developing a working relationship with every one in the allied armed forces.

Paul, the Apostle, knew this. He knew that the first thing that satan would do in his attack to weaken the Army of God, to weaken us in our aggressive offensive of overpowering evil with good, would be to get us to fight among ourselves: To "sow discord among the brethren." Proverbs 6:19

In Romans 1-11, Paul has masterfully guided the Roman mind from creation through the gift of Christ to the conclusion that God has done all on His part for us to live the Spirit-filled life. By the time he gets to Chapter 12, he is ready to make the transition from God's action to man's response.

"With your eyes wide open to the mercies of God..." (I have just spent 11 chapters telling you of His grace and mercy). Now Paul implores, "What is the most intelligent, reasonable response but to give your entire being to Him—a living sacrifice. However, you can't be thinking and acting like the world; you have to think the thoughts of God to prove His perfect will for you. Now be careful that you don't think too highly of yourself or your importance. Think soberly. Have a sane estimate of your capabilities based on the faith He has given you." Romans 12:1-3

In verses 4-8 he talks about the body functioning together, each doing its part in cooperation with the rest. (He enlarges on that in I Corinthians 12.) We should focus on doing well what He has gifted us to do.

Then! Beginning in verse 9 and continuing through the end of the chapter, Paul gives no less than twenty-five solutions to the most critical issue in Christian service: Interpersonal relationships!

Let's look at a few: "Let love be without dissimulation." Romans 12:9 Unfortunately, we are not very familiar with those King James words today. The *love* is *agape*—the deep level of God's love flowing through us. *Dissimulation* means *without hypocrisy.* God's agape love flowing through us must be real; it must be sincere (*sin*=without; *cere*=wax), uncontaminated.

Now, when we go about our busy lives isolated in our shiny, plastic bubbles of protection, we can (pretty well) control what others see of us. We can call across the foyer of the church our happy "hello." And they respond with their smile. And we feel the "Christian love of the brethren."

But get up close to each other. Take off that isolation bubble. When you ask some people, "How're ya' doin'?", and they really start telling you, your *agape* had better be sincere. When you get down in the dirt and filth of this world, pulling lost souls out of the muck and mire of sin, that *agape* flowing between you and your co-worker had better be real—without wax.

Have you ever come into a house, looked across the living room into the dining room and seen a beautiful bowl of fruit on the table? Oh! It looks so delicious. You want to reach out and taste the sweetness of that fruit.

But as you get closer, you realize it is plastic. It is fake. It is not real. That can happen when people look at you if your *agape* is not without *dissimulation.*

But that's just the first solution Paul gives to interpersonal relationship problems on the battlefield. He goes on: "Abhor that which is evil." Romans 12:9 In this case I like to stick to the KJV word, *abhor.* It is a strong, powerful word expressing the degree to which we should hate evil. It also carries in its meaning the action of fleeing the evil that we detest. May God help us to abhor evil as He does.

Next: "Cleave to that which is good." Romans 12:9 Again, *cleave* is a word not well known, but equally powerful in the opposite direction of *abhor.* The story that comes to my mind is of David's warrior, Eleazar, the son of Dodo, who "arose, and smote the Philistines until his hand was weary, and his hand *clave* to the sword." II Samuel 23:10 In battle, his hand had so gripped the sword that they had to pry his fingers off the hilt. That's cleaving! That is what we are to do with that which is good.

And Paul goes on through twenty-two more solutions to interpersonal relationship problems, solutions that will help us get along with the other people in the army. For, after all, "They (the heathen, the lost, the ones whose eyes we are trying to open) will know that we are Christ's disciples by our love *for each other.*" John 13:35

Psalm 133:1 adds another perspective to this issue. It says, "How good and pleasant it is for brethren to dwell together in *uniformity.*" Wait a minute! Is that what Scripture says? Does that sound like God? No! There is no way that a creative God who has demonstrated His matchless power of diversity would then say, "Now, conform!" He has built into each of us the uniqueness of personality and perspective. The God who has created at least 11 billion different sets of fingerprints wants diversity. Uniqueness. Individuality. But out of that unique diversity He says it is good for us to come together in *unity*. Thus, several of the solutions of Romans 12 deal with unity, such as: "Live in harmony with each other; don't be snobbish" (v.16); "Live at peace with all men" (v.18).

"But," you may say, "I *can't* be in unity with everyone on the battlefield. (I would agree that we do not want to unite with satan or his forces of evil. That would be treason!) You continue, "I know what I believe and why. I have studied the Word. I know what Scripture says. I cannot work with those who don't believe as I do." Several serious considerations are needed to modulate that attitude if we are to be effective on the battlefield.

First, let's think again about that apology statement (what I believe and why) that we talked about in Chapter 2, and the three illustrations that I used. We said our beliefs should be written in three sections. First: This I believe and here is the unequivocal Scripture to prove it. (ex: virgin birth). Second: This I have come to believe as I have considered the whole counsel of God, but I also recognize that others have studied the same Scriptures and have drawn another conclusion. (ex: pre-tribulation rapture). Third: This I believe and practice though I realize it is mostly culturally-motivated. (ex: not drinking alcohol).

I will not die for third category beliefs. Yes, I live by them and practice them. But I realize that they are culturally-motivated and I can adjust. I will not die for second category beliefs. Yes, I have studied (and continue to study) the Word, and from it I have drawn my theological conclusions. But, recognizing that others have also done *their* homework and come up with other conclusions, I hold these beliefs rather tentatively. But, I *will* die for first category beliefs! Those tenets of faith that all Christians of all generations and cultures hold true I, too, will live by—and if necessary, die for.

Now, how does that relate to working together with the other battalions in the army? I have determined that when I am on the battlefield that for which I am willing to die is the only substance for which I want to live. Where does a notion like that come from? From the Bible. Paul said, "I have determined to know nothing among you save Jesus Christ and Him crucified." I Corinthians 2:2 Does this mean that Paul knew nothing else of the teaching of the Bible? Certainly not! But at that time—for that focused point in battle—it was necessary for him to concentrate on "Jesus Christ and Him crucified."

On the other hand, as he penned Holy Scripture concerning hair and head coverings, he ended the discourse with, "But if anyone wants to be argumentative about it, I can only say that we and the churches of God generally hold to these *customs* on the matters." I Corinthians 11:16 See also I Corinthians 7 and 8 as he dealt with marriage and meat offered to idols. There were some things that Paul said he would die for (Acts 21:13); other issues were "vain babblings" that he told Timothy he should avoid. II Timothy 2:16

A Vietnam veteran once told me, "When I heard the command to advance position, I did not consider whether those working with me were white, black or green. They were carrying parts of the mortar emplacement and I was carrying a part. Our survival depended on getting that instrument of war advanced, assembled and fired."

I believe that if we are going to fight an effective war against the enemy, we need to clarify what we are willing to die for. And that is what we should be living for. But that, then, requires a tolerance for other people's opinions and beliefs—beliefs that they, too, (hopefully) hold tenuously in their second and third category. However, we cannot compromise (for ecumenical, political or any other reason) on any first category beliefs. And I realize this is no simple matter. All the soldiers on the battlefield have not placed the same issues in the same categories as you. You might have put *pre-trib rapture* in your second category of belief. Another may believe that the timing of the Lord's return is a first category belief. Thus, something he would die for!

Dealing with these issues demands the wisdom of God. However, God has not left us unequipped. In the letters of James, the Holy Spirit, through the brother of our Lord...(oops! Do we all believe that the writer of James was the actual half-brother of Jesus? Will you die for that belief? Though I *believe* it, I won't die for it.) James gives a beautiful description of the wisdom that comes from God. In verse 5 of Chapter 1 he has already said that if we don't know how to handle any particular issue of life we have only to ask of God who will give generously of His wisdom without making us feel foolish or guilty for asking. Then in verse 17 of Chapter 3 he states that one of the eight characteristics of God's wisdom is that it is "full of tolerant thoughts" (compassions, mercies).

To give some perspective on this, I will tell an embarrassing story about myself: I was the "ripe old age" of 17 (having been raised all my life in a particular denomination) before it dawned on me that there were good Christians who went to churches of other denominations. In fact, some seemed to be living a much more holy life than I was. Now, it wasn't that we were particularly taught the intolerant thought that "we were the only ones going to heaven," but it was sort of left to our imaginations to assume this (or, at least, that is the message I got).

From such a background, God had to work many experiences into my life to develop this characteristic of His wisdom: tolerance. Let me illustrate with one more story.

When I was principal of a Christian school affiliated with a particular denomination, I was privileged to notify a teacher that the Board had hired him. His first question was, "Do I have to get baptized again?" As his story unfolded, I discovered that over the years he had taught in a number of different denominational schools and that with each change, he had had to be "re-baptized" by their prescribed manner. It seems he had already been immersed or sprinkled four or five times. I told him, "No, I think that is enough." I didn't want to risk his drowning! We wanted him as a teacher. I learned tolerance for various forms of water baptism.

Soldiers, there is a war going on. There is an enemy determined to see our destruction. We need to lay aside every weight—strip off every encumbrance—throw off every impediment and the sins (including the sin of intolerance) that do so naturally entangle us...." Hebrews 12:1 We need to work together.

Think of this illustration: Brothers and sisters can fuss and fume with each other all they want to in the family room. But let little sister be hassled in the neighborhood—the family *forgets* its differences, unites and aggressively attacks anyone bothering little sister. See Genesis 34 for the story of a father, his twelve sons and their little sister!

It is measured that one horse hitched to a wagon can pull a one ton load. But if you hitch two horses to that same wagon, they will be able to pull 23 tons! Let's build a working relationship with *all* true Christians in the army. So much more can be accomplished. God's tolerance is far broader than "middle class, conservative, American Christian—or whatever economical, social, political or ethnocentric category in which you find yourself.

On the other hand (as a note of caution), we do not want to be so broad-minded that we embrace the *light* from many lamps. On a recent trip to Vladivostok, Russia, I was asked by a Bulgarian man to tell him what I believed about religion.

Knowing his religious affiliation I said I would talk with him only as it centered on one question: "What have you done with Jesus?" He agreed.

During our third meeting, he showed me his ring. He showed me the 12 rays that were leading to the sun in the center, describing them as the paths that lead to his true father, the Reverend Moon.

I took occasion to say, "Yanko, I too believe that all paths lead to God!" In light of things I had previously said, his shocked expression was expected. I continued slowly and deliberately: "All paths do lead to Jehovah God. One path leads to a God of mercy and grace through Jesus Christ. All other paths lead to a God of justice and judgment." The Gospel message is all inclusive: "Whosoever will may come." Revelation 22:17 Yet, that same life-giving Good News of Hope is all-exclusive: "No man can come to the Father but by Me." John 14:6

We need to work together with those who preach and teach salvation through Christ's life, death and resurrection. But we cannot embrace those who are teaching "another doctrine." See Galatians 1:6-9.

When does a person's doctrine become *another doctrine?* Winds of doctrine have been blowing through the Church for nearly 2,000 years. Some are rather innocuous—with little harm. But others can lead whole movements astray. Jim Jones began his efforts with the best of intentions. Love for the poor and needy motivated him. But somewhere along the line *another doctrine* allowed for grossly ungodly acts, culminating in the arsenic-laced Kool-aide mass suicide!

Listen to the *winds of doctrine*...(No! Don't!)...blowing through the airwaves by certain gifted orators. We can soon tell what are the current religiously correct terms. Each one of these doctrines usually has a measure of truth. But tragically those promoting them distort, and thus move away from, the Truth. And those not wanting to get caught in the whirlwind, also move further from the Truth—but in the opposite direction. In both movements, the enemy is the winner.

Another issue that can so easily entangle us is *doctrinal excesses.* They also usually have a solid Biblical basis. But when a Christian can speak about nothing else but his current *soap box* issue, he has fallen prey to the enemy's tactic of distorting the Whole Counsel of God.

Of course, winds of doctrine and doctrinal excesses can very easily lead to *false doctrine* which can then lead to *heresy.* We cannot deny that the trivialities of truth test us, tantalize and tempt us to turn from the true testimonies of God's Word. But eventually they become false doctrine, and can lead many astray. Or, at the least, distract soldiers from the battle that rages for the lost of the world.

These all are a part of the encumbrances we must shake off so as not to be entangled in the things of this world. At some point, by God's wisdom and a keen sensitivity to His Spirit and His Word (Paul's Letters to Timothy are a good place to start), we must separate ourselves from those who have lost Christ's Message of Love.

We must keep the Good News good news. But we must also keep God's tolerant wisdom guiding our relationships. For on the battlefield we want our lives to please the One who has chosen us to be a soldier.

Avoid Presenting Another Religion

As we move forward on the battlefield, we must be sure that we are not presenting *another religion* to the world, but that we are talking about a relationship with God through Christ. There are those expressing their concern that *Christianity* is facing a crisis. If it is the *religion* of Christianity, I can only say, "May that crisis bring death to Christianity!" In a culture of "live and let live," "do your own thing," etc., being *born again* can mean anything from a true conversion experience of eternal significance to the new vigor a football team experiences whenever they hire on another six million dollar man.

It is significant that throughout history, as Christianity finds its place of respectability in the world, it becomes a less viable force in changing the lives of its adherents. Whether it is Constantine's attempt to nationalize Christianity through mass baptisms or the current polls that say 87% of Americans pray to God once a week, the sickness of the third century and the apostasy of the current one rise as a stench in the nostrils of God.

True christianity, only *initiated* by conversion, is a radical, on-going, developing relationship with the Father, through Jesus Christ, drawn unto Him by the Holy Spirit. This radical relationship will see Christian leaders calling nations to repentance (Jonah, Evan Roberts, Billy Graham). This radical relationship will see the Church of Jesus Christ fitting into His Plan of the Ages. This radical relationship will see men of God saying, "These light afflictions are nothing when compared to the eternal weight of glory." II Corinthians 4:17; 11-12

Paul, the Apostle, said it. On through the centuries of time, thousands of saints have said it. And today, an innumerable host of Christians around the world are saying it. May we see the battle from this eternal perspective, and stick to the Truth of God's Word. It is a relationship with God through Jesus Christ that we have to offer the world, not a religion.

We Are On A Mission Of Love
Another consideration relating to battlefield living is our attitude toward our *work for the Lord.* Does the *business of service* interrupt our *mission of love?*

As part of my responsibility as Superintendent of Children's Education for Wycliffe Bible Translators in Brazil, I was asked to conduct a study on how to make the educating of our children more sensitive to the host culture. The study included interviews with many people—students, parents, and nationals who knew us and our work. One discussion was held with a national couple, Dr. and Mrs. Spadoni. Not only was he our family doctor and my tennis partner, but over time we had become quite close friends. They knew ahead of time the topic of our discussion. Yet, as we sat at the patio restaurant, watching and listening to the river cascade over the rapids, they *danced* around the subject for two and one half hours! I had written a few notes, but I sensed that they (in their gracious manner to not offend) were holding back what they really wanted to say.

Then, as if it had been pent up for years, Maggie Spadoni brought her open palm slapping down on the table. Nearly shouting, she said, "All right! All right! Do you really want to know how I feel? The whole issue lies in this question: *DO YOU LOVE US? OR ARE YOU HERE TO GET A JOB DONE?*" And, then, just in case I didn't know on which side of that question she stood, she added, "You are so production oriented. You act like you are here only to get your job done. By doing so you are running roughshod over the people. You aren't showing us that you love us." She sat back in her chair as if exhausted from an hour-long speech! But in saying that, she had communicated the essence of a major battle-field problem.

This is a cultural issue with which we Americans need to deal. We are production-orientated. We are effi-ciency-orientated. We lay out the job. We get in there. We get it done. Big! and now! We are generally reactive, responding to a crisis. We wait until it gets really bad and then we go in with our bombs or money or...Gospel! Yes, this cultural issue can carry over into Christian ministry. We develop a strategy. We establish quotas. We do our *thing.* We come back to the church in a victory celebration. Or we write a glorious evalua-tion. We have accomplished *it!* But have they seen the "love of God shed abroad in our hearts through the Holy Spirit who has been given to us?" Romans 5:5 I wonder if this is what Jesus was dealing with when His disciples returned from ministry? See Luke 10:17-20.

Battlefield living—whether we are relating to the neighbor next door or the individual around the world—requires that we do not let the business (often it is just busy-ness) of service interrupt our mission of love. As we keep our eyes fixed on Jesus, our Commander-in-Chief, we will follow His example of love as He related with people. Nothing He did was stereotypical; all was by the guidance of the Holy Spirit. What an example!

Live In The Supernatural Power Of God
Just before Jesus returned to the Father He said to His group of followers (some of whom were still doubting), "Stay in Jerusalem until you receive power from on high." Acts 1:8 I realize that our relationship with the Third Person of the Trinity is another area of "discord among the brethren."

We can relate to God, the Father. Everyone has a fa-ther. Whether he was good or bad, we can understand the Father-image of God. Jesus, the Son. Yes, we all know about sons—as children or brothers. But Holy *Ghost?* Thanks to the King James Version, just the name *Ghost* can make one shrink from a relationship with the Holy Spirit.

Though I have a fairly well-defined apology statement regarding the Holy Spirit (all based on Scripture, I trust), I believe I have put most of what is controversial in my second category. Thus, I can say, "I don't care what you call *it.* I don't care when you get *it.* Just don't leave home without *it!*" And by *it* I mean a vital, vibrant, alive, growing, developing, dynamic, powerful relationship with the Third Person of the Godhead: God, the Holy Spirit!

I cannot imagine that we have come this far in this study without realizing that without the power of God, provided to us by the Holy Spirit, we are no match for the enemy. But, on the other hand, I trust we have also come to understand that when we are "strengthened with all might, according to His glorious power" (Colossians 1:11), we are invincible!

Be Yourself
Good battlefield living acknowledges who I am—in Christ, of course—and gives me a "sane estimate of my capabilities measured by the faith He has given me." Romans 12:3 Yes, it is good to read books about the exploits of others. Ruth Tucker's *From Jerusalem to Irian Jaya*; John Woodbridge's *More than Conquerors*; the Holy Spirit's Hebrews 11! Yes, all of these are good. But in our idol mentality, we can succumb to the lament, "Oh! If only I were as good as _____ (you fill in the blank), then I too could do mighty wonders for the Lord."

A related erroneous line of reasoning goes: I never sank that deeply into sin, so I don't really have a good testimony to give. No! Stop! That is not a good line of thought. We are just to be the person God made us to be. He has created in each of us a life story. The dark and bright threads in the tapestry of our lives have been woven by a Master Weaver. And that which has been (and is being) woven is the message He wants us to share with those that we meet on the battlefield, whether they are fellow soldiers or the lost we are there to rescue.

Thy Kingdom Come
As we trod the battlefields of the world, we do need to be aware of the politics of the countries to which He takes us. But we must also keep in focus that we are not an ambassador for any earthly government. We are "Christ's ambassadors!" II Corinthians 5:20 An ambassador is one who represents the government of one country to the government of another. In spiritual terms there are only two kingdoms: The Kingdom of God and the kingdom of darkness. We are representatives of Christ's Kingdom to all ensnared in the kingdom of darkness, no matter what political lines may form their boundaries.

We are not a-political nor anti-political, but our message transcends all earthly politics. We are here to establish the Kingdom of God, not that of any country, man, denomination or non-denominational denomination.

But ethnocentrism thinks differently: "We *are* the best," it insists. "We do worship God in *the* most accurate, Scripturally prescribed manner," it reasons. Thus, it is natural to try to make them like *us* before they can *really* be Christians. Oops! Is this not exactly what the Judaizers were up to? "Yes–to Christ! But first become a Jew!" seems to be what they prescribed.

A pastor once insisted to me that a particular lady couldn't possibly be a Christian because she didn't conclude her prayer of repentance with the words, "In Jesus' Name, Amen."

In the summer, the Alps are dotted with flocks of sheep. An owner may have several flocks with different shepherds. The sheep in each flock know only their shepherd and the other sheep of their own group. As Christians we must rise above this *sheep mentality.* We must heed the voice of Jesus as He concluded a discourse on sheep: "And other sheep I have, which are not of this fold: them also I must bring, and they will hear My voice; and there will be one fold, and one Shepherd." John 10:1-16

Jesus Christ our Lord is the Good Shepherd. May we, not as hirelings, but as under-shepherds, point people to the One True Shepherd.

Be A Wise Steward
Paul argued, "Have you ever heard of a soldier going off to war paying his own expenses?" I Corinthians 9:7-14 His conclusion, as we follow through his line of reasoning, is, *No!* John the Baptist told soldiers to be content with their wages. See Luke 3:14. A final consideration, then, on battlefield living is wisdom in all financial dealings.

Unfortunately, the battlefields of the world are strewn with those who use the Gospel for their own financial gain. Again, we are not advocating a *poverty mentality* but that of a steward: "Master, it is all Yours. How do You want me to spend it?"

Though so simply stated, it is not an easy issue. Nor was it for Paul. One time we hear him saying, "I wouldn't take your money now even if you offered it to me! II Corinthians 11:7-10 Another time, he more graciously couches a *thank you* in saying, "You helped me time and again. But it wasn't so much that I wanted a gift, but that you have invested in heavenly stocks and I desire to see the dividends that accumulate to your account." Philippians 4:15-17 Yet again, he coerced Philemon into *forgiving* Onesimus' debt: "If he owes you anything, charge it to my account. Of course, I don't need to remind you that you owe me your very soul." Philemon 18-19

A good rule of thumb is to live as much as possible on the level of the people you are ministering among. One spring a Bible translator woke up to realize that while his house still had a thatched roof, all of the villagers had replaced theirs with metal! It was my privilege that summer to help him upgrade his house! On the other hand, another friend of mine had been given the distinction of ministering among the *up-and-outers* (as he called them) from Hollywood. At a time when the average American house ranged in price between $60-80,000, he was thanking the Lord for the good deal he got on a half a million dollar home! Thus, whether we live in a million dollar house ministering to up-and-outers or in a thatched-roof hut ministering among indigenous people, being a good steward of the funds entrusted to us by God, is the critical issue.

Living on the battlefield is sometimes exciting, always challenging; sometimes difficult, always demanding; sometimes lonely, yet we are never alone. In fact, how could battlefield living be summed up more eloquently than in the words of Paul, who daily lived on the battlefield: "We are troubled and pressed on every side, but we are never crushed. We suffer embarrassment and perplexities, but we are never driven to despair. We are persecuted and pursued, but we are never deserted. We may be knocked down, but we are never knocked out! Every day we experience something of the death of Jesus, so that the resurrection life of Jesus also may be plainly seen in our mortal bodies." II Corinthians 4:8-10

BATTLE FATIGUE

Editor's Note: We traversed some pretty rough terrain in the discussion about battlefield living! But as Warrior concludes in this allegory, "Where else could I be but at the side of my Commander?"

While returning to their field of service, the writer of this allegory had a dream. She put her thoughts on paper. Little did she realize that within a week, she and her family would be casualties of war. Due to some church problems back home, they were ordered off the field!

The path He was looking for emerged from between rows of tall shimmering buildings. It led onto a narrow, rocky way, overgrown with wild vines. Before He plunged into the unknown darkness, He turned. The mirrored surfaces of the buildings reflected the brilliance of the next and the next, each with the newest of modern architecture boasting its owner's name. Yet, He knew. He knew that behind those façades of tinted glass and burnished aluminum were empty rooms. Halls that echoed the loneliness of humanistic materialism.

Helper shuddered and pulled His coat more tightly around Him, as if chilled by that thought. He picked His way carefully along the junk-strewn path: Polaroid and disposable camera packaging and bubble gum wrappers—residual signs that many people had curiously come this far.

Just where the path began to become a bit rocky, Helper met a most handsome soldier. Dressed properly, his shoes were spit-polished, the creases in his uniform were sharp, his sword and shield were of a brilliant shine.

Helper, pleased to see a new recruit headed for battle said, "I'm glad we can walk to the front together. The battle is growing fierce."

"Ah...I don't think You quite understand. I have come this far. But the path is getting rocky. I have not yet been trained in 'Rock-strewn pathway walking.' I hear there is a seminar soon on the subject."

"But I'll be by your side," encouraged Helper.

"No...No...Ah...There is other training I must take. A *lot* more training! Good teaching about the history of war. And the ethics of war. And the newest in strategy and weapons. And..."

Helper turned, shaking His head, and began the long trek to battle.

The soldier, taken up in naming the classes yet to prepare him for battle, didn't notice that Helper had begun walking. Looking up, he saw Him down the path. In a final defensive tone he shouted, "I'm planning to go...." His voice trailed off weakly, "...some day."

Beyond the first ridge Helper heard a pitiful whine. "Who might that be?" He mused. He walked until he came upon the most miserable sight. There, hunched over by the side of the road, was a wounded soldier.

Whimpering and muttering to himself, he didn't even see Helper. He just sat there with his sword on the ground beside him, waving his shield above him as if to protect himself from some unseen enemy who had stopped bothering him long ago.

Helper stooped down and looked in his face. "May I help you?" He asked.

"No. No...." pined the wounded soldier. "There is nothing You can do. Can't You see that my condition is beyond help?"

"No. I'm afraid I don't see that," Helper smiled.

"Oh, You're just like the rest!" shouted the man. He finally threw down his shield and glared at Helper. "It's all their fault!" he said, pointing up the path. "They said they knew. They said they cared. They said they would support me in battle. I should have known. Oh, I'm better off without them, anyway. People like that are never there when you need them!"

"What about Me?" Helper asked. "Why didn't you call for Me?"

The soldier leaped to his feet. He shouted angrily, "Because You should have known without my asking!" His shoulders drooped as he realized the weakness of his reasoning. The soldier began to cry.

"The Training Manual says you need to ask," consoled Helper, gently touching his wounded arm.

But, at that, the soldier started to scream and wail, throwing himself to the ground. "I won't go back to battle! I can't fight again!"

Helper stood helpless as He watched in wonder. The soldier picked himself up, gave his shield a swift kick, and stormed up the path. Helper, stunned by this scene of self-pity, finally continued His journey down the lane. He could hear soldier's moaning and muttering, echoing among the buildings.

Before long, He heard someone talking. "Why, don't you fellows see? Don't you understand?" the voice rehearsed to itself. "I've suffered quite enough. I do believe I owe it to myself...." And then the man caught sight of Helper. He blushed, somewhat embarrassed at himself.

He was a soldier, and had obviously been in the battle, for Helper could see his wounds. But He wondered, because the man didn't carry sword or shield.

"Hello," called Helper.

"Who...uh...Hello," said the man. And Helper

thought his smile a bit strained.

"Tell Me," said Helper, "where are you from?"

"Oh," he said with a practiced sadness, "I am from a most terrible battle—most terrible, indeed! I saw men fall to my left and to my right. And as you can see... Well, I've suffered very much, myself."

"And where are you going now?" asked Helper.

"Well...uh," said the soldier, looking down and clearing his throat, "I expect that I shall suffer from these wounds for many years to come, and I do believe this poor old body needs a rest."

"That sounds very humane," said Helper.

"Oh, You think so?" The man looked at Helper in delight. "Oh, I'm so glad You agree! You see, there were so many that thought I was being... uh, well, You know... They just don't understand that I need to enjoy life for a while. I mean, I've already suffered so much!" And then the soldier's face took on such a fanciful gleam as he said, "Look at that," waving his arm as if to encompass the skyline of glittering buildings they could see from the ridge where they were standing. "It's all mine! Mine for the taking. Why... I can be rich! I can at last give my family all the wonderful things they need...and want!"

"And what of your comrades at the battle?" Helper asked.

At this the man's face turned white. He swallowed hard, almost choking. And Helper saw the man's eyes turn hard. "I don't need Your condemnation," he said. "Besides, I'm not made for that stuff. And...and...they don't need me!"

"You may have convinced yourself," said Helper. "But not Me. Those men at the front have suffered considerably since you pulled out of the battle."

The man's face tightened, and for the first time he looked at Helper. "It's not true," he said. "It's *not* true! And I don't need this from You. I'm finally going to get the things I deserve...all the things everybody else has.... After all, I do believe I have suffered quite enough!"

Helper stood, looking after the soldier, and felt His chest begin to tighten and tears fill His eyes. He heard the soldier's voice disappear among the buildings, still consoling himself.

Then turning, Helper continued down the path until He saw another man: Rather cold for a soldier, but very impressive. His sword and shield were polished and shiny, as was the rest of his uniform—immaculate. Yet, Helper could see that he had no wounds. As He drew close, the soldier turned to face Him. And Helper's breath caught in His throat. He'd seen those eyes before, He thought.

"I've got all I need," smiled the man. "The plans, the method, the power and the brains. Before long, they'll all be leaving the front. They will all be following me.

"They...who?" asked Helper.

"Why, the soldiers, of course! Who else?" And the man threw back his head and laughed a most hideous laugh.

"You'll be taking men out of the battle?" queried Helper. "Away from the fight?"

At that, the man's face twisted viciously; his eyes glared at Helper. "There is no fight! No battle! *No enemy!* All those stupid recruits wandering around, trying to hear the voice of the Captain. The fools! I'll make them see. I'll make them understand. They need me. I'll convince them that they are doing the Captain some great service by following me. I'll get them busy in a hundred good works. They won't have time listen to You or the Captain."

"You're not even a real soldier, are you?" said

Helper, exposing to the man what He'd known to be true all along.

Threatened, the man looked at Him with poison in his eyes, hesitated, and then laughed. "They won't believe You. I'll talk so long and hard that they'll even forget the sound of Your voice."

And with that, Helper walked away, not bothering to strive or even look back at this man. For a moment, the pity He'd felt for the first three men was almost lost beneath the anger He felt for the fourth. But soon all He knew was the ache—the piercing agony of seeing soldiers fall away from the battle.

The path was becoming increasingly treacherous. Helper walked more carefully now. Resting by the side of the trail sat another soldier. "Hello!" Helper called. "Are you headed back to the battle?"

"Why, yes, of course! You can see by my attire that I am a soldier, can't you?" A bit of haughtiness edged his voice.

"Yes, you are dressed like a soldier and you are carrying sword and shield. Yet, your wounds are few and superficial," Helper noted.

"Look, I have learned how to stay at the edge of skirmishes. I don't see why this world can't just 'live and let live'! From my vantage point I have often watched those in the thick of battle. They just seem too radical...too serious." Convicted by the sound of his own words, he grudgingly said, "OK, OK, I'm on my way."

Helper's eyes burned with tears as He continued on the path. He came upon another soldier walking wearily back to the battle; his shield hanging weakly at his side. His wounds were much deeper and more severe than any He had yet seen. His sword, Helper could see, had never been dropped. His swollen, bleeding fingers clung to it, as though it were a part of him. And as Helper neared, He heard from him a deep groaning, and then a sob.

"What is your name, Soldier; and where are you from?" asked Helper.

The Soldier turned, unsurprised by Helper's voice. My name is Warrior!" said the man. "And I am from the heart of the battle."

"Shouldn't your dwelling be in the secret place of the King?" Helper taunted.

Warrior's face lit up with such a fierce loyalty as Helper had never seen. "Yes!" the soldier said. "Yes, and where else would that secret place be other than by the side of my Captain in the midst of the battle?"

"But your wounds...?" Helper wondered.

"Wounds? Oh, they're nothing," said Warrior, grinning and waving his shield. "We're taking the land, and nothing can stand against the King!"

"But, Warrior, why are you here? Away from the battle? Were you going off to seek your own plans— your secret ambitions?"

Warrior looked away. Helper saw his face twist in pain as tears began to fall. "That's why I'm here," sobbed Warrior. "I came to find the ones who've left the battle and try to bring them back."

"And what did you find?" asked Helper.

"I found men entangled in their own plans and ambitions, like the delicate threads of a spider's web, yet binding them like bands of steel," said Warrior. "And nothing I could say would make the battle burn in their hearts again."

"And where are you going now?" queried Helper.

"Why, back to the battle, of course." said Warrior, wiping his eyes. "Where else would I go?"

"Man, you could have great power and position

among men. After all, you have already suffered so much. You could publish near and far the great exploits you have done," Helper chided.

Warrior looked deep and hard into the eyes of Helper. And then he grinned.

Helper smiled. He'd seen those eyes before. They had the look of the Captain. Warrior turned his head for a moment to look down the path. Then he looked back at Helper. "I've got to go now," he said.

Helper smiled as He watched Warrior make his way along the trail back to the battle. "So much like the Captain," He said aloud. "So much like the Captain!"

MINISTRY RESOURCES

ACTS Video/Audio Training Tapes

Prepare for Battle: Lessons in Spiritual Warfare— This 9-hour video or audio training tapes program comes with 19 pages of Student Notes and Assignments and a Study Guide for Groups or Individuals.

Building Your Support Team—This 2-hour audio training tape is the counterpart of the book, *Serving as Senders,* instructing the missionary in how to develop relationships in the six areas of support.

Solutions to Culture Stress—This 4-hour video training tape helps prepare a short-term missionary for the culture stress of going overseas and returning home. The issues raised are best discussed in the context of the specific trip.

Publications

Critical Issues in Cross-Cultural Ministry are bulletins on vital missions topics. Available back issue reprints include:

Series I: *Mobilizing Your Church* -15 Issues
Series II: *For Those Who Go* - 15 Issues
Series III: *Serving As Senders* - 12 Issues
Series IV: *Internationals Who Live Among Us* -12
        Issues

SERVING AS SENDERS : How to Care for Your Missionaries—While They are Preparing to Go, While They are on the Field, and When They Return Home. (Available in American English, British English, German, Dutch, Swedish, Spanish, Portuguese, Romanian, Czech, French, Russian, Korean, Indonesian, Sinhala, Tamil and Chinese.)

PREPARE FOR BATTLE! Basic Training in Spiritual Warfare. (Available in American English and Russian.)

THE REENTRY TEAM: Caring for Your Returning Missionaries. (Available in American English and Dutch.)

I THINK GOD WANTS ME TO BE A MISSIONARY: Issues to Deal With Long Before You say Good-bye.

Seminars

Nothing GOOD Just Happens! Seminar—This is an intense, 21-hour seminar to train church missions leadership in how to mobilize their fellowship in cross-cultural outreach ministry.

For Those Who Go Seminar—The sessions of this 6-hour seminar help the potential cross-cultural worker look beyond the "romanticism" of missions and to deal with some very practical issues of going.

Serving as Senders Seminar—The lessons of the book, *Serving as Senders,* are presented in a 6-hour seminar format.

What's the BIG DEAL? They're JUST Coming Home! The issues of reentry are presented in a 3-hour highly interactive seminar format.

Steps to the Field —Following the sequence of thought through five areas, Motivation, Confirmation, Destination, Preparation and Ordination, a lively round table discussion elicits questions with answers. 3 hours

Lift Up Your Eyes—A "painter's palette" of opportunity in at least eight avenues of missions involvement. 2-3 hours.

ACTS Training Courses (Offered by request, only)

ACTS Team Orientation—2-10 hours of cultural, interpersonal relationship and spiritual warfare training for short-term teams.

ACTS Boot Camp—One week of cultural, interpersonal relationship and spiritual warfare training for those serving up to six months.

ACTS 29 Training Course—An intensive 10-week immersion in a second culture to learn how to live and minister in other cultures. The courses include cultural adaptation, language acquisition, interpersonal relationships, spiritual warfare and unculturating the Gospel and teachings of Christ. This field training incorporates classroom study and community experience while living in the home of a Mexican national.

Mini-ACTS 29 Training Course—A 4-week modified schedule of the 10-week Course.

ACTS Ministry Trips

ERI leads three-week trips throughout the year. Prefield training, a demanding "hands-on" experience and follow through after the trip helps the church leadership develop a consistent involvement in missions.

Speakers Bureau

Neal and Yvonne Pirolo, and associates of Emmaus Road are available as speakers on a variety of subjects, all challenging to a personal involvement in cross-cultural outreach ministry.

Additional copies of this book and more information on these or other developing resources to equip you and your church for cross-cultural ministry are available through:

Emmaus Road International
7150 Tanner Court, San Diego, CA 92111 USA
Phone/Fax: 858 292-7020
E-mail: Emmaus_Road@eri.org
Web Site: http://www.eri.org